God &
Self-Realization

(A Scientific and Spiritual View)

by

Dharam Vir Mangla
M.Sc. M.Ed. PGDCA

Published by:

GEETA INTERNATIONAL
PUBLISHERS & DISTRIBUTORS

GEETA INTERNATIOAL PUBLISHERS &
DISTRIBUTORS
Phone # 91- 011²2429715
E-mail : dvmangla@hotmail.com

ISBN # 81-901604-0-0

Publishers or Distributors interested in publishing or distributing this book in different countries or languages may contact the author or GIPD in this regard.

Printed at:
Sanjeev Offset Printer, Delhi

First Indian Edition: September 2002

PRICES IN INDIA

Paperback: Rs 180

Paperback with Plastic Cover: Rs 190

Postage Charges Extra

PRICES OUTSIDE INDIA

Paperback with Plastic Cover: US $15.0

Postage charges Extra

By Sea: US $3.0

By Air: US $5.0

How to Order:

- ➢ Call 011-91-242 9715 or see website: http://www.geocities.com/godrealization
- ➢ We execute the order after receiving payment by Bank Draft or Money Order.
- ➢ Overseas payments should be in US $ only.
- ➢ We offer 25% discount to distributors or agents for minimum order for five copies.
- ➢ For an order of more than 25 books freight and transport by sea will be free.
- ➢ Send the Full Price of your order plus postage & handling to the publisher or any distributor:
- ➢ In India the book can be sent by VPP also.

GEETA INTERNATIONAL PUBLISHERS & DISTRIBUTORS
197 Geeta Apartments, Geeta Colony
Delhi-110031, INDIA
Phone # 91-0112242 9715
E-mail : dvmangla@hotmail.com
Website: http://www.geocities.com/godrealization

Also Available with the Distributors:
In USA with Mrs. Poonam Rani,
E-mail: Poonam_rani@hotmail.com

In CANADA with Dr. Ajay Kumar Gupta
E-mail: ajaygupta153@yahoo.com

In N.J.USA with Mrs. Jai Shree Garg
E-mail: jai_shree@hotmail.com

Dedicated to:

Sri Paramhansa Yogananda,
Sri Mahavatar Babaji
Sri Amar Jyoti Babaji
the Eternal Gurus

And

To all the Devoted Scientists
Doctors, Educationists, Yogis
and the Seekers of God & Truth

CONTENTS

A Word

In the beginning of the new millennium, I decided to write a book in the service of God titled as "*God and Self-Realization*" (*Scientific and Spiritual View).* There are many books written by saints about the spiritual view of God & Self-realization. There are few books by the scientists about their scientific view of the concept of the universe. But due to the limitation of scientific knowledge by the saints and the limitation of spiritual knowledge by the scientists, there are some contradictions, misconceptions and misunderstanding about each other. Due to lack of latest scientific knowledge the saints are not able to correlate spiritual knowledge with science. And due to lack of spiritual knowledge, most of the science students are becoming puzzled about God and its existence. They need some one to guide them, clarify their ideas and remove their misconceptions. Truth is always one and can never be contradictory by the two systems. I decided to correlate and remove the misconceptions between the two systems. I have tried my best not to use any mathematics or scientific equation to explain my spiritual view, so that even the non-science readers can also understand it easily.

I have written this book with the sole aim to serve humanity & to please God. I have tried my best not to twist the scientific and historical facts (as it is a general practice) to please a group of people, a religion, a country or a political party. The Truth should not be twisted to please someone.

I have been fortunate enough that I was born in India, which have given birth to so many great religions of the world. The spiritual knowledge of great *Vedas & Shastras* is available in India easily without doing any extra efforts. I have the blessings of the great saints like Sri Amar Jyoti

Babaji, Mahavtar Babaji and Sri Sathya Sai Babaji. Generally the great scientists of the west are deprived of the opportunity of the spiritual knowledge and are limited to their specialized scientific fields.

I am thankful to Sri Amar Jyoti Babaji, a most revered saint of India, who has inspired and blessed me to write this book. All of my family members have his blessings.

I am indebted for the computer help and in providing the various ideas of scientific and spiritual views of my wife Mrs. Vimla Devi, daughter Jai Shree and son Raju.

I had a lot of help, inspiration and guidance in writing this book from many God-devoted persons Sh. Ashok Verdhan Dewan Ex-Deputy Director Education from Jammu, Mr.& Mrs. Prem Bhandari Head of Third Eye Mission, Sh. R.K. Gupta Head of NIC, Dr. Archana Gupta Sr. Scientist & Addl. Director CSIR, & Sh. M.D. Goel, Assistant Director Education and many others.

I can never forget the help of all the persons in the publishing of this book, in the service of God.

--- Dharum Vir Mangla

About the Author

Sh. D.V. Mangla, M.Sc. M.Ed. PGDCA got his masters degrees from university of Delhi. Since his birth he was of scientific bent of mind. He was an atheist when he joined his Ph.D. at Delhi University. But when young he used to study the religious books. He used to discuss about God, *Shastras* and the Science with saints and learned people. In 1969 a divine miracle of Sri Sathya Sai Baba transformed his soul, life, philosophy and thinking. He became a perfect theist with a firm faith and conviction in God. He totally surrendered himself to God. After that he was fully interested in knowing and seeking God. He devoted all his energies in the pursuit of God, spiritual studies and yoga practice. During 1976-78 he served as lecturer in Mathematics at University of Aden. Since 1996 he is working as the principal of a Sr. Sec. School in Delhi.

The Yogoda Satsanga Society (YSS) of India initiated him in 1989 in 'Kriya Yoga'. He is a genius scholar of Science, Mathematics, Education and Philosophy. He has the ability to correlate the Sciences, *Shastras,* Spiritual Science and God. This book is based upon his vast studies and yogic experiences. It is useful to all categories of men, believers, non-believers and the wavering minds about God.

I hope this book will help many "Seekers of the Ultimate Truth". It is a laborious and commendable research work. The scientists will take the topics for further research work as suggested by the author throughout the book and add further to it – as it is a continuous process in the development of knowledge.

Sh. Ashok Vardhan Dewan
Ex-Deputy Director Edu., J & K

PREFACE

"God and Self-Realization" (Scientific& Spiritual View) is a rare attempt to write a spiritual book. It correlates our latest scientific researches and technological developments with the universal science of Yoga and our *Shastras.* Present is a historic times. The whole world is facing an inevitable danger of its existence due to the horror faced by intermixing of religion with politics and terrorism against the survival of humanity. Now the eternal need to understand God and Self-Realization has become more important. Due to the advancement of our scientific knowledge, a major transformation is always taking place in the minds of our men mainly the science students getting education in schools, colleges and universities.

Our system of education has become such that the most of the teachers have become indifferent, towards God while teaching their subjects to the students. The students have simply become big store - house of huge data and information supplied by the wrong educational system. They are unable to analyze and interpret correctly this huge stored data. It is puzzling their little mind day and night. The parents, the society and the governments have stopped to provide the religious and philosophical education to the students. Besides some of the governments are misusing religion to provide the training of terrorism and violence in the name of religion to their people. It is their hidden and heinous motto to wipe out all other religions of the world and to rule over the whole earth.

None has a spare time and taken the responsibility to answer the thousands of unending questions & quarries in the mind of the students. The younger generations want to know about God, the universe, dreams, death, birth, rebirth, mind, consciousness, intelligence, illusions, delusions, them. But most of the scientists and the science are intentionally ignoring the miracles performed by them. This has unnecessarily puzzled the minds of most of the persons in the world.

As the scientists verify the laws of natural sciences in their science laboratories, similarly the time has come to experiment and to verify the truth mentioned in *Shastras* through the universal science of yoga. The intentional ignoring of God by the scientists is just like the ignoring and denying the existence of the universe by a man, by closing his eyes. This is most unscientific and need to be changed.

The book emphasizes the latest researches and theories of natural science and the spiritual view of *Shastras*, especially in respect of the miracles and to understand the structure of the universe and matter. The author compared the latest concept of the universe as perceived by the scientist like Prof. Stephen Hawking and as mentioned in the Holy Vedas and perceived by the great self-realized saints at different times. The reader is open to accept the concept of the universe; whichever is more convincing to him.

Dr. Archana Gupta
Addl. Director & Scientist 'E'
Council of Sc. & Ind. Research
Govt. of India, PUSA
New Delhi.

Sh. R.K. Gupta
Sr. Technical Director & Head
National Informatics Centre
Govt. of India, CGO Complex
New Delhi.

The suggestions and comments of the readers of the book "God & Self-Realization" are welcomed by the author through the e-mail:

dvmangla@hotmail.com

Website: http://www.geocities.com/godrealization

The author will try his best to respond the quarries of readers, if any.

If you feel this book is worth reading by others for the transformation of their soul, it will be your greatest service for God in this life to recommend this book to others or gift it to your friends, relatives and the seekers of God. There cannot be any other gift better then a soul-transforming book in their life, which can bring joy, bliss and happiness in their lives.

NEXT EXPECTED
FUTURE BOOKS BY THE SAME AUTHOR ARE:

1. ***How to Know God?***
2. ***Awakening of Kundalini (The Journey Back to God)***

ILLUSION OF HUMAN FACE

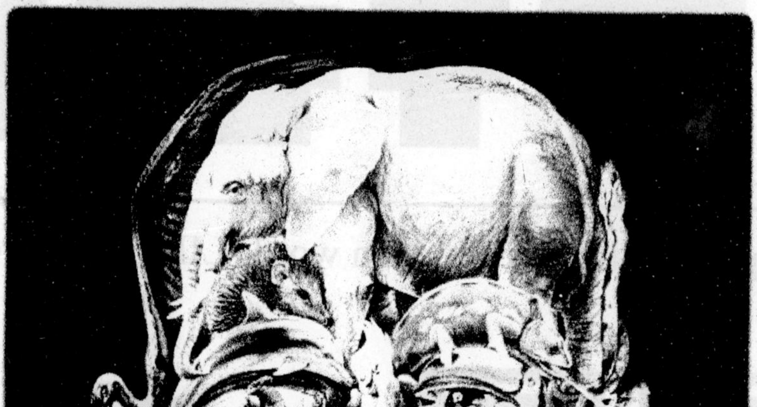

IN THIS PICTURE THERE IS NO TRACING OF ANY LINE. IT IS SIMPLY AN ARTISTIC ARRANGEMENT OF LIVING CREATURES GIVING US A FALSE ILLUSION OF HUMEN FACE.

Swami Vivekananda

Jesus Christ

Yogananda Paramhansa

Swami Prabhupada

LORD KRISHNA

SRI SATHYA SAI BABA

SRI MAHA-AVTAR BABAJI

SRI AMAR JYOTI BABAJI

1

Illusion, Delusion and Maya

Men's Unending Enquiry

What is Illusion?

What is Delusion?

What is Maya?

Anything Exist only if its Thought Exist in Our Mind

General Knowledge Tests are Not the Tests of Knowledge

Knowledge of God is Self-Explanatory

Illusion, Delusion and Maya

Prayer

O Divine Mother, teach me to understand Thy great mystery of the spirit, mind, matter, energy and the wondrous universe around me. Since millennium and in my numerous past incarnations, I might have forgotten Thee, but I am sure, you have not forgotten me even for an instant. Now I am in search of knowing Thy reality and nothing else. I am crying to find & meet you since my first breath in Thy delusive universe. Father, by your *Maya* Thou hast separated me from Thee. I was busy with Thy enchanting creation and had forgotten Thee.

O Divine Father, Thy creation is already entrapped in Thy great Illusion, Delusion and *Maya.* Our limited senses, intelligence and mind do not perceive Thy absolute reality and Truth, but only glimpses of Thy great Dream-Drama projected through Thy Infinite Great Mind. O Creator of Lives, help us to know Thy Drama.

Men's Unending Enquiry

Om Poornam-Madaa, Poornam-Midam,
Poornat-Poorna-Mudachiate;
Poornasia, Poorna-Madaya,
Poorna-Meva-Visisyiate.

... *Isho-Upnishada*

This means: O, God Thou art infinite and complete. Out of Thy Infinite formless existence, the Infinite creation (universe) has come out from Thee as Thou manifestation. Thou art (the left-after) still infinite i.e. nothing has been reduced from Thee. Nothing can be added to Thee.

This nature of God exactly tallies with Mathematics. Mathematically this means if we subtract infinity from infinity it is still infinity and not less. ($\infty - \infty = \infty$). Conversely, if we add infinity to infinity it still remains infinity i.e. ($\infty + \infty = \infty$).

Since birth man observes so many illusions & delusions around him. His mind is generally befooled by his five senses & commonsense. He tries to understand all these delusions. To understand this there is a good example: man observes his own image hidden inside a plain mirror. His commonsense & mind interpret that the image is inside the mirror. After his investigation he finds that there is no such real image inside the mirror. A virtual image simply appears inside the mirror. In fact no such image exist, and his mind wrongly interprets it as a real image inside the mirror. Since a mirror affects the minds of all the human beings and of all the animals for quite a long time, they think that there is no delusion in this phenomenon. On the other side if the mind of an individual or a few persons misinterpret some phenomenon for a short duration of time, it is called an illusion. It is also interesting to understand the misinterpretation of the senses. On the basis of so many examples I have explained it later and hence we can conclude: The information reported by our sense organ may not be correct or absolute truth. It is a misconception among the scientists that our five sense organs provide us absolute truth.

What is an illusion?

Illusion means *'ill-vision'*. An error entertained by one or more persons (but not by the whole humanity) for a short duration of time is called *'avidya'*, or illusion. The person suffering from the illusion misinterprets the object. He can remove it by applying his own correct senses, reason, mind & intelligence. Illusion is not permanent. For examples:

- To presume a rope as a snake, by a person in the dark.
- To presume a devil or some mysterious object, in the dark, which does not exist.
- A mirage of oasis in the dry desert etc.
- The color blindness and visibility of two or more objects instead of one due to defect of vision.
- Deceptive visions in illusion pictures. The cover picture looks like a human face, although there are no tracing lines by the artist in the picture.

- As it is self-evident from the picture of human face created by the arrangement of living creatures given on page 5, that the pictures of animals cannot arrange themselves automatically, to look like a human face. It needs, the intelligence and creativity of an expert artist. Similarly all the atoms and molecules of the whole universe, cannot arrange themselves of their own, to give the required forms to the galaxies, stars, planets, living creatures, plants, animals, solids, liquids and gases etc. It needs the infinite intelligence of God to arrange all the microscopic particles, in the form as they are in the universe.

What is a Delusion?

Delusion means '*dual-vision*'. It means seeing every thing apart from God. In delusion both ego 'I' and God exist. Delusion separates ego 'I' from God. The observer knows that every thing else is God, but still he feels his separation from God due to delusion. A delusion is an error entertained by the whole humanity for a long duration of time. Our intelligence, mind, senses and reason can partially interpret the phenomenons and the appearance of substances. But most of the time our senses report falsely. The correct scientific investigations and interpretations by our own intelligence can remove our delusion and inform us about the correct phenomenon or substance. A few examples of delusions are:

1. All human beings observe that '*Sun revolve around the earth'*. Which is false. In fact the earth revolve round the Sun and about its axis.
2. 'With our naked eyes the s*tars look like the tiny bright objects suspended in the sky and appear a few kilo meters away from earth'*. In fact they are heavenly bodies like our Sun and are thousands of *light years* away from us.
3. Every body appears to fall towards the earth. But it is strange that the heavenly bodies like the stars, the sun and the moon do not fall on earth.
4. We feel that we are now observing the ***present*** positions of the stars like other objects. But in fact we observe them not of their present positions, but of many years past, depending on their distance. The nearest star we observe now is of at least four and half years before. The Sun we observe now is of 8 minutes and 20 seconds before as light takes this much of time to reach earth from Sun.
5. The surface of earth seems to be flat. In fact the earth is spherical. The Euclid Plane Geometry, which we teach in our schools and colleges, is not true even on the surface of our earth. The sum of the angles of a triangle on the surface of the earth we live on is not 180°, but more than 180°. Similarly the space around us is not linear as predicted by Einstein's General Theory of Relativity. Space has got a curvature due to

gravitational field in it and the Euclid 3-D Geometry does not hold true exactly in space around us.

6. The color of the sky seems to be blue is an illusion. In fact sky has no color etc.
7. The depth of the bottom of a water tank looks less then the actual depth.
8. In a motion picture the motion of the image appears to be in continuous motion. In fact it is a series of still pictures projected more then sixteen images per second of a moving object.
9. There are all kinds of electromagnetic waves like Radio, TV, Wireless, X-rays, Ultra Violet, Infrared and Ultra-sonic waves etc. around us. But our five senses fails to detect these waves without proper scientific instrument.

Now it is clear that all these optical delusions are due to the misinformation or misinterpretation reported by our sense organs to our mind. From time immemorial the whole humanity has been suffering from all the above delusions. The science & technology are continuously helping us to understand and remove these delusions. It is significant to note that the human mind & intelligence is able to correct and remove these delusions. We view things around us according to our different mentalities and moods. Our eyes are unable to see the subtle astral bodies and subtle astral colors, which are hidden in every thing around us. Our ears are unable to hear the supersonic & ultrasonic sounds, astral sounds and the *Anahat* sounds. Our nose is unable to smell the astral fragrances due to its limitations. The taste of a patient is changed during and after his disease. During the paralysis the skin looses the sense of touch of the body does not obey the orders of mind. It appears that the sense organs do not report the mind the absolute correct information. The diluted mind is not able to report the signals received by it correctly to the ego 'I'. It is known as diluted-vision or delusion. *We conclude that the whole humanity is under the influence of delusion.*

What is Maya?

But *Maya* is different to some extent from illusion & delusion. *Maya* is our ignorance and a cosmic delusion created by God. It is a cosmic force by which *Brahman* has separated Himself from His own creation. The power of consciousness to separate & divide is called *Maya Shakti*. Before the creation of universe God was alone. When God started the creation, He became the Creator. All our educational systems, throughout the world are simply busy in studying and getting more & more information or Vidya (limited knowledge) about the creation and ignoring the Creator. Sciences & Technologies can simply answer the *how* of a question but ignore the *why* of question. The Creator is waiting, whether his best creation the human being will ever start thinking about their Creator.

Our universe is not an ultimate reality, but it is just the God's dream or a thought of His Mind. God is dreaming the dream of cosmic motion pictures on the delusive human consciousness. *Maya* is responsible for the manifestation of 'formless' God to provide different "forms". *Maya* reduces the omni powers of Cosmic Consciousness to limited existence of matter, mind, intelligence and soul. Due to Maya we have forgotten that we were God in the beginning and we will again merge in God in the last. Due to *Maya* we also feel our association with the ego 'I'.

The universe is just a great thought in the mind of God. If God just stops His dreaming, the universe will dissolve immediately in God. For a child the motion pictures on television screen appears to be true and real, but that the pictures on television screen are only images created by light and nothing more. Similarly the universe is just a motion picture or a dream of God on a four-dimensional screen of space & time by a universal hidden projector.

For a dreaming man the dream appears to be a total reality. The dreaming man forgets every thing of this awakened universe and even the existence of his physical body in this world. Man has the power to dream and create his own dream universe. Similarly this universe is simply a great dream of God and the creatures are just active images or puppets in His Universal Dream.

The following *fundamental law* is acceptable to both the physical and spiritual science: '*if there exist anything, it must have been created by someone and cannot come into existence itself out of nothing. There cannot be anything without any creator or without any cause.*' Another *fundamental law* acceptable to both is the ***Law of Cause & Effect*** i.e. to every effect there must be a cause. If there is any thing in the universe it must have been created by some one. Nothing can be created out of nothing. Even the thoughts coming to the mind must have a cause. Thoughts cannot come out of nothing. How the thoughts are coming? What the science has done in this regard?

A Thing Exist only if Its Thought Exists in the Mind

We know that from the beginning of the universe, there exist cosmic rays, X-rays, radio waves, gamma-rays; electromagnetic, gravitational and magnetic fields & waves; hundreds of fundamental atomic & subatomic particles of matter & anti-matter and all the laws of natural sciences governing this universe including our earth. But until few hundred years before, man was not even aware of any of these things. And a few hundred years back there was no existence of all these things in the mind of man at all. If some body or a scientist or a saint or any body else, would have talked about the existence of these things, he might have been humiliated, punished or hanged or become a laughing stock in the world. So many people have already suffered and faced the cruelty of world in the past history. All the above scientific findings do not exist even today or have any meaning, in the minds of the millions of illiterate people and other living beings.

For example: If some body has not heard or has no concept of bacteria, virus, atoms and subatomic particles then all such things does not exist in his mind for him. Even today we may not know about so many wondrous things already existing in the universe about which we are not aware of. Daily we experience that during our sleep and dream this world does not exist at all. The thought of this world melts away during the dream.

At a particular instant of time we are aware of only about a single thought existing in our mind at that particular instant of time. We forget the rest of the things of the universe & even about our physical body at that instant of time. We have only one mind and can have only one thought at a particular instant of time, in our mind.

Our past concepts about the soul, physical body, matter and the universe are always constantly & rapidly changing. After so many achievements, can we claim that nothing more is left to find about? Absolutely not. Uptill now we have found only a very few things out of the infinite unknown things. Is there any way to find out and know everything instantly at a time, in our lifetime? As per the *Vedas & Shastras,* you may not believe that, *the answer is*

'yes'. Accordingly, there is a big difference in the mind & intellect of human, as compared to all other living beings on earth. Similarly there is a big difference in the mind and intellect of man, as compared to the Cosmic-Mind and Infinite-Intelligence of God. God has given the power to man only to think about Him and to none else. Will you believe that after the self-realization, a man become one with God and he achieves everything, including all the super-powers of God?

***Maya** is different from an illusion or delusion. Maya* cannot be removed by our human intellect and without the grace of God. The human mind & intelligence are not able to overcome & remove the ignorance due to *Maya. Maya is the power of God, which creates an illusions and delusions, to **separate** the creation from the creator.*

We know fog vanishes before the Sun. Similarly our ignorance due to *Maya* vanishes before the knowledge of God. We remove the husk that covers the rice or wheat. Similarly we remove the ignorance, delusion and *Maya* that adheres to the mind of man by the regular practice of meditation, introspection and *Samadhi.* During *samadhi* we realize the absolute Truth and Knowledge face to face and nothing else is needed to explain.

General Knowledge Tests are not the Tests of Knowledge

All over the world in almost all the countries there are General Knowledge Tests and there are thousands of books written on General Knowledge for the preparation of these tests. In fact neither of these tests measure knowledge nor the books are about General *Knowledge.* In fact all these books and tests are about General *Information* only. These tests measure the information stored in the mind of the candidates by his power of cramming the information. A really knowledgeable man like a great scientist or a saint or a writer may utterly fail in these information tests. Does it mean that they do not have General Knowledge? The incorrect name of these tests misleads our students about the correct concept of knowledge. So our educationists should do something to change the name of these tests to avoid confusion between the meaning of words knowledge and information. You will agree that nearly all the researches and discoveries in the field of sciences are information only.

The Knowledge of God is Self-Explanatory & Self-Evident

A blind man by birth can never understand the true nature of light. We may try our best to explain, define and clarify about the light to the blind man, but it will be all in vain. The blind man by birth will never be able to understand light however efforts we do. He will always think that we are just befooling & wasting his time. But if anyhow, we are able to show him the actual real light and the glimpse of our world for few seconds, it is sufficient for him to understand light & its importance without any explanation. Similarly a dumb & deaf man by birth cannot understand the concept of sound till he really listen the sound. Hence, God has made the things self-explanatory.

The conflict between the believers and non-believers of God is never ending. The believers declare that God is to be found at this place and everywhere. The non-believers says that God can be found nowhere at any place. This fight between the two has been throughout the past ages.

Our two eyes gives us the view of the vast expanse of the universe and space; but our eyes cannot see our own face to which they belong, without a mirror. However the two eyes are the part of our body, the eyes cannot see the back and the inner parts of our body. Even the outer and inner visible parts of our body are not same as visible through the powerful microscopes. Whatever is visible through the naked eye is an illusion or delusion, not the absolute reality. The spiritual science tells us the ways to get rid of these illusions and delusions. Therefore the person who has no experience or knowledge of the spiritual science and the divine concepts cannot comprehend God even if he is a scientist.

Our eyes can see but cannot talk or hear. Our tongue can talk but cannot see or hear. Similarly our ears can hear, but cannot talk or see. One sense organ cannot do the work of the other organ. The God and the Divine can be grasped only through universal love, through faith, through devotion and true *sadhna.* Love and devotion unites us with God, but *Maya* separates us from God. To verify the truthfulness of God or the *Shastras*, the scientists have to follow the spiritual laws. If they fail to verify, there is something lacking in their *sadhna or practice,* but not in God.

We have been born inside the universe and the omnipresent *ether.* We can never understand both these fully, unless & until: we observe both these from outside the limits of the universe or become one with the ether and the universe. To understand this think of a fish, which is born inside the deep sea, and has never come out of the seawater in its lifetime, to look the outside world or the universe. Such a fish can never understand the presence or the existence of seawater around it and the universe out side the water. Similarly we are born inside the omnipresent *ether* and the universe and we can never go out of the universe & *ether.*

According to spiritual sciences the universe and *ether* are inside our mind. During meditation we can go beyond our mind and then we can understand both the universe and the *ether.* Do not doubt upon this.

As per the famous French Mathematician Rene Descartes, if human can conceive the idea of God, God must then exist, for whatever the brain can think of must have a basis in Truth. "*A clear and distinct idea of an absolutely perfect Being contains the notion of actual existence; therefore since we have an idea of an absolute perfect Being such a being must really exist.*"

Remember: "Our proud of little learning and sallow knowledge is our biggest enemy, to learn more and to know the absolute reality of the universe. Through the science whatever we have learnt or learning is only about the creation. It is just a glimpse of the dream of God, which provides a little information. The whole universe and all the creatures are the images or puppets on a 4-dimentional screen of space and time, projected by a universal stereoscopic holographic projector in the mind of God. Due to Maya, we are misinterpreting the dream images as the reality, which is false."

2

Who am I?

Who am I?

Prayer

O, Divine Consciousness! O, Ocean of Bliss! Since millennium I do not know myself, because I have forgotten Thee due to my ignorance. I am taking pangs of joy and sorrow, life after life and from birth till death. My greatest ignorance puzzling me throughout is: Who am I? I have realized that I am neither the physical perishable changing body, nor I am brain, nor the life force, nor I am mind, nor I am intelligence and nor the thoughts. Also I can never be anything, which belong to me and is mine. I am the king of all such things.

O Mother Divine, in the false changing world everything is changing continuously, but my ego 'I' remain the same throughout my life in the same body. I am the same witness & the same observer during my awakening, sleep, deep-sleep and meditation states of consciousness. I am eternal, unchangeable, imperishable and deathless soul.

O Giver of our life & death! From where, I came in this world? Where will I go, after my death? Why I have to experience the horrible dreams during my sleeps? Why I do not have a freedom to decide to have a body of my choice and sweet will? Why my birth and death are not in my control? Why I am made sick all of a sudden without my will and how I am cured of the diseases without my knowledge? How to remove the ignorance of my soul and to know who really I am? What is my relation to Thee?

Who am I?

This is the greatest puzzling question, which is hunting the whole humanity since time immemorial. Can there be anything more important then to know our ego 'I'? From where I came to this earth and where I will go after my death? Who gave me this body and forced me to live in it? Do I have any freedom in selecting a suitable body of my own choice and design? Such questions are hunting the mind of the seers. The humanity on earth has always been busy in learning about the history of creation, solving the human problems & sufferings and to understand the mysteries of the universe, but ignoring the above questions.

We know only a little bit of our body, but do not know any thing about our ego 'I'. We are sure that we possess a physical body and there is an ego 'I' which exist in our body. Our ego 'I' is the most important thing among all, in this universe. We can sacrifice any material thing even the dearest thing for the sake of this 'I'. A mother can sacrifice her dearest child to save her own life in a sudden accident. Since birth our ego 'I' is trying to learn about so many things of the universe including the puzzle '***Who am I***'? This is the question where the sciences and philosophies have not helped much. But the holy Vedas & *Shastras* starts with this basic question.

There have always been some changes in our body since our birth. Science has informed that all the present cells of our body are being replaced by, some new cells after some time. It means we have an entirely new body made up of new atoms and cells after some time. But our ego 'I' does not change in the new body. Our ego 'I' remains the same in the body throughout our life, till death. No other 'I' of someone else can replace our ego 'I' during our lifetime in our body and vice-versa. Due to *Maya* we are completely ignorant & have forgotten about our own 'I'. We don't know from where this 'I' came? What shall happen to this 'I' after my death? Will 'I' exist after my death or not?

Who gave me this body and forced me to live in it and to act in the world? Why I am forced to dream the dreams, I don't like? Why do I suffer and made sick? Why I have no complete freedom & always happy? What is the real source of my happiness?

How to know Ego 'I'?

If we want to understand our ego 'I', then our own 'I' should become the object to be known the observer also. Remember our ego 'I' is not our physical body. It is different from physical body. Our 'I' do not possess any sense organ, brain, mind or intelligence. 'I' is different from physical matter even the *ether*. In the process of knowing our ego 'I': 'I' become the object to be known, and 'I' become the observer & 'I' becomes the senses to report. All these three become one during the meditation state. In that state there are no sense organs, no vibrations emitted by the object, no brain, no mind, no intelligence, nor anything else. When the object, senses and observer become one, then and then only we can understand our ego 'I'.

There are some interesting examples of strange personalities in the world. The *Puranas* and the Holy books are also full of such strange personalities:

- Some individuals have been found with two or more brains instead of ordinarily one brain. They can do two or more different works at the same time. At present there is a lady who can write two different letters with her two different hands at the same time. But she has only one ego 'I' in her personality. Ravana is said to have ten brains and ten minds in a single body.
- Some snakes and some extra ordinary persons have been found with two or more heads in a single body. The famous Lord *Seshnag* (The King of snakes) is said

to have one thousand heads. Most of the Hindu Gods have more then one head on their body. But all of them have single ego 'I' in their personalities?

- There are examples of twins having two heads with one lower body. They have two different egos 'I' sharing one physical body.
- There are historical examples that an advanced yogi leaves his old diseased body and enters his ego 'I' in the body of some other dead body of healthy young man. Mysteriously the dead body of the young man became alive with a different ego 'I' of the yogi. The yogi lives his later life comfortably in the new body of the other person.
- The Hindu *Puranas* and many others are full of miracles that some of the men were able to transform their body into any other form of different creatures at their will. It is said that even some of the snakes have this power to assume any form of any creature, even the human form.
- But there is not even a single example that the ego 'I' of a man in his body is changed during his life. There are changes and variations in the physical body throughout the life, but the ego 'I' remains unchanged. Since it is immortal and eternal. No scientific theory of evolution can explain, how this ego 'I' was evolved in the living beings or in the living organism.

The Story of a Shepherd Lion Cub Under Delusion

There is a good illustrative story from great saint Kabeer of India about the ignorance of our soul: Once there was a shepherd in a village. One day he caught a young lion cub in the forest. He brought the cub to his house and kept him among his sheep. In a sort time the lion cub mixed with others and acquired all the traits of sheep. He used to love, play, eat and sleep with them. As the lion cub grew up, due to his ignorance he forgot that he was a lion. He was convinced that he was also a sheep like others. After few years the lion cub became a full grownup lion, even then he began to behave like a coward and a non-violent vegetarian sheep. He had lost all his original characteristics and qualities of a lion in the jungle.

After some time a full-grown up lion came to the village from the nearby forest & met the lion living with the shepherd. The lion of forest wondered & shocked to know that a full grown up lion like him was behaving like a coward sheep and was also a vegetarian & non-violent. Immediately he understood the cause of his strange behavior. He tried to convince him that he was a lion and not a sheep. He tried his best to remove his delusion and ignorance of lion but failed. Then he asked the shepherd lion to accompany with him inside the forest, where there were many other lions. When the shepherd lion saw the other lions of the forest, enjoying, killing, eating other animals, he at once realized his ignorance, laughed at his own folly and changed immediately into a strong and normal lion like others. After that there was no need to teach him that he was not a sheep, but a lion.

In the same way the human children are brought up with the men, who are ignorant about their real nature of soul or God. The children associate themselves with their physical body and behave like an ignorant man when grown up. But when an ignorant man met with a self-realized Guru, who removes his ignorance and *Maya*, and make him to realize that he is infinite, immortal & cosmic consciousness and not the perishable body. He makes him convinced that his soul is nothing but God. His ego 'I' and God are the same. Only *Maya* has separated both. You now have a little glimpse of your ego 'I', but still you have not realized the truth of it.

With the Increase of Our Information, Our Ignorance is also Increasing

How do the illusion, delusion and *Maya* affect our understanding of the universe? When a child is born & takes his first breath in the world, he cries, because he has been imprisoned in a physical body. The child is surprised to know that he possess a physical body. His body has some of the basic needs to sustain, depending upon the outside world. He has no knowledge, who has given him his body and why it has been given to him? He knows that he has not come to this world out of his own choice and will. It appears that somebody has imprisoned him in his body to achieve some hidden objective from him. What does He want from him? Science has yet to answer to this question.

It is observed that a newly born baby has already learned so many hereditary behaviors, without learning them from outside world. Since birth the baby knows how to breathe, how to drink, good or bad tastes, how to smile & weep, instinct of hungry & excretion, sleeping, sense of touch & pain and so many other inherited human behaviors. Is it not miraculous, how a child learns, all these inborn human behaviors? Science has yet to do further research work to answer this question.

Further as the body of the child grows he realizes that there exist a mysterious and a wonderful universe around him. His little mind is unable to understand & grasp the delusion and *Maya* around him. He is unable to understand his mysterious and wonderful physical body, the people, the world and the universe around him. He tries his best to understand the universe, the different organs of his body and their functions inside and also about the world outside his physical body. But his little intellect fails to answer his numerous quarries.

Due to delusion the child observes that every thing falls from above to below. But he does not understand why the sun, moon & stars do not fall on the ground? He also does not understand why earth attracts every thing? What is the cause of gravitational force? How do actually the two heavenly bodies attract each other from such a great distance? Do the science really knows the cause of gravitational force of attraction & how actually the gravitational forces affect the other bodies in the universe till now? Why the gravitational force has no repulsion force, like magnetism and electricity? What exactly causes two heavenly bodies to attract each other at an enormous distance of billions of light years? What really is a gravitational field? What changes it brings in space between two bodies. Is there any kind of exchange of gravitational particles called *gravitons*, which are still unknown to science?

Just like gravitational field we also do not know much about electric and magnetic fields. All these 'fields' are still mysteries for us. Till now we simply know the mathematical formulae searched by Newton or Einstein about the gravitation, nothing more.

Child Wonders About his Mysterious Physical Body

Regarding his little physical body the child wonders as: Who is palpitating his heart, which needs a tremendous amount of constant energy? Neither he can stop it nor he can run it at his own command. His heart is functioning regularly since his first breathe in the world and it will continue palpitating till death. He has no control over his heart. His stomach or his digestive system is digesting all kinds of food, which consists of millions of complex chemicals. His body is manufacturing thousands of complex chemicals, needed for its sustenance, without his slightest knowledge of these chemicals & their need? He has absolutely no control and no knowledge of thousands of complex chemical actions and reactions, taking place in his small body. Most of the time he is not even aware of his body at all, as during the sleep.

The child further wonders after knowing that there is a world's biggest industry of manufacturing complex chemicals and thousands of organs are functioning in perfect order in his small body. He also learns that he has many wonderful sense organs, which produces special signals & reports the information received instantaneously to his brain. But he fails to understand how these complex signals of sense information are reported correctly to the brain? How his brain further interprets them correctly & reports these signals to his mind? And how his mind further reports these signals to his ego 'I' instantaneously? Does science know the answers of these till now?

Sense Organs → Special Signals → transmit signals through neurons & nerves → special faculty in the brain → brain interpret signals & report further to the Ego 'I' i.e. the soul → Soul is the ultimate observer, record & experience all kinds of signals → soul further stores these experiences in its memory and has the ability to recollect the experience from memory.

Due to *Maya* he is ignorant & has absolutely no knowledge of the exact phenomenon of all these happenings in his body. But about one thing he is sure that all these are happening without his control and efforts. He is unable to stop or activate any of the functions of his body organs.

Due to the strong impact of *Maya* he associates his ego 'I' (*Ahankar*) with his physical body. As his information about the creation around him increases, his ignorance also increases tremendously. More and more questions daily arises to his mind, the answer of which he does not know. A young child has got only very few questions in his mind whose answer he does not know, but a learned old man has got millions of questions in his mind the answer of those he does not know. So we can rightly say that:

"*To every new answer you can always ask at least two or more new questions. So although our information is expanding rapidly, but our ignorance is also expanding more rapidly.*"

As the knowledge of our Science & Technology is progressing, we are exposed with more & more mysteries of the wonderful universe, about living, non-living and heavenly bodies around us. Now we have billions of questions about the unexplained known & un-known mysteries, the answer of which we do not know. We are not leading from un-known to known, but:

form ***un-known → known → more unknown.***

Unknown or ignorance + Scientific Research → more known information → more known information leads to more unknown questions and ignorance → Never leads to complete known Knowledge.

A General Knowledge Test is not a test of knowledge. It is simply a test of general *information.* Knowledge does not mean information. If some one is not informed of the question asked in G.K. test, it does not mean that he is not a knowledgeable person. If some one has stored by cramming a lot of information in his mind, it does not mean that he is full of knowledge. The educationist should change the name of the General Knowledge tests to General Information test.

It is strange that all the Fundamental Atomic & Subatomic Particles are Exactly Alike

In school child learns that matter is made up of atoms & molecules and further these are made up of subatomic particles like electron, proton, neutron and so many other elementary particles. But do we know every thing about these particles? Do we know what are their colors, shapes and sizes? By which material, the particles are made up of? Is it not miraculous why all the trillions & trillions of the sub-atomic particles are exactly same and alike individually, throughout the vast universe? For example, why all the electrons are exactly same in size, color, charge, mass and all other properties? There is no difference at all between any two electrons throughout the universe. Why there are not different types of electrons manufactured by nature? It means all the electrons and other sub-atomic particles had been created and controlled by one individual throughout the universe under the exact mathematical laws. It is a limitation of science that it can never make any two things exactly alike in all respect.

The Universe is made from Only One Material

It is a common delusion of the mind that the universe has been made up from billions of different kind of materials and things. But according to science the matter can be converted into energy and the energy can be converted in to matter. An atomic and sub-atomic particle is inter-convertible by nuclear reaction. This shows the equivalence between matter and energy. The great scientist Albert Einstein has given the famous formula $\boldsymbol{E=mc^2}$. Where $\boldsymbol{E}$ is the energy created, $\boldsymbol{m}$ is the mass of the matter disappeared and $\boldsymbol{c}$ is the velocity of light. This equation proves that the matter and energy are the different physical forms of the same thing (God). It is just like that the ice, water and steam are the different form of same thing i.e. H_2O at different temperatures. All the fundamental particles consist the same material inside them.

Ice, water and steam appear to be different due to delusion. Science & Technology can now say with a great confidence that the whole universe including the '*ether*' and space are made up of only one material. But they don't know, what is this material? How much do we know about it? From where, this material came? What are its properties? Was it present before the creation or not? Who decided to create such atomic and sub-atomic particles? Who designed this wonderful universe providing us all kind of comforts, without expecting anything in return from us? Who created all the laws of science, before the creation started?

How Much We Know About`something?

It is a common paradox that we say that we know most of the things. In fact we know only a little bit or just nothing about any thing. To illustrate my point I would like to tell you the following talk between a saint and his disciple. Once there was an interaction between a saint and his disciple as follows:-

Disciple: Guru Ji, what is God? How can I see God?

Saint: Have you seen India?

Disciple: Yes. I live in India and I have seen it.

Saint: Have you really seen the whole of India?

Disciple: No Guru Ji, I have seen only few cities.
Saint: Have you seen Delhi?
Disciple: Yes. I live in Delhi.
Saint: Have you seen each and every part of Delhi?
Disciple: No Guru Ji. I have seen only a few places in it.
Saint: Have you seen your house in Delhi?
Disciple: Yes. Naturally, I live in it.
Saint: Have you really seen every part of your house and its household goods etc?
Disciple: No. I have not seen everything in my house. There are still some places in my house, which I have never seen. I do not know all the things in my house.
Saint: Have you seen your own body?
Disciple: Yes. I daily see my body?
Saint: Your body is made up of billions of cells. Have you seen all those cells of your body?
Disciple: No. I have not seen the cells of my body. They are very small.
Saint: Have you seen the structure of all the body cells?
Disciple: No, I have heard that the cells have beautiful structure and can be seen though a powerful microscope.
Saint: Have you seen all the components of cell in your body? What chemicals are contained in the cells? How does they multiply each other? Do you know about the functioning of the sense organs, nerves, brain, mind, heart, kidneys and stomach etc. in your body?
Disciple: No, Guru Ji, I do not know all these.

The saint smiled and explained when you have not seen each and every part of an object, how can you say that you have seen the object completely? Also to see an object is totally different than to know an object. When there is ignorance about the subsets of a set, how can we say that we know the whole set? In fact we have only a little spark of information or a little bit of knowledge about something in the universe. We do not know any of the physical thing completely. Remember, it is not scientific to say that we know an object completely.

We are trying to know God, but it is something different from all the material and immaterial objects and our ownself also. The God is the totality of both the manifested universe including us, and the un-manifested remaining part of God. Unless and until we know everything about both, we cannot say we know God completely. *Nothing remains to know further, after knowing God or our ownself.*

The saint further explained: A tree consists of many different parts like its roots, stem, branches, leaves, flowers, fruits etc. We cannot say that a particular portion or a part of the tree is the tree. Similarly we cannot say that any part of our physical body is our ownself. The totality of all the parts of a tree arranged in a systematic organized manner (already designed by God) can be called a tree. If someone knows little bit about the leaves of a tree and say that he knows the whole tree is neither scientific nor logical. To know a tree we have to perceive it as a whole and also every particle inside it, all at a time and not in parts. Similarly to know God we have to perceive God as a whole & every part of it, all at a time and not in parts at different times.

Wonderful Arrangement of Atomic And Subatomic Particles in Living & Non-living Beings

Atoms and molecules in living or non-living matter are not scattered in a haphazard manner without any order, but are systematically arranged in a beautiful & well-defined network, which needs infinite intelligence to arrange. The arrangement of electrons, protons and neutrons in atoms of the same element anywhere in the universe is always exactly same. Further the atoms & molecules are arranged beautifully, in elements, compound and crystals. The molecules of water (H_2O) and other fluids are always arranged in their solid, liquid or gaseous forms. There is not even a slightest amount of matter which is not arranged, any where in the universe, to give it a proper form & shape.

The complex molecules are further, beautifully & systematically arranged in living cells, body cells, viruses or bacterias. The arrangement of molecules in all the viruses or bacterias of the same kind is further exactly same. How the arrangement of billions of atoms and molecules in a cell, virus or bacteria can be done exactly same without the infinite intelligence (of God)? Science has to accept the existence of God for these arrangements. Who is arranging all the particles and giving them shapes. What is His aim?

Microcosmic View: Due to the great delusion or Maya, man is unable to see, through his naked eyes the arrangement and motion of the atomic and subatomic particles inside the matter around him. If he could see the matter through a powerful microscope he will find the atomic and subatomic particles are spinning in circular motion and also vibrating. No particle is at rest in the universe. His naked eyes are unable to see the actual shape, motion, color and arrangement of the particles. The objects visible through a powerful microscope are entirely different than what the man sees with his naked eye. The naked eyes see the objects in the shape the God want the man to see due to his delusion or *Maya.*

All the atoms or molecules of one substance are exactly alike in all respect all over the universe. There is no difference between any two molecules of the same substance anywhere. If we mix a drop of water in the sea, it is impossible to search out and collect the original molecules of the drop of water again by any scientific method or procedure, because all the molecules are alike and indistinguishable.

Further the microscopic living body cells, bacterias and viruses etc are made up of billions of atoms, complex molecules like RNA & DNA, chemicals, genes and other things all arranged in a beautiful organized manner. The living body is made up by the complex arrangement of billions of living cells of different kinds. All these arrangements can't be done by the inert nature itself without infinite intelligence to organize. Blood cells are constantly doing their great work of supplying the oxygen and heat energy to different parts of our body, which we are unable to know and control. Similarly in living plants: water, fertilizers, chemicals and so many other things are constantly supplied from its roots to different parts of its body, not visible to eyes. So all the microscopic particles are doing a huge work continuously without any break, rest or knowledge of our mind to keep the world alive. In fact God is doing all these works secretly, without men's knowledge and control. Due to delusion men are unable to see the actual shape of non-living matter & living beings.

Whatever is visible is exactly what the God wishes it. Without delusion or Maya the universe and the world have been observed entirely different then what is seen with the naked eyes. It is the will of the God that He wants everybody to see the world in the manner, he likes and as it looks. If God stop the motion and arrangement of particles even for a second there would have been no life at all.

Macroscopic View: Our naked eyes are able to see only the moon, planets, Sun, few thousand stars, Milky- way, few galaxies and some other heavenly bodies. But now with the help of a powerful telescope like Hubble Telescope, we are able to see more and more mysterious heavenly bodies like neutron stars, red-giant stars, black holes, quasars and billions of stars and galaxies in the universe. So whatever is visible through the naked eyes is not a reality, but a misleading delusion.

Our common sense interpret or misinterpret that the thousands of small tiny bright stars are suspended in the sky mysteriously and they do not fall on the earth like other worldly objects. Star looks to naked eyes a few kilometers away. The sun, moon, planets and stars seem to revolve around the earth in a day and the earth seems to be at rest and also seems to be the centre of the universe. The earth looks flat. But we know that whatever the common sense interpret is not true. This is due to the delusion and *Maya.* Whatever the common sense interprets is exactly the God wants us to observe, through His great delusion and keeps our mind away from the reality.

Question arises: can we know the reality? To know the reality God has given us the power of intelligence, through which we are able to remove our delusions. The science, technology and education are exposing the recent new discoveries of heavenly bodies and the new structure of our universe. The model of the universe designed by scientists is totally different than the model of the universe in the mind of an ordinary man, a child, a newly born baby, an animal, an insect and other living beings. Truth is always one and same it cannot be many. If the universe is real it can't be interpreted by different beings in different manner. The universe should have been looked the same by every body at all times.

But due to the delusion of God it looks different to different individuals and creatures. God is controlling the minds of all the living beings. The concept of the universe is exactly the same in the mind of a living being, which the Almighty God wants it to interpret. Our different interpretations of the universe are exactly like the different interpretations of an elephant's shape given differently by the totally blind men by birth. No blind man can tell the structure of the universe correctly. It is a well-known story.

The Concept of the Universe is Different in Different Minds of the Living Beings

If an object or the universe looks differently to different individuals it can't be real. The universe visible to us is simply a concept in our mind, which differ from person to person. It differs even among the different scientists, since they are also under the same delusion as we are. The self-realized yogis (spiritual scientists) who have a victory over the great delusion and Maya of God have told us differently. According to them the universe is just a great dream or a condensed thought in the mind of God. All of us are simply images and the actors of a film in the world, just like on the screen of a T.V. or cinema projected by a universal projector.

We also know that the concept of the physical universe is also not same to an individual at different times. When a man go to a dream-sleep or a deep-sleep, he completely forgets even the existence of the awaken physical-universe. During sleep man is not aware of his physical body and he does not care and bother for the same. It remains lying in the physical universe unattended by him. During dream the mind of the man is tuned to different cosmic viberation and creates a dream-universe, which is different from the physical-universe. The human brain is just like a T.V. tuner. It catches different receptions like different T.V. channels.

During dream the man creates a body for him to act, which is not made up of physical matter. He has no control over the dreams during his sleep. He generally forgets the relationships with his acquaintances. His dreams are totally irrational. Generally when he sees his dead near & dear ones in dream, he forgets that they are already dead. Some times an old man dreams that he is a child. He forgets his past history & experiences that he is not a child but an old grown up man. It is wrong to say that these dreams are the manifestations of our past memories, stored in our mind just like computer memories in a hard disc. If it had been the repetition of the past memories, it would have been rational & just the same replica of the past memories. But it is not so.

About Sleep
Dreams and Death

When we go to sleep we have to detach our mind completely from every thing of the physical awakened world. We have to completely forget our body and leave it unattended for some time by us in this world. Even a single thought of attachment to this world will be a hindrance to go to sleep state. After enjoying dream or sleep we come back again in the awakened world. By these dreams and sleep daily Almighty God is trying to realize us that we are under delusion and the physical universe is not a reality. But we are ignoring his efforts.

The ***dreams*** we are going to experience tonight can never be predicted. The dreams are irrational in nature and have negligible relation with our physical world. Generally the dreams are such, which we have never thought of in advance. Some times the dreams may give us glimpses of our past lives and some times of our future life. But the dreams may or may not be true. A dream universe is the creation of our own mind or the mind of God, just like the God has created the physical universe in His mind. But it is certain that we are helpless to dream as per the choice of God and cannot dream as per our own choice or will. We are forced to experience the pain & pleasure, laugh & weep, fear & joy, falling from a height, excitements, our own death and accidents etc. as per the fruits of our past actions or *karmas.*

What Happens at Death?

At the time of our death, we leave every thing permanently in this world included our physical body. But if we have desire or attachment to anything in this world at the time of death we will come back to this world again to fulfill our desires. Death is never instantly. It takes some time by the soul to leave the body. At the time of death our sensations in different parts of the body is lost one by one slowly. Sense organs are lost one by one as during meditation. The hearing sensation remains in a dead body for quite a time after death. After our death our soul is given another ethereal or astral body for some time to act, just like we get a body in our dreams. This body possesses sense organs, brain, mind, intelligence etc. We live in this body, in some other astral universe that is obtained by tuning our mind to a different cosmic frequency, till we find a suitable womb to take birth again in this world.

But if we don't have any attachment or desire at the time of death, and have a strong desire to merge in God or to know God, we get *Moksha* after death. Moksha means no births or rebirths and merge in God forever, like a water bubble merge in sea.

When we are awakened after the sleep, we are astonished to find ourselves in this awakened world. We analyze that dream world is not real and we were under a great delusion and *Maya* during sleep. But it is again due to the influence of *Maya* on our mind that we do not analyze that the physical world is also *Maya* just like the dream universe. Our brain and mind are like TV tuner, tuned to different channels.

Our universe is not a reality. The whole universe has been projected in the great mind of God just like a universal four-dimension projector projects on a 4-dimensional space-time screen. Whatever is visible or happening in the universe is not real but false images. We can realize this if we go out of the delusion and *Maya.*

The deep sleep state is different from dream sleep state. In deep sleep our mind is tuned to different cosmic frequency. In deep sleep state there is nothing to interact, no time, no place, no space and nothing else etc. After enjoying deep sleep we report that there was nothing in the deep sleep. But we cannot say that we were not in existence during the deep sleep state. We are the observer, a witness and have experienced the deep sleep. It means where there was nothing in deep sleep, we must be there in that nothing as a witness to observe it. In this state we are very near to God and very near to our own true self 'I'. If instead of sleep, we could go to this deep sleep with an awakened consciousness, we are under meditation and can know our own self. Through the deep sleep God is showing us a path to know our own self.

The universe appears to us exactly what Almighty God wants us to see. We all are His children. *God never takes rest and never go to sleep even for a second.* Out of His divine love, He is constantly taking care of all of his children without any break. But due to His infinite love and kindness, He daily provides us sleep, to recharge our tired body, and also give us experience of the non-reality of the physical universe.

Our scientists are ***not exceptions*** to this delusion and *Maya* of God. They are as much under the delusion and *Maya* as we are. Scientists will not be able to know the absolute reality of the creator and his creation, unless they remove their own ignorance, delusion and *Maya* as advised by so many self-realized saints, who have realized God. For any scientific experiment a well-equipped lab, a thorough knowledge of the experiment and the guidance of the learned scientists are required. Similarly for a spiritual experiment, the yogic scientists require the purification of body, mind and sprit. No scientist can enter the kingdom of God unless he strictly follows the path of spirituality. It is unjustifiable and unscientific to declare the non-existence of God, without proper experimentation. If the sea-divers do not go the deep bed of sea, they may not get even a single pearl from sea. How can they declare that there are no pearls in the sea without reaching and searching seabed?

This can be explained through the ***story of frog inside well***, which has never gone out of the well in his life. For the frog the well is the whole universe and nothing is outside the well. But if he gets a chance to come out of the well his concept of the universe is totally changed. Similarly our universe is like a cosmic dark well or ocean of ignorance (*andhakoop*). We (including our scientists) can never go out of this *andhakoop*, till we get self-realization. Till we are in the *andhakoop* and *Maya* we can never understand the reality of the creator (God) and the creation (universe). Our *Shastras* has given the scientific methods to go out of the *andhakoop*.

The Great Dreamer Nostradamus

Nostradamus was a physician of France born in 1555 A.D. He is the finest example of a miraculous man who dreamed about the important events of the future world. He had predicted many thousand great events of the world out of which nearly half the predictions has come out to be true. The rest of the events will occur in the next few hundred years or so. There are so many saints in the world that had the ability of most accurate predictions. There arc so many genius astrologers in India and other countries who are able to predict on the basis of astrological mathematical calculations. There are so many ordinary persons whose dreams come out to be true many times.

As per mathematical and scientific logic *if even one such prediction has ever come out to true* in the history of earth, it is sufficient to prove that the events or the dream drama of the universe is pre-planned or a stored programmed in the mind of God. All the events in the universe are happening in a systematic pre-planned manner, except the man has been given a freedom to act to some extant. The universe is not just a *random accidental happening* or creation, out of nothing, without any purpose. But it is well planned, fully programmed and well organized, beautifully arranged and has a great purpose behind the creation. The human life is also not just purposeless, fruitless and aimless. The creator has a purpose to send us on this earth. ***What is that purpose***? Is it not true that we are terribly busy with the studying of the creation only and ignoring the study of the creator intentionally?

The Universe is Not Eternal. It took Birth and will Vanish at the End

It is now almost certain with a great accuracy that the age of the universe is between 16 to 20 billion years. Hubble Telescope has verified it. It means that our universe did not exist before 20 billion years ago. It has taken a birth, and before that there was no time, no stars no heavenly bodies, no earth, no water, no air, no fire, no space, no *ether*, no matter, no energy, no fields, no rays, no particles and no human beings and no other living creatures. It leads to so many eternal ***unknown questions*** before the humanity, which are still unsolved?

It is just logical & acceptable by all the scientists that *there can't be any creation without any creator.* To every effect there must be a cause. ***Cause & Effect Law*** must hold. Was there some thing or many things or nothing before the creation of the universe? It is just logical and mathematical that if there was nothing before the creation, then the universe can't be created, of its own, out of nothing or without any cause? There must be some body, which has created the mysterious universe.

Science has observed that not even a single particle can be created or destroyed in the universe. It can be changed into one form to another form. Not even a single atom or a particle can be created of its own. Science has also observed that the universe has been made up of only one material and not two or more materials. The whole universe is made up of the same kind of matter throughout, which obeys the same laws of Natural Sciences, everywhere. How wonderful it is that the same laws of Natural Science are applicable in this vast Universe having a diameter approx. 20 billion light years. No scientific laws of natural science can be created of its own. Scientists are busy only to search or to find the laws, which already exist in the *ether*. So there must be a creator of all the laws of natural science we have searched through our scientific & technological researches. The scientists are further puzzled with great questions like:

- Who created the universe?
- Why the universe was created? What is the purpose behind the creation?
- For whom it was created, when there was none other?
- What material was used to create universe, as there was no material available before creation? How the heavenly bodies, matter, atomic and sub-atomic particles and living beings came into existence?
- How the non-materials like Ego, Mind, Intelligence, Pain, Pleasure, Sorrow, Bliss, Joy, Sex, Senses, Prana (Life Energy) and other Cosmic Energies came into existence?
- When there was a beginning of time?
- Will time run backwards from future to past?
- Is the universe finite or infinite or does it have boundaries or limits?

Due to the strong impact of Maya and delusion our scientist are unable to answer these questions correctly.

It is well known that the Natural Sciences can give answer of only to ***how*** of a phenomenon or an event and cannot answer satisfactorily the ***why*** of a phenomenon or an event. The questions mentioned above are beyond the preview of the Natural Science. The explanation to these has been given in our *Shastras.*

What is Brahman?

Brahman is the name for the ultimate, unchanging, reality, composed of pure being and consciousness. *Brahman* lies behind the apparent multiplicity of the phenomenon world, and is ultimately identical to the *Atman* or inner essence of the human being. *Vedas* have declared "***Braham vidam brahamaive bhavati*** (the knower of Brahman becomes Brahman).

Before the creation of the universe there was only one thing i.e. *Brahman (God alone).* He was in His absolute state of rest, *i.e. Sat, Chit and Ananda* (Truth-Consciousness-Eternal Bliss). There was no other individual or material or immaterial to share his infinite powers like Omnipotence, Omniscience, Omnipresent, Infinite Intelligence, Mind and Love. As sugar cannot taste sugar itself, some one else is needed to taste sugar. One cannot love oneself; someone else is needed to love. Similarly God also needs some one else to enjoy and experience his Super Powers and Supreme-Love. So He decided to create the universe from Himself and also created *Maya* or ignorance to divide and separate the creation from Him, into so many individual souls.

There was no other body, material, energy or field except God alone. So through His delusion & *Maya,* He decided to convert Himself into different kind of living beings, space, ether, air, fire, water, materials and heavenly bodies. All the different kind of matter and energies are nothing but God Himself. Since there was none other, He created the universe for Himself, by Himself and for none else.

So it is self evident that the He Himself is the whole universe. ***Whole Universe is God's Physical Body***, made up of Himself and for Himself alone. He has a full control on each and every atom of the universe. It is strange that we human beings have no control or a very little control on our physical body. Due to the delusion we don't know even what are the different parts and organs inside our body and how they are functioning inside our body? What chemical actions and reactions are always going on in our body? We can't change our body system as per our own sweet will, choice or desire.

All the atomic and sub-atomic particles are ***manifestation of 'Shiva & Shakti'***. *Shakti* means power or energy. *Shakti* is the manifestation of Godess *Mahakali* or *Durga (wife of Lord Shiva).* The centre of each atom known as the nucleus is stationary, which contains protons & neutrons. The electrons revolve & whirl around its nucleus with a very high speed. It is miraculous & strange that all the particles like electron, proton & neutrons spin billions of times in a second around their axis. The electrons revolve billion times in a second around their nucleus. Inspite of such a large number of revolutions inside the atom no particle collide with each other. The nature without an infinite intelligence can't do it. This can only be possible by accepting the infinite intelligence of God working behind the nature. Only God can do it. The nucleus of each atom is relatively stationary is *'Lord Shiva'* and the electron revolving round the nucleus (*Shiva*) is vibrant nothing but '*Shakti*'. Therefore all the atoms in the universe are nothing but a divine manifestation of '*Shiva & Shakti'*. '*Shiva*' is sitting at the centre of each atom and the '*Shakti*' is revolving round the '*Shiva*'.

Microscopically due to great delusion or *Maya,* human beings are unable to see actual motion of the atomic and sub-atomic particles and the reality. Due to delusion we see only what the almighty God wants us to see. The human mind is under the direct control of the Super Mind of God. ***On the other hand the microscopic structure of a living body is also a well organize arrangement*** of billions of microscopic living organism known as cell. These cells in a living body are not randomly or haphazardly placed but are further beautifully arranged in an organized network. As the blood cells are constantly moving and doing the great work of supplying oxygen, heat and so many chemicals to different parts of the body. Similarly in plants and other living bodies water, food, minerals & chemicals are supplied to its different parts by living cells. All these microscopic fine works are not visible to human naked eyes due to the delusion and *Maya.* If the human eyes could have seen the motion of these tiny particles and the living cells, the world would have been looked quite different to us and not as beautiful and attractive as it is now. It is the great ***Will*** of the God that we see the world as He wants us to see.

Macroscopically: Human eyes are unable to observe the whole universe all at a time. The human eyes can look only a tiniest and negligible portion of the universe at a time. We can never see the whole Sun or the whole Earth at a time. But God can see not only the whole universe but also each and every atomic and subatomic particle all at a time forever. Every thing is under His full control. Each Galaxy consists of billions of stars like Sun and each star has so many planets revolving around it. There are billions of such galaxies in the universe. Each galaxy has thousands of Black Holes, Novas, Super Novas, Neutron Stars, Red-giant stars and Quasars etc. There may be so many other heavenly bodies about which science does not know even today.

A Neutron Star is the Condensed Form of Dieing Matter

A Neutron star has a very small size of few kilometers only, but has a huge mass and huge gravitation. Its mass may be much more then our Sun and the gravitation on its surface is millions time more than the Sun. The matter inside this is in the neutron state of matter. In a neutron state of matter the space inside and outside the atomic & sub-atomic particles is minimized. In this state the whole galaxy may be reduced to a size of few meters and our earth will reduce to a size less then a football.

Any thing that takes birth in the universe must die one day. The matter inside the Neutron Star is in its dieing state to be finally digested by God.

Black Hole is the Mouth of God to Digest the Creation

A Black hole is a huge dead star in neutron state of matter. It has much more mass than a neutron star. The gravitation on its surface is so huge that nothing can escape out from its surface, while radiations can escape from a neutron star. Even the radiation of any kind or of light cannot escape its surface and again falls back into it. So nothing can come out of it. We cannot get any information of the object, which have fallen into the black whole. It simply stops existing for us forever. If by chance any object or a star comes under its gravitation, it will fall into it and we can never know any thing further about it. These black wholes are nothing but the ***Mouths of God*** through which the

Almighty God is digesting and annihilating its creation. In one portion of the universe new stars and new galaxies are created, in another portion so many stars and galaxies are disappearing through these black wholes. This creation and annihilation of anything can never be without the Super Powers of God. (Bhagwad Geeta Chapter XIII).

The computer is the great gift to man from God. But most of the non-believers think that one-day man will be able to manufacture a man from robot in the factories. This is a great misconception that they think that a computer has got an ego 'I', infinite intelligence and feelings too. They do not know that a computer has got zero or no intelligence. It simply computes very fast. It has no mind, no intelligence and no soul. It can never differentiate between beautiful and ugly; or good & bad. It can never have feelings of worries, happiness & sorrows, pains & pleasures, sleep & dream, joy & bliss, and laugh & weep etc. A computer is only a 100% obedient idiot servant but computes very fast.

We will never be able to create, any living being, without taking anything or something originally as the cause of life already existed & created by God.

Remember: "A little knowledge is a dangerous virus in your brain. It creates a false pride, kills our curiosity to know further, due to the influence of Maya. We should never be satisfied with our learning and knowing of new things. Also never be proud of your vast learning and knowledge. More we know about known, more we came to know about the unknown. Known is always finite, but unknown always remains infinite and increases too."

3

What are Miracles?

What are Miracles?

Prayer

O Mother Divine, teach me how to remove my ignorance and delusion due to Thy *Maya?* O Cosmic Sprit, reveal the great mystery behind Thy creation. There have always been great self-realized saints to prove Thy existence in most of the religions in the past and present. I humbly bow to all the saints, of all the religions. Tell me more about the saints who performed miracles to create a firm faith in Thee. Teach me how these saints were able to perform the miracles, to their disciples? O Beloved Mother, I know these are due to Thy powers, Thy infinite energy and Thy infinite divine love, which have been flowed out and expressed through them. Thou art behind all the saints of all religions and all their miracles. Divine Spirit what glory and what joy Thou art!

Miraculous Saints and Avatars

In this chapter we will learn about ***some of the miraculous saints and avatars***, all over the world, belonging to different religions and sects. The Holy books, the *Shastras & Puranas* and some history books are the proofs and witnesses of the recorded miracles performed by the numerous saints during and after their lifetime. It is our own limitation that, out of the millions of miracles performed by the saints so far; we have been able to record only a few. Other un-recorded miracles have been forgotten in a large time-span of the world history.

The saints have always performed so many miracles before the world, with their ultimate divine motto to make the people of the world to have an un-shakable faith in the

Almighty God. Their aim to perform a miracle was, never to get the benefits of publicity, money, fame or any petty material things, but to create a firm faith of the humanity in the creator God, His *Dharma* and His miraculous super powers. Such saints have no worldly desire of any kind.

The Bible, Hindu *Shastras* and the *Puranas* are ***not myths*** as claimed by some non-believers who have no knowledge of God and the *Shastras.* All the facts mentioned in all the Holy books or *Shastras* are verifiable and can be realized through the yogic science. During yogic *Samadhi* and the rise of *Kundalini-Shakti* the truth and every thing mentioned there in Shastras is fully revealed. The curtains of our ignorance and *Maya* are opened, and the delusion melts away. It is not justifiable or scientific to call the *Shastras* as mythology, as declared by some non-believer of God and biased historians who are unable to understand them. Most of the ***non-believers*** have a little or no knowledge of the holy books and *Shastras.*

The comments of a person, about something on which, he has no knowledge, is generally misleading, non-sense and of no value, however educated, prestigious and renowned he may be. It is similar to an illiterate man who has no knowledge of high tech researches of science and technology, scientific facts appears to him as false and myths. The understanding of the scientific facts is beyond his comprehension.

Similarly a person illiterate in Yogic Science, who has no faith in God cannot believe or comprehend the concept of miracles performed by so many saints and avatars. So, they have no right to give their comments without the complete knowledge of the holy books and about the yogis (religious scientists) and the practice of yoga. Generally their comments are misleading and biased against the religions they don't respect. Such non-believers have also a tendency to hide their comments against the miracles of the saints of their own religions, inspite of the fact they do not believe in their miracles also.

Who can deny the existence of the Shastras like the Ramayana, the Mahabharata, Vedas, the Bhagwat, 18 Puranas, the Upanishads, the Bhagwad Geeta and the Bible etc? Remember the Shastras are the reality and not Myth.

Bhagwan Ved-Vyas
(The Creator of most of the Shastras)

Who can deny the greatness of the greatest writer of most of the *Shastras* known as ***Bhagwan Ved-Vyas*** at the time of the Mahabharata nearly 3500 yrs B.C? He has written most of the above *Shastras* except the Bible. All the *Shastras* constitutes a huge writing in Sanskrit as original text in the mantra form, which are much more than a poetic language. In these *Shastras* the absolute truth is written in words arranged in a beautiful and scientific manner. These Holy *Shastras* are not copied from anywhere and cannot be a human creation unless God has transferred their contents directly to the mind of the writer internally. The content and the quality of these *Shastras* are beyond human thinking. An ordinary man can never write so many Holy *Shastras* in his short span of life, by his ordinary intelligence. If a man could write such huge *Shastras* in his lifetime then there would have been so many other writers like Bhagwan Ved-Vyas, but there is none else.

It is well known that Ved-Vyas was not physically present in the battlefield of *Kurukchetra* along with Arjuna and Krishna. And there was none who reported all the events to Ved-Vyas. How did Ved-Vyas, Sanjay and *Dhristrashtra* were able to listen and see the vision like a live-telecast and could remember each and every word of the talk between Lord Krishna and Arjuna in Bhagwad Geeta? Ved-Vyas knew everything about every body and every event during the Mahabharata. No doubt he had super powers and was omniscient & omnipresent.

It is false and childish to say that the natural science was highly advanced at the time of Krishna and the Mahabharata. The instruments like the TVs., airplanes and rockets were already invented. So many miraculous deadly weapons were used in the great Mahabharata *Kurukchetra* battle. In fact the people at the time of *Mahabharata*, were not as educated as we are today but they were much more ***spiritually advanced*** then the people in *Kali-yuga* and not at all more technically advanced.

Ved-Vyas was omniscient and must have the miraculous spiritual power of divine vision to see and to listen everything. He knew about all the events happening in the universe, sitting at his own place. A spiritually advance yogi knows each and everything happening in the universe and he does not need any scientific physical instrument for this purpose, just as God is omnipresent and omniscient and does not need any physical organs like eyes, ears and other sense organs to know about all of us.

All these Holy *Shastras* must have been transferred to Ved-Vyas by the Almighty God to provide the knowledge of His *Dharma* to humanity. This is a clear-cut proof of God's existence on earth. What else the man want to have a proof from God about His existence. Should God come to each and everyman's home, keep standing at his door and request like a beggar, till everyman accept Him as God or asks Him to run away from his door?

What are Holy Shastras?

Can we call any ordinary book written by any learned man as the *Shastras* or the Holy Book? Can we call an ordinary book as a Holy-Book, simply because it has been declared as a Holy-Book by some of the elected leaders or its religious head? Should there be any criteria to know whether a book is Holy or not? At present most of the writers of the world simply collect some text material to write their book from here and there. Such writings or the literary books collected from here and there cannot be an original literature created from God's power. A collection of historical events by a group of historians is generally biased and manipulated. Their writing is influenced as per their whims and choices. You may call them simply the historical books but not the *Puranas.*

A critical review of other writers is so simple to write by anyone. Also a biography of a man written by others cannot be called an autobiography. The collections of spiritual sayings, songs and writings of so many saints from here and there, by someone cannot be categorized as a *Holy Shastras.* All such types of collection books are just ordinary books available in the world. Some of the organizations may declare their ordinary books as the holiest book on earth. But these are excluded in my definition of *Holy Shastras in this book.* Whatever is written in *Holy Shastras* must be a changeless and timeless absolute truth and should be verifiable through the science of spirituality i.e. yoga. The *Shastras* must have come direct from God, but may be written through a human media.

Difference between the Belief and Faith

Belief: A belief is a statement or an event or a *hypothesis assumed to be true without verifying it.* We presume and accept that our belief is true. But a belief is *subject to change on verification and experimentation.* If the experiment regarding our belief is in favor, our belief becomes stronger, but if the experimental outcome is against our belief, the belief is shaken and discarded. After that, we may become non-believer in our belief or we may reject the hypothesis. Most of the scientific researches and the Laws are simply beliefs as follows:

1. If there is a hypothesis that some body believes that there are snakes in a house. But if after a through search it is found that there is no snake in that house. The belief of the man is shaken and changed. He will not believe further that there are snakes in the house.
2. If we have a hypothesis or a belief that a new medicine or herb cures the cancer. But after giving the medicine to many cancer patients it is found that it has no positive effect and have not cured any patient. After the experiment our original belief that the new medicine or herb cures the cancer will be discarded.

Faith: But a faith is much more than a belief. It is a statement or a hypothesis or an event, which is presumed to be true beyond its verification. Our faith is unshakable even if the outcome of the experiment or an event is against the faith. Faith does not depend upon the outcome of an experiment whether it is against or in favor. Faith is unchangeable and unshakable forever. For example:

1. If some one has a firm faith in God. If some accident or a bad incident happens in his life and his life becomes miserable. Even then his faith in God is not shakened. Even if the whole world makes a propaganda

that God does not exist, his faith in God is not changed at all. It remains the same unaffected by anything. *Bhagat* (disciple of God) *Prahalad* is a finest example.

2. A child has a faith in his mother and father. If by chance some accident happens, which harms the child due to the fault of the mother. The mother may be the cause of the accident even then the faith of the child in his mother is not shaken and his love for the mother will remain the same. Faith does not depend on the happening of the events in our favor or against us.

Difference between Miracle and Magic & What is Magic?

Magic is an art of performing hidden tricks, used by an individual (magician) to deceive the observers and viewers, before whom he performs a mysterious performance. The magician always uses some special objects, which he keeps with him for his help and uses them on the stage in the performance of his magic. Without such helping objects, magician cannot perform his magic. A magician cannot perform his magic in the absence of the viewers i.e. far away from a remote place. Magic is performed generally to extract money, from the ignorant viewers by pleasing them with hidden tricks.

Generally the observers are unable to detect the hidden tricks, used by the magician. It remains an unsolved mystery, till the tricks used by the magician are revealed to the observer. Magic is performed with a narrow aim of earning money, by pleasing the observers. Magic is simply a trick and not a miracle. It is not justifiable to say that there are no miracles, all are magic.

A magician cannot know your inner thoughts, your past and future events and your dreams. A magician cannot create any thing in your house from a distant place.

What are Miracles?

On the contrary, a miracle is not magic at all. In a miracle no trick is used, to deceive the observers. In a miracle there is no aim of earning money from the viewers and observers. The miracle is performed to create more firm unshakable faith in the existence of God and to have more devotion to God. The observer cannot understand the miracle, till he achieved some *siddhies* or self-realization.

Miracles are nothing but the operation of super-mind and super-conscious cosmic laws by someone who has mastered these laws. A miracle is a mysterious phenomenon or an event performed by someone including mother Nature, God and saints, generally seems to defy the known laws of our physical, natural and life science. No hidden tricks or special trick-objects like that of magician are used in their performance. The observers are unable to understand the unknown science behind the miracle, since the mind of the observer is under delusion, therefore the miracle is beyond his comprehension to understand. Examples of some of the miracles are:

Creation of an object out of nothing, without using any tricks or objects by so many saints.

- Few saints are found at different places at the same time, without using any transportation media. Some times a saint keep his existence even after his *Mahasamadhi* (death) and used to appear before his disciples after his death.
- A saint sitting continuously inside water for months together, meditating without any breathe, food and heart palpitation.

❑ Creation of *Vibhuti or Amrita* by Sri Sathya Sai Baba inside the homes of the millions of his disciples all over the world. Baba has never gone out of India except once in South Africa long back.

❑ Knowing everything about your life, past, present and future, even your dreams by a saint, whom you have never met earlier.

❑ Prediction of the date and time of their own *Mahasamadhi* (death) by the renowned saints. Non-disintegration of the body of Sri Paramhansa Yogananda for 22 days after taking his *Mahasamadhi* in California on 7th March 1952. It is a certified recorded event.

❑ Curing the patients from the incurable diseases and inabilities like blindness, deafness & dumbness, leprosy, lameness and TB etc. instantaneously, by the spiritual healers and saints. Jesus Christ and Sri Sathya Sai Baba are a great spiritual instantaneous healers.

❑ There are so many examples of rebirths remembering their past lives by so many children in the world. This confirms the rebirth of soul.

❑ Communication ability by so many telepathically.

❑ The art of Hypnotism.

❑ There are so many levitating saints, who raise their body suspended in the air. Many ordinary persons also posses this mental power and lift the body of others suspended in the air without any base. Body becomes weightless and regains weight at the will of their command.

❑ Many people and the saints in the world can walk bare footed on red-hot burnt wood-charcoal openly in front of thousands of people. They ask the viewers also to walk on the fire and assure them that they will not be burnt and harmed. Miraculously none is burnt out from viewers. Is it not a miracle?

❑ Many people have developed their mental powers to cut some of their body organs openly in front of others with knives, like their tongues and nose for some time. The observers without any doubt openly view the separated bleeding organ. After some time they again reattach the cutout organ with their body. Miraculously the cut organ is healed and cured immediately.

"*I will remember the deeds of the Lord;*
yes I will remember your miracles of long ago.
I will meditate on all your works
And consider all your mighty deeds.
Your ways, O God are holy.
What god is so great as our God?
You are the God who performs miracles;
You display your power among the peoples."

--- Psalm 77:1-2a, 3, 7-9, 11-14

The present is the historic times, when a major transformation and changes are taking place in the mind of human beings. Old ideas are replacing and the new ideas are born. Scientific laws are continually changing or modified by new researches. There had been so many instances in the world history about rebirth, reincarnation and re-getting life after death of a human soul.

We have now started to believe that our basic identity is not simply a physical body, having five senses, a mind and intelligence and which requires many things to keep it fit. But more fundamentally our basic identity is that our soul is a spark of the Spirit (the infinite Soul), which is pure infinite consciousness, universal and eternal.

Mind is the Creation of Super Consciousness of God

Due to the misconception most of the people thinks that mind and brain are same. But these two are totally different things. Mind is a cosmic energy. It is universal, eternal and one. Brain is simply a physical organ, an instrument of nearly 500 grams weight inside our skull. When mind-energy function in our brain it works. Without mind-energy the brain cannot function, as an electric fan cannot function without electricity. Doctors can operate the brain but not the mind, since it is not a physical thing. Our consciousness is beyond the death, time and space. Due to our *Ahankar ego* 'I', we feel that we have different minds. In fact there is only one mind energy throughout the universe, functioning in all different brains. There is a growing scientific confirmation that our mind is under delusion and our mind deceives us often believing otherwise. The material world is a manifestation of Spirit.

The great Jesus Christ performed so many miracles in his life. Thousands of his followers and many saints, who used to travel with him, witnessed his miracles. Due to his deep prayers many of the dead men got their lives again and many sick people were cured spontaneously from their deadly diseases like leprosy and others. The Bible is full of such miracles. We must not doubt upon such a great personality of Jesus who was the Son of God with super powers.

The Hindus are counting and celebrating their festivals like *Deepawali* and *Dussraha* every year after the Lord Rama. Not even a single festival has ever been missed and ignored. Similarly Hindus are celebrating Sri Krishan *Janamashtmi* festival each year after the Lord Krishna. Do not doubt upon the existence of Lords Krishna and Rama. Krishna was there in the human form 3251 yrs before the Jesus Christ. The comments of some of the western Europeans and historians who doesn't know the abc about Lord Rama and lord Krishna are not correct. Lords Krishna and Rama are not Myths. Since these people are not spiritual scientists, so the Lords Rama and Krishna are beyond their comprehension.

The *Shastras* like the Ramayana, the Mahabharata, the Bhagwad Geeta, the Bhagwat, the Puranas and the Bible are the great reservoir of thousands of miracles performed by Lord Rama, Lord Krishna and so many other great *rishies* and saints. At the time of the Ramayana even the *Rakshasas* like *Ravana, Kumbh-Karan (brother of Ravana) and Meghnath (son of Ravana*) and non-human beings (like *Hanuman, Jatau, Sampati and Jamwant* etc) had the power to perform miracles. They had the power to fly, magnify or diminish their physical bodies. They could fly and travel with a tremendous speed, create their weapons at their will during the battle etc.

At the time of Lord Rama the animals had the power to speak and learn the languages and knew the *Shastras*. They were having their own kingdoms like men. Most of the weapons, used by the warriors during their battles were divine and created spontaneously by their will power in the battlegrounds. The weapons used by them were not ordinary but divine weapons. Man had the miraculous power to create many things at his will in the past, which has been lost in *Kali-yuga* now, due to the ignorance and change of Yuga. We must try to regain our lost spiritual powers. Believe me it is possible.

The *Vedas* and *Shastras* like the *Ramayana*, the *Mahabharata, The Bhagwad Geeta, the Bhagwat* and the *Puranas* are ***not just myths***, fictitious and false imaginations. These are the reservoir of the absolute knowledge of God and His *Dharma* (religion). In these *Shastras* the words are so beautifully arranged in a poetic language, which no human being can write with ordinary human mind.

This is open challenge before the world. How these *Shastras* were written? Is it possible to write the *Shastras* without the grace of God? Certainly it is not. Vedas are the ***undisputed*** the oldest literature in the world. Vedas are ocean of knowledge of pure Spirit. In Vedas there no stories and no mention of any individual like lord Rama and lord Krishna or any other existing literature. But in all the *Shastras* there is description of Vedas. The Vedas are the storehouse of absolute truths (the truths which are independent of place, time and space). No human history is mentioned in Vedas. Vedas describes the creation of universe by God, when no human being was there in the universe. Vedas cannot be a human creation, but it must be a super human creation. Vedas were created before the creation of the life on earth and are also found in the hands of *Brahma (one of the Trinity) appeared in the beginning of the universe).*

Before Mahabharata Vedas were not available in written form. Vedas were use to be transferred orally from one generation to the next generation, by the gurus to their disciples. Later they came into written form by Bhagwan Ved-Vyas during the time of the Mahabharata. Bhagwan Vedvyas also wrote many Shastras. One can write such a huge literature only due to the transfer of knowledge, thoughts and ideas by the mercy of God directly to the writer.

There is a good example of transfer of knowledge by God to his disciple or a saint in our own times: ***Swami Ramakrishna Paramhansa*** (guru of swami Vivekananda) was neither educated nor literate. But he had a great devotion to God. His school education was negligible and he had never read books. One day he was taunted by one of the saint, who was educated, that Ramakrishna will not be able to get self-realization or knowledge of God, due to his lack of education.

By his comment Sri Rama Krishna was so much depressed that he went before the idol of goddess *Mahakali*, and decided to end his life. He whispered that O, Divine Mother, my birth is useless if I can't realize Thy Knowledge. I have no other purpose of life except to know Thee. As he was ready to cut his head by a sword, the goddess *Mahakali* appeared before him stopped him to suicide and blessed him with Her grace of Divine Knowledge. Miraculously he knew every thing in no time. Next day his disciples were exclaimed with wonder to note that Sri Ramakrishna knew so many languages and almost all the *Shastras* including Bible. Goddess *Mahakali* directly transferred the divine knowledge to him. In the similar way the *Shastras* were transferred to Sri Ved-Vyas and other saints to write.

During this event there were so many miracles: appearance and disappearance of goddess Mahakali out of nothing and transfer of the divine knowledge instantaneously to a human being. As per scientific logic only one miracle is enough to disprove the authenticity of the science. This miracle proves that there is much more to know beyond the science. The history of earth is a witness of millions of such miracles.

A Historical Recorded Miracle of Swami Haridas

This great miracle was historically recorded when Swami Haridas permitted and offered himself to be buried alive underground, for six weeks continuously before the court of Maharaja Ranjit Singh of Patiala, in Punjab. The miraculous performance was historically recorded under the seal of French and European doctors. The body of Swami Haridas was waxed and sealed inside a sack and kept in a stone chest, before the court and his body was buried several feet below the earth in the royal court. His body was fully secured and carefully watched for six weeks. The stone chest was opened. The sack and wax was removed. The doctors examined his body and declared it dead. But after few minutes the life again came into his body, eyes opened and Swami Haridas stood before the court and thousand of people as a witness. *It should always be remembered that a man of self-realization does not perform any miracle unless he has inward permission of God.*

"*Our mouths were filled with laughter,*
Our tongues with songs of joy…
The Lord has done great things for us,
And we are filled with joy…
Those who sow in tears will reap with songs of joy.
He who goes out weeping, carrying seed to sow,
Will return with songs of joy, carrying sheaves with him."

--- Psalm 126:2-3, 5-6

Remember: "Do not doubt upon the Holy Shastras created by God. They are not myths as said by some ignorant men. Each and every word of the Shastras is a truth and can be verified through deep communion with God. The collections of the various statements, facts or the writings by a man or group of persons from various sources are not Shastras or holy books. Shastras are revealed to a self-realized writer, directly from God and can't be written by a man of ordinary intelligence, however great he may be."

"As per our past actions (karmas) in this or previous lives, we may have some problems, diseases and difficulties in this life. But we shouldn't worry; these are the tests of our patience to have the firm & unshakable faith in God. Never doubt upon the existence of Almighty God, if the events in our life are not in our favor as per our desires. We do not know our future. But we also do not know what is the best for us. Only the God knows our best requirement and needs."

For example: Inspite of his best efforts, once a man could not get a seat in the air-flight in which he was very much interested and was in need of it. He was cursing God and everyone for the non-availability of his seat. Later on, that unfaithful flight was crashed and every body on board died. This was a great lesson and enough for him to have an unshakable faith in God.

4

Saints Seem to Defy the Laws of Sciences

Miraculous Great Saints

Swami Pranavananda Saint with Two Bodies
Levitating Saint Negendra Nath Bhadudi
Blissful Saint Master Mahashyia
Perfume Creating Ghandh Baba
Sleepless Saint Ram Gopal
Miraculous Adi Shankaracharaya
Vedvyas the Creator of Shastras
Ram Krishan Paramhansa, Swami Vivekananda
Guru Nanak Dev & Other Sikh Gurus
Nostradamus the Dreamer of the Future
Tralinga Swami & Lahari Mahasyia
Sri Paramhansa Yogananda
Non-Eating Saint Giri Bala
Saint of Extreme Devotion Meera Bai
A Child-like Saint Sri Anand Mai Maa
Sri Aurobindo, Srila Prabhupada
Maharishi Mahesh Yogi, Jesus Christ
List of few Miraculous Saints one should know further
There should be no Contradiction Between the Religions
Misconceptions about Gurus & How to Select a Guru?

Saints Seem to Defy The Laws of Science

Prayer

O Spirit Divine, Come Thou in my temple of silence. Thou art just behind the curtain of *Maya.* Thou art my Creator, my Guru, my Teacher, my Soul, my Friend and my Love. Thou art the saint of all religions. Thou saints are Thy incarnation doing Thy work. I bow them all.

Divine Mother, Thou all the laws of science are miraculous, but Thou saints are more miraculous. The each phenomenon of Thy wonderful universe is also miraculous. But my little mind is unable to understand Thy miraculous creation fully and their mysteries unless Thou help me to understand, through Thy infinite vision.

Thy saints know Thy reality and are beyond Thy *Maya.* Thou hast revealed them Thou secret of wonderful creation. Thou art the Creator of all the laws of nature, science and the universe. Nothing is beyond Thy omnipresent omni-power and nothing is impossible for Thee.

Miracles by The Great Saints

Sri Paramhansa Yogananda was a great seer & yogi-saint of India who lived his later life in USA. He has written a detailed description about himself & so many miraculous yogis and saints from all over the world in his famous book "***Autobiography of a Yogi***". Sri Yogananda has mentioned about some of the miracles performed by some of the great yogis and saints. The greatest of them is ***Sri Mahavtar Babaji***. All the yogis mentioned in his book were pure, simple, renounced and honest men. None of them was interested in moneymaking or any kind of self-publicity or intellectual dishonesty. They were not interested in taking anything from their disciples. All these saints are miraculous. Their simple aim to show the miracle to their disciples was to change their shakable belief into a firm & unshakable faith in God. For the spiritual awakening and to transform your soul & previous beliefs I would like to acquaint you with some of the miracles performed by these saints. The science has till now *ignored the miracles* performed by all the saints during their lives. Probably it is due to their own limitations to explain them scientifically. But it will be interesting and worthwhile to know about their miracles.

1. ***Swami Pranavananda*** the saint of India had the ability to materialize his two physical bodies, at two different places at the same time. It is just impossible as per all the existing laws of science and is really a great miracle, if it is true. Pranavananda seems to violate the famous Law of conservation of matter and energy and most of the other existing scientific laws. He had the power to disintegrate and again integrate the atoms, molecules and living cells of his body as per his simple desire. To perform such a miracle he did not need any laboratory equipments, materials or instruments. It is really unbelievable, how the same person can exist at different places at the same time? How he can walk, talk, think and perform all the functions of a human being in two different bodies at different places at the same time? How he is able to materialize and dematerialize another body and further transport the same to other place instantaneously? How he is able to create the duplicate of his soul or two of his egos 'I' in two different bodies at the same time?

Space, time and place have no meaning for such a yogi. He seems to be the master of physical matter, time & energy and their governing laws. Not only Pranavananda but also so many other yogis are also able to do the same miracles in their lives in past and present. If it is true, which I am sure is really true, then why the scientists are silent about it? Why do they not confirm the happening or not happening of these miracles and enlighten the world through their further researches by clarifying these miracles?

2. ***Sh. Negendra Nath Bhadudi*** was an Indian levitating yogi saint. He was the master of art of *pranayam i.e.* the science of controlling the *prana* (life force) and recharging the body at our will. During pranayam his body automatically used to levitate & lift from the ground and remains standstill, hanged in the air, many feet above the ground. His body used to become weightless. There have been always so many yogis and some of the magicians too, who have this power to make the human body weightless and keep it suspended in the air by simply controlling their mentai power.

This miracle is against the existing law of gravity. A human body is much heavier then air. How a heavier body can become lighter then air and is lifted above the ground without any base and remains suspended into the air for quite a long time without any support? Further he was able to bring back his weight and his body on the ground as per his will, without using any scientific instrument. In doing all this, he had not to do any effort or to use any trick. It was just simple at his will and command of his mind. He never used any trick to perform this miracle.

To understand better and deeper about the gravitation, the scientists should not shy but learn from such yogis and other persons who can also do the same. It may solve our so many problems and the great problem of fuel requirement in the transportation of vehicles from one place to another.

3. ***Ever Blissful Master Mahashyia*** was a great yogi saint of India. He was always in p*armananda* (eternal bliss) & joy. The joy, bliss and p*armananda* are the ultimate aim of achievement of all the human beings. All the actions of our life are based to bring in life more and more joy & bliss. The parmananda of Master Mahashyia was much more then a multibillionaire's state of bliss. Some of the men are ready to spend even billions of US $ to achieve this state of bliss in there busy, sad and boring lives. Master Mahashyia has proved that the permanent joy and bliss are not to be achieved from outside our physical body, but it is hidden inside our soul. We should know the actual yogic scientific techniques to explore out our hidden ananda, joy and bliss. If the scientists are able to understand the real source of *eternal bliss & ananda*, the world will entirely change and will be peaceful.

4. The saint ***Ghandh (perfume) Baba*** from India was able to create any kind of perfume from a flower or even without flower. He had the power to convert an old decayed flower, which has lost its perfume to make it fresh and full of fragrance. Such a yogi is able to create a complex chemical of his own choice at his will, without any equipment? How he could do it?

It is a miracle violating the laws of chemical combinations, 2nd Law of Thermo-dynamics and many others. One cannot produce any perfume out of nothing. One cannot convert an old thing into a new thing. It is against the 2nd law of thermodynamics i.e. time cannot flow from future to past. Even today we do not know much about the fragrances. Why the scientists are silent and ignoring this miracle? The study of this miracle can enhance our knowledge of natural science that how the complex chemicals are formed in plants and animals and many unsolved mysteries of the Mummies of Egypt.

5. ***A sleepless saint Ram Gopal*** lived in Himalayas and had a victory over his sleep. He did not need to sleep for years together. Generally every body needs a sleep when our body is tired and exhausted due to the discharge of stored life energy in the body cells. Sleep is needed again to re-charge the body cells and refresh our body with life energy. But due to the advance meditation the yogi like Ram Gopal was able to recharge his body with life energy, so that sleep was not required. The medical science is unable to understand fully this achievement. It needs further research work by the scientists on sleep, reception & exhaustion of life energy and how to recharge our tired body?

6. ***The Miraculous Revered Saint-Avatar Adi Shankaracharaya:*** Adi Shankaracharaya was a rare spiritual incarnation of Lord *Shiva.* He took birth in south India some time after Lord Buddha and before Christ. He was a genius and miraculous child by birth. At the age ***one*** only he was fluent in his mother tongue. At the age of ***two*** he could read and memorize the stories from *Puranas* in Sanskrit. When he was ***five*** he joined his Guru's *ashram.* At the age of ***seven*** he returned to his home after completing the studies of all the *Vedas, Upanishads, Vedangas, Puranas and Vedanta* etc. Every body was surprised to

observe his extraordinary power of learning and his achievements.

After his studies he took *Sanyias* at the age of seven in his childhood and left his house. But he assured his old mother to come to her at the time of her death. He got his *Diksha* from a renowned Guru named Gobind Bhagwatpad. Very soon he achieved self-realization. Before him all the *Shastras* were written in Sanskrit and it was not a common man language at his time. He translated and interpreted all the *Shastras* in the common man language. Very soon he became famous all over India. God Shiva also gave him *darshana (appearance) blessed* and advised him to translate and interpret *'Bhramsutras'. Bhagwan* Ved-Vyas also appeared before him blessed and advised him to propagate the *Adwait* (non-duality) Vedic-philosophy i.e there is nothing other then Brahman in the universe..

He established so many *Matths (ashrams)* in different parts of the country. He had the power to appear and disappear at any place at any time. It is miraculous that he traveled throughout India without any transport vehicle and roads in his very short life span of 32 years. He is the founder of the institution of *Shankaracharaya Maths* (The highest adorable post of Hindus) tradition in India.

After Buddha, so many kings like Ashoka in India and of many other countries adopted Buddhism as the royal religion. Most of the forefathers of Hindus were converted to Buddhism through those rulers. The whole of India became just a Buddhist country before the time of Adi Shankaracharaya. But it is miraculous that due to the great extraordinary powers & spiritual personality of Adi Shankaracharaya, the forefathers of Hindus surrendered at his feet and again converted themselves as Hindus at his revered feet. It was due to his miraculous divine personality & not due to any coercive force or power.

No body can deny that the Adi Shankaracharaya is a miraculous historical fact. How a child at such an early age of seven years can learn all the *Shastras* and also translate and interpret them? How he was able to travel throughout India without any road and any transport vehicle and any communication at that time? How Shankaracharaya alone was able to convert the whole of India again from Buddhist to Hinduism? How he achieved the ability of appearing and disappearing at any place? Adi Shankaracharaya is neither a myth nor any fiction. Why the science has not studied his miraculous personality and not clarified such a spiritual event to the world? A scientific study of such a saint can definitely help a lot in the development of the human personality. India should come forward to start with such studies.

7. ***Vedvyas: The Saint-Avatar & Creator of so many Shastras***

Bhagwan Vedvyas was the grand father of Arjuna nearly 3500 B.C. He was the son of *Satiyawati*. He took his *Sanyias at early age* and lived a renounced life in forest away from the palace & the crowd of the people. He was an incarnation of God and Knowledge. He is the creator of the most of the Hindu *Shastras*. Before Vedvyas all the Vedas were used to transfer orally from the Gurus to their disciples & from one generation to next generation. He divided the Vedas into four parts. He has the honor to write all the four Vedas first time in Sanskrit in the book-form and that is why his name is Ved-Vyas. He is the originator of *The Great Maha-Bharata, The Bhagwat Geeta, The Srimad Bhagwat* and the eighteen *Puranas*. He is the writer of so many, *Brahamsutras, Upanishads and Vedangas*. He is undoubtedly the greatest writer on the earth. No human being can write so much as the original literature or text of such a high quality in his short lifespan. It is said that these *Shastras* were written with the cooperation of the Lord *Ganesha.* Vedvyas used to think and speak and the Lord Ganesha used to write simultaneously. How Vedvyas had the knowledge of every thing without any investigation, recording, collection, searching and listening about the incidents and events happened from others during the Mahabharata? It is said that he was *omniscient and omnipresent* and need not to ask anything from any body.

It is said that Bhagwan Ved-Vyas is still alive and in his physical body. He has given his *Darshan* (appearance) to so many. Adi Shankaracharaya is one of them. He is undisputedly the greatest writer on earth, till now. If science could understand Ved-Vyas, it would definitely change the future of the world. There cannot be any doubt in this.

8. ***Swami Ramakrishna Paramhansa:***

Sri Ramakrishna Paramhansa was a great saint of modern India. He was born in India on 17th Feb. 1836 AD in *Bengal* state. *Paramhansa* is the highest order degree in spiritual achievement. It is much higher then the degree of *Swami.* His childhood was also full of miracles. He first achieved *Samadhi* at the age of four and after that it was his usual daily practice. He could get only the primary education. He had all the qualities of a devotional saint. He was the Guru of the famous saint Swami Vivekananda. The world knows him due to his disciple Vivekananda.

He was appointed as the priest (*pujari*) of the famous Dakshineshwar Temple in Calcutta. His Guru was Totapuri who gave him *Diksha* to seek God. Very soon he achieved selt-realization. Later Totapuri and so many other saints considered him worthy of *Paramhansa* order after his thorough spiritual tests. He had the ability to convert sand into gold and gold into sand. He had the miraculous power to provide a spiritual experience of God and raising their *Kundalini* by the simple touch of the body of his disciples. Vivekananda was one of them. Only very few yogis can do it. He had a great regard for all women in the world. He used to worship the women as goddess and his wife too.

He was not much literate and did not read any book. Once an educated person taunted him that he will not be able to achieve self-realization, since he was illiterate. He went before the idol of Goddess *Mahakali* in his temple and said that it was useless for him to live any more, if I cannot achieve self-realization. As he was just ready to cut his head by a sword at that moment Goddess *Mahakali* appeared before him and blessed him with divine Knowledge of God. Next day he knew miraculously all the Shastras including Bible and Koran and so many languages. Every body was surprised, from where he got the knowledge of all the *Shastras*, without even reading anything? If it is true then we can say with a great confidence that the knowledge comes from within & our soul is omniscient. There is ignorance over it. Science has to do further research work on such a saint to find out, how to explore the knowledge from within, for the benefit of the humanity?

9. ***Swami Vivekananda:***

Swami Vivekananda was a great famous saint of India. He was disciple of great saint Ramakrishna Paramhansa. He was a graduate from Calcutta University. He took spiritual education and practice from his guru from 1881 to 1886 A.D. He took *Sanyias* later and never married. He had an extraordinary strong will power to achieve his aims. He faced many problems in his life including money. After his *Sanyias* he worked hard to achieve self-realization.

From 1886 to 1893 AD Swami Vivekananda was on tour throughout India. He studied a lot about the Indian culture and the difficulties of the people of India. He worked a lot to eradicate the difficulties of people. He attended the World Religious Conference at Chicago, USA in 1905 and represented Hindus. He was considered the best participant and the most advance spiritual personality in the conference. Everybody was looking for him after the conference. He had all the qualities of an ideal personality like very good health, handsome, genius, spiritual teacher, leadership, devotion to God, knowledge and the nation builder. He died at an early age at his Bellure ashram.

10. ***Sri Guru Nanak Dev Ji & other Sikh Gurus***

Sri Guru Nanak was the first Guru out of the ten Gurus of Sikh *Panth* (religious path) in India. He was a self-realized saint. He was born in Punjab state in India on 15th April 1469 AD. At that time, India was under the cruel Muslim rulers. Other ten Sikh Gurus created a history and sacrificed their children & their own lives for the survival & sake of Hindu *Dharma* against the cruel Muslim rulers in India. From the very childhood Sri Guru Nanak Dev was peaceful and used to sit alone and devote most of his time to meditate on God. He also ignored his parental business & earning money. Soon he achieved self-realization. He is famous for the performance of many miracles in his lifespan in the world. He was embodiment of peace and love.

Out of so many miracles one of his famous miracles is: Once he was sleeping in Mecca with his feet towards the famous *Kaaba Mosque* (said to be the house of Allah), in the direction towards which Muslims used to offer their *Namaj*. This was objectionable to *Kaji* (police man) of Mecca, who asked him not to keep his feet towards the direction of Allah. Guru Nanak said politely to the *Kaji* to rotate and correct his feet in the direction in which there is no house of God or Allah. It is said that when his feet were rotated in any other direction, the *Kaaba* of Mecca was also rotated in that direction. The *Kaaba* of Mecca was found in all the directions. Through this miracle he convinced his disciples that God is omnipresent in all directions and there is no fixed particular direction for offering our *Namaj* (Muslim prayer). The list of other gurus in chronological order is:

Sri Guru Angad Dev Ji	Sri Guru Amar Daṣ Ji
Sri Guru Ram Das Ji	Sri Guru Arjun Dev Ji
Sri Guru Har Govind Ji	Sri Guru Hari Rai Ji
Sri Guru Hari Krishan Ji	Sri Guru Teg Bahadur Ji
Sri Guru Govind Singh Ji	

All the ten Gurus were the followers of Sanatan Dharma & had faith in Lords Rama, Krishna, Vedas & all the Hindu Shastras. They even sacrificed their lives for the sake of these. But the tenth and the last Guru Sri Guru Govind Singh started the new Khalsa Sikh Panth in 1659 A.D. The cruel Muslim ruler Orangjeb crucified two of his sons, by cementing them alive inside a wall of bricks openly before the public to create terror. The other Gurus also faced the cruelties of Muslim rulers; they fought and sacrificed so many things in their lives for the sake of *Sanatan Dharma* (The Eternal Hindu Religion).

The followers of Sikh *Panth* were assigned to wear five specific kinds of things such as turban, beard, kada (iron bangle), keep a kripan (small sword) & follow the *Guru-Granth-Sahib*. Later some of the followers started ignoring their faith in Lords Rama, Krishna, *Vedas* & other Hindu *Shastras* due to some of the temptations of minority rights provided in the Indian constitution. In the beginning the Sikh *Panth* was a sect (part) of Sanatan Dharma, but now some of them call themselves separate from it. As per the definition of Hindu word in UNO all the followers of Sanatan Dharma, Sikh *Panth*, Jainism and Buddhism are Hindus. Before the independence of India, all the four used to call themselves as Hindus.

15. Nostradamus:
(A miraculous dreamer of the future of the World)

Nostradamus was the famous French physician who made thousands of major world prophecies. He saw the future of the world as a great prophet or dreamer. He was a great saint from France. He was born in 1555 AD. He was a miraculous man and has predicted thousands of main events about the future of the world. It is a strange that thousands of predictions have already come out to be true. He had the ability to saw the great future events of the world in his dreams and visions. The great future events used to come to his mind as vision just like a drama in a dream or a movie film on the screen. Nearly half of his predictions have come out to be true and the rest are also supposed to be true. Among his great predictions are the two world wars, the freedom of India by Mahatma Gandhi. The world has still to watch & witness the truthfulness of the rest of his predictions, which will occur in the next few hundred years.

In India there have always been numerous distinguished astrologers, who have the ability to predict accurately about the future of a man on astrological mathematical calculations. Astrology is an exact mathematical science, but it depends upon the experience & the mastery of the astrologer on his subject.

How a man is able to predict the future of the world so accurately? How the exact picture of the future events, which has still not occurred, comes to the mind of Nostradamus so accurately? Who projected these future movies to his mind? How he was able to receive the future dream vibrations from the Mind of God, but others are not able to do so? Does it not prove that the whole universe is not a reality, but it is just a great dream or a thought or a pre-planned idea in the Mind of God as informed by the Hindu *Shastras* and the great saints? All the past, present and future events are already stored it *ether*. Only we have to learn to catch these vibrations stored in ether. Every event in the world is already pre-decided.

Why God chose to show the miracles through its saints for the benefit of the world? The aim is to create a firm faith in Him. Why our learned scientists are silent and ignoring these great miracles. If sciences accept the existence of God, what is the harm in it? Will the science not remain as science after accepting the existence of God? In so many scientific theories, scientists have already accepted & presumed so many imaginary hypotheses and presumptions without any basis and without verifying their validity. As in the past, some of the hypotheses may be wrong and will change in future. Why should not science accept the existence of God, which is an absolute Reality & Truth? It will answer so many unanswerable questions of science.

16. Sri Tralinga Swami & Sri Lahari Mahasyia

Tralinga Swami was a famous saint of Varanasi in India in the end of the 18th century. He had a mass following of thousands of disciples all over the country. He was well known to millions of disciples as a miraculous saint. He was nearly 300 years old and had nearly 300 lb wt. His weight was increasing by one pound every year. He used to eat very little after weeks of fast. He was habitual to break his fast with some curd and juice only and used to perform so many miracles openly. He didn't like to wear clothes on his body even in winters and preferred to be naked. He was in the habit of taking his *samadhi* by levitating on the surface of water or inside the Ganges water for weeks continuously. During *samadhi* he didn't take any food or any breathe for weeks altogether and used to sit stand still, breathless in lotus posture before every body.. Tralinga Swami always used to keep *Mauna* (do not speak to any body).

By these wondrous miracles Tralinga Swami was able to convince his disciples that the oxygen, water, food and clothes are not necessary to survive and sustenance of life. Our physical body is sustained by some super vital energy, cosmic energy or *prana*. Tralinga Swami had a victory over the physical matter & death. Instead of food he used to live on cosmic consciousness.

As per the laws of British Government, it was an offence to be naked openly in public. But Tralinga Swami was not conscious of his physical body and the laws of the government. For him to wear or not to wear clothes had no meaning. The British police officers put him behind the bars and locked him inside the jail so many times for his offence of wearing no clothes in public. But it was always miraculous to find out that he was out of the locked jail room, without opening the locks by anyone. For him locked rooms of jails had no meaning. He had the spiritual power to transport his body to any place without any obstacle.

Deadly poisons had no effect on his body. Many times he drunk the poison publicly but was never affected by it. How he was able to do all these miracles, without using any trick or equipment? Clearly he was a *sidhpurusha* who had a victory over his physical body & physical matter. He had also mastered many other super-powers. Although he was a great *sidhpurusha*, but still he could not achieve self-realization, for which he was doing these best efforts. It is clear from the following incident:

At his time there was a great saint of Varanasi, known as ***Sri Lahari Mahasyia***, who was also his neighbor and a good friend. Sri Lahari Mahasyia was a *grahasthi* (one who is married and living with his family) and was not so famous and known to the public. But Sri Lahari Mahasyia was a self-realized saint and direct disciple of Sri Mahavtar Babaji. Tralinga Swami used to pay Lahari Mahasyia an extraordinary high respect & reverence. Once Tralinga Swami honored Sri Lahari Mahasyia publicly. He even broke his habitual *mauna* (silence), and spoke few words of honor for Lahari Mahasyia. Many of his disciples didn't like it, and many of them objected to it. One asked Tralinga Swami, "Swami, you are a renowned *Sanyiasi of high fame,* why are you paying so much respect to an ordinary *grahasthi* man, who is not well known to any body?"

The reply of Tralinga Swami was remarkable: He said, "My child, Lahari Mahasyia is a divine genius child of the Divine Mother, and he has achieved self-realization of the highest order. It is only to achieve self-realization that I renounced my family, my village, the world, and even my clothes long ago. I used to keep m*auna,* remain nude, keep fast, and meditate above or inside the water for months together only to achieve self-realization. I am still trying my best, but Sri Lahari Mahasyia has already achieved self-realization. That is the reason why I bow my head to him and have left my mauna for him"

No doubt that Sri Lahari Mahasyia was a God-realized saint with miraculous powers also. He was poor and had a big family to support. He had the liability to fulfill many social responsibilities. But he demonstrated for the modern world, an ideal balanced life that can be achieved by combining meditation i.e. our duty to God with the worldly duties.

17. Sri Paramhansa Yogananda:

Paramhansa Yogananda was born on January 5, 1893 AD, in Gorakhpur, India in a Bengali family. He has been recognized as one of the greatest spiritual teacher form India to the west (USA). His yogic teachings are universal, timeless and a great inspiration to all the God-seekers of all races and creeds in the world.

Since his childhood he was recognized as a great spiritual seeker of Truth and God. When he was young, he was in search of a self-realized Guru. His father helped him and he met so many great spiritual saints of India in his spiritual quest. Ultimately, Swami Sri Yukteshwar Giri, who was a great spiritual yogi. He accepted Yogananda as his disciple in 1910. Sri Yukteshwar Giri was the disciple of Sri Lahari Mahasyia. Yogananda did his graduation in 1915 from Calcutta University on the advice of Mahavtar Babaji.

In 1920, Yogananda was invited to International Congress of Religious Leaders convening in Boston (USA) as India's delegate. He addressed there on the topic "The Science of Religion". Every body enthusiastically received his lecture. In the same year 1920 he also founded Self-Realization Fellowship (SRF) in USA to disseminate his teachings on India's ancient science and philosophy of yoga and its time-honored tradition of meditation, throughout the world. During the years 1920 to 1935, he delivered his extensive lectures on yoga to full capacity audiences in major cities of the United States. *The Los Angeles Times reported,* "The Philharmonic Auditorium presents the extraordinary spectacle of thousands being turned away an hour before the advertised opening." There were writings on the walls of USA, " A Hindu has attacked America, to bring God here."

In his lectures Sri Paramhansa Yogananda emphasized the underlying unity of great religions of the world. His teachings are mainly concerned with the direct experience of God through Yoga, mainly meditation. He revived and gave *Diksha* for the soul awakening techniques of *Kriya Yoga* to his disciples. This technique was lost in the dark ages of time. His great Guru Sri Mahavtar Babaji is said to be many millenniums years old and still alive, initiated his Guru's Guru Sri Lahari Mahasyia in Kriya Yoga.

Sri Paramhansa Yogananda has written his famous books: ***Autobiography of Yogi***. This is the only autobiography of a yogi available. Others are biographies written by others. His autobiography is full of his interaction with the so many great miraculous saints of the world.
The Men's Eternal Quest, The Divine Romance, Journey to Self-Realization and God Talks with Arjuna (Two Volumes) are the books for advance spiritual seekers. These are the collection of his lectures delivered in USA.

Lessons in Self-Realization:
These are nearly 200 lessons. In these lessons Paramhansa Yogananda has written and arranged systematically the instructions of the art of *Kriya Yoga* to be followed by his disciples, which compliments the need of a self-realized Guru not easily available these days.

Among his great disciples were:
Mahatma Gandhi, C.V. Raman, Luther Burbank, George Eastman, poet Edwin Markham etc. In 1927, the President of USA Mr. Calvin Coolidge officially received him at the White House.

On 7th March 1952, Paramhansa Yogananda entered *Mahasamadhi* (knowingly leaving the body by the soul and a permanent communion with God after which the soul does not come back to the body again) in California USA. His passing away was marked by an extraordinary phenomenon or a ***miracle***. His body was fresh, peaceful & smiling even after more then 20 days. A notarized statement signed by the Director of Forest Lawn Memorial-Park testified: "*No physical disintegration was visible in his body even twenty days after death.... This state of perfect preservation of a body is so far as we know from mortuary annals, an unparalleled one... Yogananda's body was apparently in a phenomenal state of immutability.*"

17. A Non-Eating Saint Giri Bala
Sri Giri Bala was a non-eating lady saint from Bengal in India. Sri Paramhansa Yogananda visited her place during his visit of India pilgrimage in 1935 AD. From the very childhood Giri Bala used to eat too much and was a cause of great worry to her parent. After her marriage her in-laws mentally tortured her, due to her excessive abnormal diet. Her life had become very much miserable & difficult to

live in family. She tried her best but she had no control over her diet.

One day she was very much depressed and prayed to God, "*O, Lord, please send me a guru who can teach me to live by Thy light and not by Thy food*". Instantly her prayer was heard and a guru was send to her by God. Her Guru appeared before her and blessed her with some sacred mantras. She was taught *Kriya* technique and some special breathing exercises that made her body free from dependence on food. From that very day she was free from her hunger and quest. She didn't take any food, water or fluid till her death in old days. Giri Bala used to materialize the chemicals and energy needed by her body direct from the cosmic life energy (*prana*) received from the medulla oblongata.

There have been so many saints like Giri Bala in India & other countries who never ate or drink anything in their lives. *Giri Bala & Neumann of Bavaria* are two rare examples of saints who are a clear proof of the fact that our physical body does not depend solely upon food and the life force is the essential energy for the body to sustain and to depend upon.

Since there has been a small number of such non-eating saints, science have wrongly declared that human being cannot live very long without eating food & drinking water. We ordinarily think that we cannot live without breath also. But when we go in deep meditation or a *samadhi* we do not need any breath for a long time. We know it can be done by so many. Even our heart may not palpitate for long during deep meditation.

But by the examples of the non-eating saints, I do not mean to ignore food by anybody. Food is the most essential ingredient to keep our body healthy and free from diseases. What I mean to say is, along with our balanced diet full of vitamins and minerals, we must also energize our body with the life force received by the medulla oblongata from the cosmos by deep meditation.

18. Meera Bai:
(The Miraculous Saint of Extreme Devotion)

Meera Bai was a great lady saint of India, born nearly 450 yrs before, in a royal family of king Rattan Singh at the time of the renowned saints like *Tulsi Das* and *Soor Das.* Since her childhood, she was a faithful devotee of Lord Krishna. She was married to the prince Bhoj Raj of Chittorgarh in Rajasthan. But even after her marriage Meera was too much devoted to her *Sadhna* to seek God. She ignored her daily routine & duties of royal life of queen. She used to call so many poor fellows who were devoted to God, right inside her palace. She used to dance with them for long in the glory of God. She was fond of *Satsanga* with them throughout the day.

Due to her abnormal behavior and actions, which were not upto the standard of a queen, her in-laws became deadly against her extreme *bhakti* (devotion) and worshiping of Lord Krishna throughout the day. A royal queen was supposed to be a symbol of luxury, a ruling power, a prestigious living and to have a life-philosophy for eat, drink and merry. A queen was not supposed to be mixed with ordinary poor public men. Her in-laws tried their best to change her but failed as Meera had already lost her consciousness in the bliss and joy of God's devotion. She didn't bother for their objections.

Having no other alternative the in-laws decided to kill her. They began to torture her in so many cruel ways. She lost her husband only five years after her marriage at a young age. Once she was sent a cup of deadly snake poison to drink. Having unshakable faith in God, Meera drunk the poison cheerfully & miraculously, but nothing happened to her. A deadly cobra was sent to bite her, but that too hadn't done any effect of poison on her body. She had extreme devotion to Lord Krishna and had completely surrendered to Him. It is said that lord Krishna used to appear and dance with her.

She had written hundred of *Bhajans* (songs in the glory and devotion for God), which are not ordinary songs but are expressions of her rare and true inner experiences. Only a self-realized saint can write such *Bhajans* (sons in the glory of God). Her *Bhajans* are of greatest help in creating a true love and devotion for God to the yogis. She was a true saint and always preferred God, in place of enchanting temptations & distracting material things of the world.

Ultimately, she left her palace. She preferred as a beggar in search of God instead of luxurious life of a queen. In her times it was most difficult for a queen to leave her palace, to live outside home alone and become a poor beggar. She traveled many religious places in India on bare foot, met so many great saints like Sri Tulsi Das & Sri Soor Das to establish that the men and women both have the equal right in search of God. Women cannot be deprived from the Knowledge of God.

Meera is a historical fact. What researches the scientists and psychiatrists have done to study deeply about such a miraculous personality? Why should we ignore Meera? Is it not a scientific biasedness?

19. Anand Moyi Ma (a Childlike Saint)

Sri Anand Moyi Ma was a Bengali and great lady saint of India. She was always a joy-permeated and a blissful saint. It is said that in the past incarnation Sri Paramhansa Yogananda was his father. The Blissful Mother had a mass following of her disciples and she had many good Ashrams in Banaras, Kankhal (Haridwar), New Delhi, Calcutta and all over India. Most of the times she used to remain in ecstatic state of *samadhi.* Her eyes usually remained fixed at eternity, glanced heavenward, half opened and standstill. She had an aura around her body.

As she was always in *samadhi,* she was not able to look after & took care her body and food. A group of her disciples always used to travel with her, to feed and look after her comforts. She never demanded food or anything for her. Her disciples used to feed her with their own hands like a child. Even when meals were placed before her, she was not able to feed herself. She was not aware of her body and its needs.

She was a God-realized soul & had the miraculous power to cure the sick by simply touching with her hands. She traveled widely all over India and had the power to transform and create love & faith in God in her disciples.

20. Sri Aurobindo

Sri Aurobindo was born in Calcutta on 15th August 1872. He got his early education in England at King's College Cambridge. He had learnt so many languages like French, Latin, German, Greek Italian & Spanish. He was a great scholar. He took part in the freedom struggle & movement of India and the Indian politics. He went jail many times in 1906, 1907 and 1909 AD. During his jail he has written so many spiritual books of high order.

Sri Aurobindo started his practice of Yoga in 1904. He got his first realization of silent, spaceless and timeless Brahman or *Nirguna* (unmanifested) Brahman. The second realization was of *Sugun* (manifested) Brahman. Later he got many realizations. According to Sri Aurobindo "Mind is an ignorance seeking after Truth and though the highest yet reached in the evolution, is not the highest of which it is capable. The created world is not a mistake or a vanity or illusion to be cast aside by the soul returning to heaven or *Nirvana.* There is a Super-mind or eternal Truth-Consciousness which is in its nature the self-aware and self-determining light and power of a self-existent Divine Knowledge."

21. Srila Prabhupada

Srila Prabhupada was the founding spiritual master of the International Society of Krishna Consciousness. He translated over 40 volumes of most essential works of Vedic literature. Srila Prabhupada delivers transcendental knowledge with maximum impact of wisdom and precision.

In 1966 he came to America and started Hare Krishna movement. He imparted the Vedic knowledge to the contemporary world addressing the spiritual needs of the people confronting the frustrations of modern life. Srila Prabhupada has said to the physicist Gregory Benford, "We don't say that scientific knowledge is useless. Mechanics, Heat, Electronics & others are also knowledge.... But the central point is *Atma-jnana* (self-knowledge), the knowledge of the soul." After this we understand the soul and the quest for the knowledge continues.

The real key to happiness and satisfaction is discovering the eternal and personal link between the Super-Consciousness and our consciousness. This state is called Krishna Consciousness. He was a great spiritual teacher from India.

22. *Sri Maharishi Mahesh Yogi*

Sri Maharishi Mahesh Yogi is a great saint of 20th century from India. He is widely regarded as the foremost scientist in the field of consciousness, and is considered a great teacher of Vedic sciences in the world. He spent his early life in remote areas of the Himalayas with his guru. He learnt the ancient lost knowledge of Vedic sciences from his guru. About forty years ago, his great love for the humanity forced him to come out of the Himalayas to serve and remove the sufferings of humanity. He has completely revived the practical, ancient Vedic science that is capable of creating perfect health and the enlightenment for any individual & society of happiness and peace.

Maharishi Mahesh Yogi has given wondrous ideas and practical management programs to the people of the world in his tremendous task of creating heaven on earth. He is the founder of the worldwide program of Transcendental Meditation & Spiritual Regeneration Movement in 1957.

He introduced scientific research in the field of seven states of consciousness from 1957 to 1967. He created a new science – '*The Science of Creative Intelligence*' and trained 40,000 teachers of this science. He has established Maharishi Vedic Universities, Maharishi *Ayur-Veda* (the Veda which deals with health & cure) Universities and Maharishi Universities of Management throughout the world to offer mastery over Natural Laws to every individual and to perpetuate life in accordance with Natural

Law perfection in every profession and government with the ability to prevent problems and to eliminate the problems of management every where.
For more of his program detail you may see his website http://www.alltm.org/Maharishi/Maharishi achieve.html.

Lord Jesus Christ

The Christian era was started after the crucifixion of Jesus Christ at the age of 33 years in Jerusalem. He was a miraculous incarnation of '*Son of God*'. He was an ideal miraculous saint and performed numerous divine miracles in his short life. He cured so many men suffering from incurable diseases like blindness, deaf and dumb, leprosy, lame and paralysis by his divine miraculous powers. He gave life to dead persons. He had control and powers over the Nature. He was able to control the dangerous tornados and floods. Who can deny his so many miracles 2000 years back? But all these miracles are beyond the understanding of our scientists till now.

As the childhood record of Christ is missing, it is said that he was in Himalayas for many years during his childhood as a disciple of a great Guru. He was a self-realized saint of the highest order. He was always one with God. But he never claimed or said that he is God. He always used to say that he is 'not God' but '*The son of God*'. At the time of his crucifixion he said, "*O, God forgive them, as they don't know what they are doing.*" His last words were, "*O, Father, I surrender my soul to Thee.*" Jesus was nailed to the cross and had to pass through a dream of great suffering. Yet before his crucifixion he said, "*Destroy this temple, and in three days I will raise it up.*" (John 2:19), 'not as I will but as Thou will' (John 10:30) this shows that he was one with God.

Jesus let himself crucified even though he had the power to destroy the world with a glance. He had the ability to raise the dead; certainly he could have annihilated all his enemies by a single thought at his command. Before his crucifixion Jesus was forced to wear the crown of thorns. He said, *"My God, my God, why hast Thou forsaken me?"* ...(Mark 15:34)

But quickly he realized that he was "*Son of God*" and can never be destroyed. And he proved it. Miraculously after three days Jesus was able to resurrect his body. Many of his disciples saw him again after three days. How it was possible, without super powers?

How Jesus was able to resurrect & materialize his body again after his death? It is a historically recorded world miracle. Jesus knew that this world is a dream of God. He knew that his crucifixion to the cross and death were all but dreams. Because he realized this, he could recreate life in his dream body again after his death. There are so many other saints all over the world, who have been seen by their disciples after their deaths. Master Lahari Mahasyia and saint Kabeer also appeared before their disciples after their death. How it was possible? Science has no answer.

Jesus could walk on water. But, how he could? Jesus had realized that both water and the body are the dreams of God. And one dream form can walk on another dream form. There is no barrier of difference between different form of the matter i.e. solids, liquids and gases. But we have to realize this truth. Mere imagination will not be sufficient.

There are cases throughout the world and especially in India that the people have ***walked on water and walked on fire bare footed, without a single blister.*** Such persons even do not claim that they are self-realized or yogis; still they have convinced their minds that the fire or water is nothing but consciousness or dream of God. Therefore these cannot harm their bodies, because body is also dream of God. Will our worthy scientists, enlighten the masses, to explain these miracles, how do the people are able to walk on water and fire?

List of Few Miraculous Interesting Saints one should further know

There have been millions of saints all over the world in almost all the religions. I am suggesting and providing a list of few saints for further enlightenment. If possible one should know more about them. The life of all these saints was mysterious and miraculous.

1. Mahaveer Swami	2. Lord Bhudha
3. Sri Hanuman Ji	4. Saint Moose
5. Saint Suleman	6. Saint Socrates
7. Saint Aristotle	8. Saint Daiojenees
9. Prophet Mohammad	10. Sri Lahari Mahasyia
11. Saint Kabeer	12. Sri Soordas
13. Sri Tulsi Das	14. Saint Paul
15. Saint Augustine	16. Saint Luis
17. Saint Pluto	18. Chataniyia Maha-Prabhu
19. Saint J. Lynn	20. Saint Therese Neumann
21. Swami Shivananda	22. Swami Ram Tirth

There should be No Contradictions Between the Religions

There is only one God throughout the universe. He is the same God for all the religions. Two or more Gods cannot exist at the same time throughout the universe. All the religions teach us to have a firm faith in God and to lead a spiritual life to seek and to know God. All the religions tell us almost the same truth but different paths to know God.

God is one, but His religions can be many depending upon the place and time of origin and the founder. But God has created only one religion to which He has given the Shastras and used to take Avatara to re-establish it. Some of the holy incarnations, holy saints and messengers have also given births to other religions in different parts of the earth at different times.

It is true that there may be some differences in the teachings and the religious paths of the religions, due to the cultural, geographical, historical and other reasons. But there should not be *any self-contradiction* between any two religions. If there is any contradiction, than at least one of the religions is not true. For example, some religions believe that God takes human form descend to earth as an Avatara. But some of the religions don't believe on it as their founders were not Avatara of God. It is not clear that how men the creation of God can put a condition that God Himself cannot assume human form? Such a condition puts a restriction on the omni-powers of God. It doesn't seem to be correct. Some of the religions believe in existence of soul, some do not. Some religion believes in rebirth, some doesn't. There are religions, which doesn't believe in God even.

No religion teaches us hatred, violence, terrorism, un-tolerance and aggressiveness to other religions. No religion teaches us to kill the people of other religions, convert the religion of people by applying force, temptations and monetary helps. No true religion teaches us to make the lives of the citizens of a particular religion hell and difficult to live in. No religion allows living of only the people of one faith comfortly in a particular country etc. Even then some of the people under the garb of their fanatic religion are teaching hatred, violence and exporting terrorism to kill the people of other religions in other countries. Due to some of the selfish diplomatic reasons some super countries might support them.

The cause of these contradictions is not due to God or due to any religion, but due to the selfish motto of few misguided people. There may be the following reasons like:

- There may be some mistakes done by the founder of the religion. The founder may not be a fully self-realized person and might have not fully purified his soul, before starting a new religion. Naturally he may commit some mistakes.
- The absence of the *Shastras* with the religion. The *Shastras* are the philosophical & logical base of a good religion and save it from the selfish motto of its followers.
- The absence & lack of self-realized saints in a religion.
- Some of the powerful elected heads of the religion, who are not usually self-realized saints, might have introduced some anti-religious concepts, to achieve their own selfish interests.
- Biasedness and un-tolerance of the followers of one religion against the followers of the other religions.
- Some philosophical, political and historical reasons.

In the past most of the wars and battles in the world had been due to the un-tolerance of the other's religion by the people of one religion. Inter-religious wars in the name of God have done the biggest harm to this peaceful world. Now many of the politicians have started the intermixing of the religion with the dirty politics. This is the most dangerous thing and will harm the world in the near future, if unchecked and not controlled right now. Why the followers of the peaceful religions should tolerate the cruelty of the fanatic religion forever? Time has come now to stop these with a firm determination. The delay will be dangerous.

The United Nation should do something unbiasly & sincerely so that no country in the world is able to declare itself as a religious country exclusively belonging to only one particular faith or religion. No religion should be allowed to make the life of people of other religions difficult and hell to live in their country. Some of the religious fanatics are killing and forcing to leave the people of other faiths from their country and are forcing to convert their religion. No religion should be allowed the forcible conversion of the people of other religion to their religion by offering temptations at any cost. No religion can tolerate it.

There should not be any country exclusively as a Hindu country, a Muslim or Islamic country, a Christian country or a Buddhist country any where in the world. No religion or a country should be allowed to kill the innocent people of other religions due to hatred and selfish interests. No government should be allowed to support one particular religion and work against the other religions.

No religion or a government should be allowed to instigate the followers of one religion to unite on a false religious cause all over the world and to kill the innocent people of other religions and to become terrorist & anti-national even against their own country. This is the worst thing a religion or faith can do in the world in the name of God. If any religion/ country does so, then its entire followers should be considered as the warring terrorists all over the world and not as civilian peaceful people during any war or attack against them.

It is true that the followers of some of the religions are peaceful but the followers of some of the religions are fanatics and terrorists, with their hidden intention to rule all over the world on religious base. The UN must take strict action against such terrorism in the name of religion. The joint UN forces of all the countries should take action against such a religion or a country.

A terrorist has no religion. His religion is only violence. Terrorist has no sympathy for the life of a man & do not want the development of the world. The religion of a terrorist is only to spread terror and to get the money he receives from his terrorist organization. If the followers of a religion or any government helps to instigate & allow its people for terrorism under the garb of a particular religion or faith then it is not a religion of God. The whole world and all the religions of the world should fight against such terrorism unitedly.

Some Misconceptions About Gurus & How to Select a Spiritual Guru?

Due to the mass publicity of media, a person may create his huge following. He may be simply an ordinary spiritual teacher (preacher) and not a self-realized Guru. A real self-realized Guru has no desire to get any fame or anything from the material world. He may sit alone in his cave at a lonely place unknown to the world and its crowd and may have no following at all. But he has mastery over the super divine powers and is able to do any thing for the benefit of the world just by his super-will, by sitting alone in his cave. By a single thought he can do any thing in the world. Generally, he does not interfere with the day-today world affairs and prefers to be sitting alone, then to be active inside the crowded world. But do not think that such a Guru is useless to the world. He is very much involved in the worldly development as per the will of God.

It is also true that there may be some self-realized Gurus having mass following and mass publicity. One has to check and test thoroughly his prospective Guru, before becoming his disciple. A Guru must have achieved the miraculous powers of God, which the disciple has to test. A real Guru never expects any material thing from his disciples except their love. He guide, council and transform his disciples in the spiritual path without taking any money. He loves but ignores the shortcomings of their disciples. If any of his disciple is not faithful to him, even then he continues to love him as before and do not punish him.

***Remember*:**

"God is the ultimate source of all our joys and cause of all the manifestations in the universe. God has not to earn, anything. "Seek ye first the kingdom of God... and all these things shall be added unto you. Nor be ye of doubtful mind." *... Matthew 6:33, Luke 12:29*

"Everything can be sacrificed for the shake of Truth and God, but not the vice-versa. Our seeking of God should be first; every thing else can be later. Although everything comes from God but hiddenly, God never claims it."

"Just as every leave, stem, flower and root are the integral part of the whole tree, so the whole universe including galaxies, stars, planets and all of us are the integral part of God. Just as nothing other then the own parts of the tree can exist in the tree so nothing other then God can exist simultaneously in this universe."

!Om Peace, Peace, Peace!

5

Life Force Doing Infinite Works

Many Folds of Men's Nature

Physical Body is not as it looks to our Senses

Physical & Mental Works are Different

Do not Over-eat but must Do Regular Exercises

Body Cells Need Regular Recharging

Our Body has been Given an Ego 'I'

Types of *Pranas* and *Sub-Pranas* in body

What happens to *Prana* After Death?

Medulla Oblongata and Seven Chakras

Reception & Distribution of *Pranas*

Sahasrar (the Reservoir of Life Energy)

Picture of Position of *Nadis & Chakras* in Astral Body

How to Increase the Reception of the Life-Force?

Vegetarian Food is Full of Life-Energy

What is *Om* Sound and what are Anahat Sounds?

Life Force Doing Our Infinite Works

Prayer

O Cosmic Father, O Divine Mother of Creation, teach me to understand Thy secrets, Thy great mystery of creation, the Spirit, mind, intelligence, matter and the wondrous universe around me. Since my birth I am not only curious to know Thy wonderful creation but also Thee the Creator.

O Cosmic Mother, teach me to heal from various diseases of my physical body, by recharging it with Thy cosmic life energy. Make me realize Thy presence beneath the waves of creation. How Thou art constantly working and arranging the atoms, molecules and the subatomic particles to create the living cells? How the living cells are further being arranged themselves as building blocks of matter inside the living bodies?

Teach us how our five enchanting senses, my heart and digestive system are working continuously with what kind of energy? How can I be able to control my sense organs at my sweet will through Thy energy and will power? Teach me, why my body is tired during my awakening state, even if I do not work at all and take plenty of food to supply the physical energy to my body? And how my body is recharged again and becomes fresh during the sleep when I do not supply any physical energy to it through food?

O Sustainer of Life, millions of complex chemical actions and reactions are always going on inside my body, even without my knowledge. No body is worried and responsible for all these actions & reactions, except Thee, not even my ownself. I bow to Thee.

Many Folds of Men's Nature

The nature of Man is of many folds: physical, mental, intellectual and spiritual. For the perfect development of human personality, a proper balanced development of all these factors is necessary. The present system of education emphasis more on mental and intellectual development and storing all kinds of huge information in the mind and ignore the others. So the development of man's body, mind, intellect and spirit is unbalanced. The development of one factor effects the development of the other. They are interdependent. Mahatma Gandhi stressed on three harmonious developments i.e. development of the body, mind and spirit.

In this chapter we will learn more about the life energy known as ***prana.*** The life energy controls the whole universe including all the livings, non-livings and inert matter. It is a wondrous kind of energy and has infinite intelligence. The other physical energies like heat, light, sound, magnetism, electricity and mechanical etc. are inert without any intelligence. The natural physical energies have no intelligence, cannot think and cannot take its own decision to work or not to work or how to work?

Physical Body is not like as it Looks to Our Senses

Our Physical body consists of five sense organs, five work organs like digestive system, excretion system, nervous system, blood circulatory system, spine and brain etc. All these systems are interdependent and inter-connected with each other in a perfect network. Understand that each of these organs is further made up of billions of tiny living cells. The cells in each organ are well organized in a beautiful design and in a network, which comprise our flesh and bones. All the organs are well arranged in a well organized network and working in perfect co-operation with each other to form the physical body of different shapes. *Remember a human body consists of nearly twenty eight thousand billion cells of many kinds, well connected in a network.* Our ordinary commonsense does not inform all these.

All the cells are further made up of so many complex chemicals, molecules and whirling atoms all in motion. None of the atom or molecule or anything is at rest. Each cell is composed of complex chemicals, proteins, genes and RNA & DNA molecules etc. Miraculously the atoms and molecules are dancing and vibrating in circular motions without colliding with each other.

The atoms are further composed of electrons, protons, neutrons and so many other elementary particles. These elementary particles are nothing but *tiny sparks of thought* in the Mind of God. These particles are arranged in each cell and further these cells are arranged in the physical body. These arrangements need infinite intelligence of God. No inert physical energy can make the arrangement of these cells since it requires intelligence. *Hence it is clearly evident that infinite intelligent life energy is doing all kind of arrangements and fine works. The whole universe is fully controlled by the Infinite Intelligence of God.*

The bodies of man and other living beings are the biggest chemical industries. To design, install and run such a huge chemical industry with an infinite intelligent network, running inside man and other living beings, *the whole surface of earth is not sufficient.* It is impossible for the engineers to design it in such a small compact body, which does not need a huge number of workers and management force inside.

All the human body organs are constantly working in perfect co-operation in a network, continuously day and night. It requires an intelligent energy to run and manage it in the small compact physical body. This huge factory inside the human body does not affect whether we take food or not. The food and fluid we take in, simply supply heat, electrical, chemical and mechanical inert energies and a few complex chemicals the body needs. If we stop taking food at all, all our body organs and systems like heart, sense organs, brain, digestive system, excretion system and nerves systems etc. will still continue to work as usual till our death. None of the body system stops working due to the lack of food energy. But all the body organs stop functioning instantaneously just after our death when the life force leaves our body.

It clearly shows the body is not running by food alone, but it is working due to some infinite intelligent energy known as life energy or the prana. Strength comes from within, not from the muscles alone. Life of a human body is sustained from our power within. It does not depend solely on food.

The Physical & Mental Works are of Different Kinds

Our body does both *the physical work and mental intelligent work.* A physical work needs only some kind of physical energy to perform it. As per the scientific laws "***No physical work can be done without any physical energy***: like Mechanical, Heat, Light, Sound, Electrical, Chemical, Nuclear or Magnetic energy etc." According to physics a mental work done by a person is ***not a physical***

work in real terms. It is a great illusion and misunderstanding among people that a mental work is also a physical work and requires physical energy to do it, and it is supplied by the food. A mental work does not require much of physical energy. The brain (which is a physical organ of our body) and the mind energy of cosmos together do the mental work. There is only one mind energy throughout the universe, which works in different brains of all the living beings. It is just like the same electrical energy, which works in millions of electrical equipments.

The brain requires only the omnipresent cosmic mind energy to function its different faculties. Remember that ***Mind is not the brain***. A doctor can do the operation of brain, but not of the mind. Mind is not a physical thing, but brain is. Mind is a cosmic energy of God & it functions on brain when the body is alive. It is true that we are tired after both the physical and mental works. Physical energy is required to do the physical work and is supplied by food (chemicals & nutrients etc.). But the life force comes from cosmos. By doing a mental work no food or chemical energy is consumed or required, and only the life force and mind energy are used. *So the person doing only mental work should not overeat when he is tired rather he should do regular exercises to consume the surplus calories supplied by the food.*

We Must Not Over-Eat & Do Regular Exercises

So it is important and necessary to *take less food and do some exercises or asanas* daily and regularly for the persons who are always busy to do some kind of mental work in their offices or work places. Because due to the lesser physical work the amount of calories or energy supplied by the food they have taken in, is not consumed properly by their body. When people get tired after their mental work they usually take rest instead of doing some exercises or physical work. A mentally tired person should not think that his body should take physical rest and consume more rich food to get rid of the tiredness. This is a delusion and cause of their overeating, overweight and disfiguring of their body. Hence the persons doing mainly the physical work require more rich food to supply the extra physical energy and chemicals they consume.

It is a misconception that thousands of our body organs like heart, stomach, kidneys, sense organs and so glands are functioning due to the energy supplied by the food. The food mainly supplies the heat, chemical and mechanical energy to do the physical work by living creatures. The entire body organs functions regularly, even if we stop taking any food, till death the death of the body. The scientists still does not know exactly by which energy all the body organs are functioning. None of the body organ including the sense organs & brain can function without some kind of energy. Remember, the entire body organs functions due to life-force received by the medulla oblongata & not due to the energy supplied by food or breathing.

Body Cells are like Battery Cells and Need Re-charging.

A living body cell is just like a battery cell. It consist of hardware i.e. a physical outer container and a few chemicals inside it. The chemicals or fluids to the cells are supplied by the food we take in. As for a battery cell, these two are not enough. A battery further needs charging by the electrical energy. Similarly the body cells further need charging by the life energy just like energizing the battery with electricity. Without charging, the battery is dead or of no use. A dead battery cannot do any work. Similarly in our body, living cells also need energizing or charging by life energy. When the life energy of the cells is exhausted we are tired. *Always remember when the body cells get fully charged body becomes fresh and active. When the body cells are discharged, body is tired, exhausted and need to go to sleep to re-charge it, but there is no need to overeat.*

Ordinarily most of the people think that our body simply depends upon on food, water, air, heat and some physical exercises. *But remember our body is sustained not by food alone. No amount of food given to a dead body of a man can make the body alive, not even a single body organ will function, since the four out of five life forces are missing in the dead body.*

Our Body has also been given an Ego 'I' or Ahankar

All mighty God has also assigned each soul with a physical living body and by His delusive power a separate ego known as 'I' or *Ahankar* is also assigned. God has separated each soul from Himself due to his delusive power of *Maya. Maya* separates the creation from the Creator by creating ignorance. Our soul is associated with an ego 'I'. The ego 'I' is not our physical body. Any thing, which is mine, can never be 'I'. I am always different from my things, which are mine. All the things like my shirt, my car, my ears, my nose, my tongue, my hands, my legs, my brain, my mind, my intelligence are mine. None of these is my real 'I'.

No part of my physical body is 'I'. Our ego 'I' is surrounding by the ignorance due to *Maya* created by Almighty God to separate us for Him. Only by our continuous efforts of yoga, love & devotion and the grace of God, we can remove this ignorance of duality ('I' & God' are different) and our separation from God. We must remember that *Maya separates us form God, but love and devotion unites us with God.*

During ***samadhi*** when ignorance is removed our ego 'I' is dissolved in the ocean of cosmic waves of God. We realize that there is no difference between my 'I' and the creator Almighty God. Our 'I' merges in God and it becomes one with God (*Advaita* Philosophy). We realize the absolute state of *Sat, Chit* and *Ananda.* During this state we experience and realize the great powers of God i.e. omnipresence, omnipotence, omniscience etc. We realize that the whole universe is my physical body. We will experience that I am present everywhere and all living beings are inside me. Further there is nothing other then me in the universe. We will come to know each and every thing about the whole universe. Remember it is only in this state of consciousness that we can really realize the great statements of Vedas like: "You and 'I' are One" or "*Aham Brahmashmi*" or "*So-Ham*" or "*Tatvamasi*". *Remember without the victory over the ego 'I' one can't realize the truth of above great statements of Vedas.*

Five Types of Sub-Pranas are Working in our Living Body

Generally we know that the food, sunrays, air, fluids & juices etc. sustain a living body. But the most important apart from these is *the vital infinite intelligent life force **(prana)**.* There are two kinds of '***prana***':

(1) ***Main Life Force*** (*Main-prana*): It is the cosmic vibratory energy. It is present throughout the universe even inside the living cells, atoms, molecules and elementary particles etc. It structures, organizes and

sustains every thing in the livings and non-livings throughout the universe.

(2) ***The Specific Life Forces*** (sub-*pranas*): It prevails and sustains our physical body. These are of five types of life currents depending on their functions in our body. The following are the five *sub-pranas*:

- *Prana* current controls crystallization.
- *Vyana* current helps circulation
- *Samana* current helps assimilation.
- *Udana* current helps metabolism.
- *Apana* current helps elimination.

All the above five *sub-pranas* have further five, *sub-sub-pranas.*

What happen to Prana after Death?

At the time of our death, four out five sub-*pranas* left the dead body. Only the *Udana sub-prana* remains in the body to destroy the dead body into further five elements: earth, water, air, fire and space from which it is made up of. Nothing can perish automatically without this prana. The dead organic materials are destroyed due to this prana, but the plastics are not due to its absence. This is a great ecological problem of the world. Our earth would have been a hell or a big storage of dead bodies in the absence of this important *Udana sub-prana.* Remember that *the injuries or diseases of a dead body can never be repaired or cured by any medicine given after the death due to the absence of other four sub-pranas.*

Even the injuries of a living body are not repaired by any medicine however costly it is. It is the life force inside the living body, which repairs the injuries of the living body or cures the body. The medicines simply help and protect the body from the infection caused due to external or internal bacterias. The medicines may also cure the deficiency diseases. Most of the medicines and the treatment simply help in activating the life force in the sick part of the body. The body is repaired and cured by the life force having infinite intelligence and not by the medicine and the treatments given to the body.

In physiotherapy treatment life force is activated in the required organ of the body. No physiotherapy can help in a dead body where four of the life forces (sub-*pranas*) are missing. *Remember it is the infinite intelligent life force, which knows what to do and knows how to cure a diseased body and not the inert blind medicine, which is void of any intelligence.*

It is now clear to us why we are tired during the awakening state, even if we take enough food and do not work throughout the day? Further why we become fresh and energetic again, in the morning after a peaceful sleep during night, without taking any food? ***It seems to be a paradox. But what is our tiredness exactly?*** Science needs to do further research work to understand it deeply.

To understand the above paradox, we have to understand first, how our body is receiving the life force and how it is stored, consumed or spend by the body? From where the life force is coming? Which organ of our body receives the life force? How & who distributes this life-force in different parts of our body as per its requirement?

Medulla Oblongata & The Seven Chakras in the Body

The most important part of our body ***is the medulla oblongata***. It is also known as '***mouth of God***' or '***the seat of soul***' or '*Atam-singhasan*'. It is situated at the top end of our spinal cord, at the centre of cerebrum. For safety a fluid surrounds it. It is said that a surgeon can operate all the parts of our body, but cannot touch medulla oblongata. Why? The reason is: it is the centre of all the centers of life, in the brain and spine. Medulla oblongata is like the radio or TV antenna or the receiver of the life force from the cosmos. The other centers of the body are not the receiver but the storehouse & distributor of the life force, which has been received by medulla oblongata.

There are seven important centers of distribution of life energy inside our Astral or Ethereal Body, which is not the physical body. But the doctors cannot find these centers, inside the physical body, as these centers are not the physical things. The advance yogis can experience these centers of life forces, during deep meditation state. These are known as *Chakras.* There are seven *Chakras* corresponding to seven life-force centers inside our brain and spine. They are as follows:

	Physical Body Organ	***Corresponding Chakra in ethereal body***
1.	Sacral or Coccygeal	*Muladhar*
2.	Lumber	*Swadhisthan*
3.	Dorsal	M*anipur*
4.	Heart	*Anahat*
5.	Cervical	*Visuddha*
6.	Fore Head	*Aggyia*
7.	Top of Brain	*Sahasrar*

Reception & Distribution of Life-Energy (Prana)

Sahasrar: It is the most important thousand-patelled lotus 7th *Chakra* situated at the top of the brain. It is like the *reservoir or the storage of the cosmic life force* for the body. It is experienced as the thousand-patelled lotus at the top of the brain to the yogis. From this life force is released or supplied to the body whenever it is required.

THE POSITIONS OF IDA, PINGLA, SUSHUMNA NADIS & SEVEN CHAKRAS IN THE SPINAL CORD OF HUMAN ETHERIAL BODY

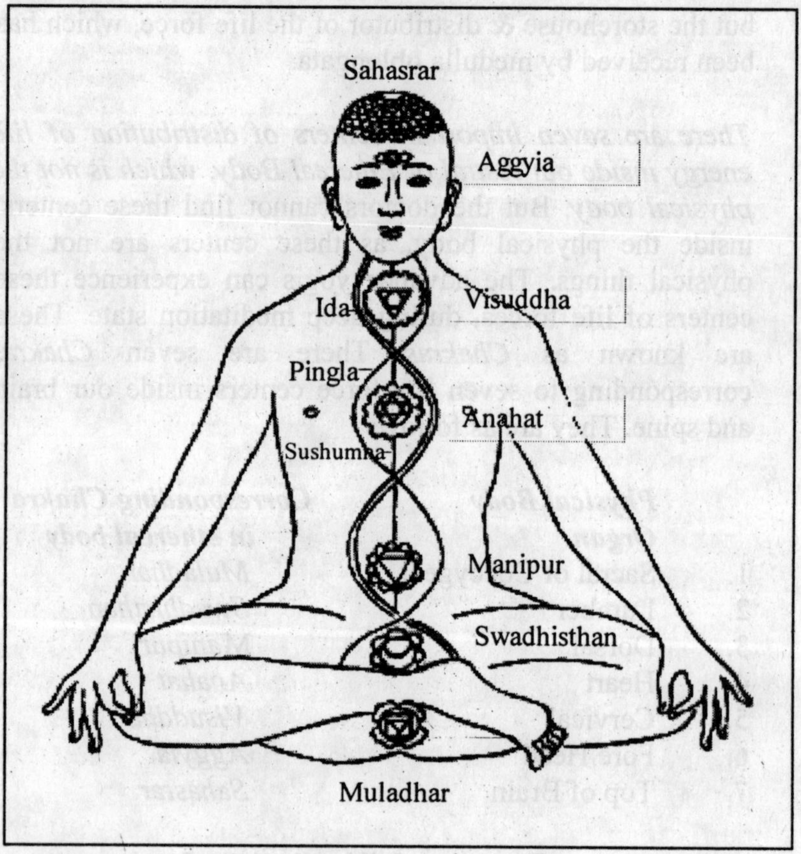

Some times a person with a heavy blow or injury in the head may see the thousands of stars of light, due to the forceful displacement of this stored energy in *Sahasrar.* At the time of death, the soul of some of the advanced yogis leave out their physical body through this *Sahasrar Chakra* by breaking the top of their head. The soul of such a yogi is merged with God after leaving the body.

Our brain and mind are like *TV tuner*, which tunes our mind to different cosmic wavelengths or states of consciousness like awakening, dream sleep, deep sleep & meditation etc. But the medulla oblongata is like a *TV antenna,* a receiver of the cosmic life currents. After receiving the life energy vibrations, these are reflected at the *Aggyia Chakra* situated in our forehead.

The next 6th ***Aggyia chakra*** situated at our forehead is also called 'centre of command', 'the eye of Shiva' or 'third eye'. It converts the main *prana* into five types of sub-*pranas*, reflect and distribute the sub-*pranas* to different parts of the body organs through other *Chakras* as per their requirement. *Aggyia chakra* is like the *power supply* part of the personal computer, which converts the 240V main current into other currents at different voltages as per the requirement of the computer parts.

The 5th Chakra known, as ***Visuddha Chakra*** is the 'centre of purification' situated at cervical. S*huddhi* means purification. Awakening promises freedom from 'worldly desires'. The 4th Chakra is known as ***Anahat Chakra*** is located at the level of heart is associated with love and compassion. With the awakening of this chakra one can here with the inner ear the ten *Anahat* sounds including Om. The 3rd Chakra known as ***Manipur*** is located in abdominal area. The 2nd Chakra known as ***Swadhisthan*** is located at the level of sex organs. It is responsible for our source of creative power. The 1st Chakra is known as ***Muladhar*** situated at the lowest point of spine. It is the seat of ***Kundalini Shakti***. *Kundalini* is energy distinct from *prana and ether*. It is the creative power of God, kept in dormant state. Without the awakening of *Kundalini Shakti* the journey of involution (back to God) can never be started.

Ida, Pingla and Sushumana are the main *Nadis* (Nerves) in our ethereal body. The doctors cannot find these *Nadis* in the physical body. Advanced yogis experience these *Nadis* by the practice of pranayam and the victory over the prana. Ida is cold represent *Moon Nadi*. Pingla is hot represent *Sun Nadi*. Sushumana has the equilibrium of both represent *Brahman Nadi*.

How to Increase the Reception of the Life Force?

During the day in the ***awakening state*** of consciousness (when mind is not tuned) the reception of the life force is less and the consumption is more. *During awakening* state life energy is spending in digestion, blood circulation, in sense organs, excretion and even in thinking etc. Hence till night our body cells are exhausted of their charged life energy, and they need further re-charging by the life-energy. *Remember due to the exhaustion of life-force in the cells, we feel drowsy and it is also the cause of our tiredness.*

But ***during the sleep at night*** the function of all our body organs becomes very slow. The connection of our sense organs or sense telephones is cut off from the brain. The beats or pumping of heart and the digestive system becomes dead slow. So the expense of life energy in different body organs becomes negligible. But during sleep the reception of the life force by the Medulla oblongata becomes very high. Our mind is more tuned & is nearer to God, who is the ocean of the life energy. So our body cells get re-charged again during night sleep. Further *during the deep sleep,* our soul is still *more nearer* to God and the reception of life energy is many folds. This is the reason why we are fresher in the morning after enjoying the deep sleep instead of the disturbed night. During a *disturbed night*, which is generally full of dreams, we are less tuned with God and the reception of life energy is low.

During the ***deep meditation*** we are perfectly tuned with God and there is a *resonance* of reception of life energy. The reception is thousands of time more, then the awakening state. Our sense telephones are cut off from our body and the brain. Hence a yogi who practice deep meditation, either need no sleep or a short sleep for few hours is enough for him. Such yogis are less tired and need less rest. Their intuitive & thinking power increases manifold tremendously.

Among the so many body systems the *digestive system* consumes the maximum amount of the life energy. It requires nearly 25% of the total life-energy received. The instant we put any food in the stomach, whether the body needs it or not the digestive system begins to work. It keeps pending all the other important works of the body. Otherwise the body will become sick immediately.

But whenever the life-energy is free from the digestion, then 25% of this important life-energy is saved. Then it is available to do more important works, like the repairing of the injuries in the body, fighting with the bacteria of diseases, cleaning of the digestive system and the blood circulatory system and so many other important works. We all know whenever our body falls sick, our hunger gets automatically reduced to save the expense of the life energy and we need bed rest. The nature warns us not to eat much to save the life energy from digestion. That is why during our sickness, we should eat the minimum. The fluids are easily digested and keep the life energy free from digestion, and to fight against the disease. Very soon the doctors will realize this truth.

Hence remember a *weekly fast, limited food and no overeating is the essential requirement for maintaing a healthy body free from diseases*. There have been so many ***non-eating saints*** in the world from time to time to further affirm this.

Vegetarian Food is Full of Life-Energy

Food contains only a limited supply of life energy. A vegetarian food like the fresh milk, vegetables, fruits and pulses contain some amount of life-energy. The vegetarian foods are generally the things from vegetation including milk and contain all the five sub-*pranas*. But a non-vegetarian food comes from dead creatures excluding vegetation thing and contains only one life energy i.e. *Udana* sub-*prana*, which destroys the body after death. The other four types of life energy (*sub-pranas*) left the dead body (all kinds of meat).

We observe that only a small portion of a vegetarian thing is spoiled, if infected by the bacterias or germs. The infected portion can be removed easily from it, as it is generally visible through eyes. But a non-vegetarian food is completely infected by the harmful bacterias & germs throughout the dead body and is not visible through the bare eyes or our senses. The infection of a non-vegetarian food is neither traceable nor can be removed.

It is totally a false misconception, if we eat meat or blood it will directly go to our muscles & blood. Remember not even a single atom or molecule can directly go inside our inner body, unless & until it is fully digested by our digestive system. The vegetarian foods are generally much easier to digest then the non-vegetarian foods. Therefore our body gets more out of a vegetarian food then a non-vegetarian food.

A non-vegetarian food is of *tamsic* nature. But a vegetarian food is of *Satwic* nature. *So a yogi should avoid eating the non-vegetarian food to achieve early success by fewer efforts.* There have been some non-eating saints in the world who never ate or drunk any thing in their lives.

Hence, learn the art of ***Pranayam*** i.e. the techniques of charging our body with life energy. Learn to control the life energy at our will and then we can achieve an excellent health, mental power, victory over diseases and many other important things. This is possible only through the science of *yoga*.

The Holy *Shastras* says that God is beyond the comprehension of mind and senses. Unless we detach our mind from the senses and make the mind peaceful without any thought of distraction, we cannot know God. God is knowable not by our intelligence, but through the intuitive perception in man. ***Intuition*** is beyond the five senses. Intuition can comprehend the facts, which are beyond the five physical senses. Intuition is the sixth sense of all knowing faculty of soul. By continuous and regular meditation, we have to increase our power of intuition and make the mind peaceful.

What is Aum or Om? & What are Anahat Sounds?

Om or the *Word* or *Amen* or *Amin* is the first vibratory manifestation of the almighty God Brahman. Before the creation of the universe only God (Brahman) was there in unmanifested form. Om is the first cosmic viberation of God. It is the sound of the whirl of the universal cosmic motor of creation. The cosmic creative motor is working in the universe and Aum is its resulting sound. The sound of Aum is not audible by the human ears. The frequency of Om sound is beyond the audible frequency range. Ordinary sound created by a vibrating object is known as *Ahat* (sound which is produced by striking an object with another and due to the vibration in the object). In all there are *ten* different types of sounds audible by the inner ears during deep meditation known as *Anahat sounds* (sound which have no physical source of viberation). Has any scientist ever do any research work on these ten Anahat sound? Probably no.

Out of ten *Anahat* sounds two or three Anahat sounds are easily audible by every body during the peaceful nights and meditation. But the others are audible only during the deep meditation. If we are awakened suddenly during night, try to listen these *Anahat* sounds immediately. You will listen many of these *Anahat* sounds even if you close your ears. These are the inner sounds of consciousness and not external physical sounds. The technique of meditation through the concentration of our mind on these Anahat sounds is known as ***Laya Yoga.*** The seekers of God should try it.

Aum sound is all pervading in the universe, but is different from the physical sounds. Any physical sound cannot travel in the vacuum or space, but the Aum sound can. Remember that the Aum sound is subtler than the ether, intelligence, cosmic forces and our thoughts. ***Aum created the ether. Ether created the space. The space throughout the universe is filled with ether. The space is not a vacuum. Space created fire, fire created air, air created water and water created earth.***

Om → Ether → Space → Fire → Air → Water → Earth

Our body is made of these five elements i.e. Earth, Water, Air, Fire and Space. Since Aum sound is the subtlest of all these elements, therefore it cannot be detected by any physical scientific instrument and is unheard by our ears. But the yogis can listen *Anahat* sounds during the deep meditation. These *Anahat* sounds are not detectable, as a doctor cannot detect the pain, joy, pleasure and sorrow by any physical instrument. Aum sound develops the intuitive (sixth sense) power of man. There is little intuitive power already in all the men, but it is not so developed that it can be used frequently. But by deep meditation the intuitive power of man get fully developed.

The chanting of *Aum* with human voices is not actually the Aum sound. It is just the imitation of the real cosmic vibratory Aum sound. Chanting of Aum sound helps us in listening the real inner Aum sound. We can know God, if we can utter or repeat the *Aum* sound mentally (*Japa*) during meditation. *Remember Aum is the best name of God.*

Prayer

O, *Omnipresent Cosmic Sound of Aum,* open my sixth sense of intuition, to know Thy secret of creation, savoir and destruction of the universe. How Thou art creating & rearranging the five elements? And how these five elements again dissolve into Thou art at the end of the universe? Heavenly Father! Make me understand your secret of *creation and annihilation.* Reveal Thyself. Make me understand my role to play in your divine universal drama of cosmic dream.

Remember:
"We are not alive only due to food and breath alone. We should know the technique to increase the reception of life-force to develop & to vitalize our body-cells, mind, spirit and intuition."

"A deep state of meditation activates the reception of the life force by medulla oblongata. It revitalizes the human body cells, the nerves and keeps all the body organs in perfect harmony with each other. The human body then functions in a better routine without any distortion, keeping a firm control on the healthy development of body, mind, spirit and intellect."

6

Avatars: The Reincarnations of God

Avatars:
The Reincarnations of God

Prayer

O Heavenly Father, O Cosmic Mother, Thou art omnipresent, omnipotent and omniscient. Thou art the creator of the universe, controlling, arranging, beautifying and looking after every thing. Thou art One, and hast one religion. Whenever Thy *Dharma* (religion) is declined or eloped and forgotten by Thy children, Thou come to the Earth to play Thy *lila* (God's play), perform many miracles, to re-establish Thy *Dharma* (religion*)* in the world, which Thy children have forgotten. Father, whenever Thou come to this world as an Avatar, punish the guiltiest, responsible for *Adharma* (non-religion) and re-establish a firm faith in Thee. Now the time has come, as there is so much *Adharma* everywhere in this world that only Thou can re-establish *Dharma by taking an Avatar.* Thy devoted children are waiting impatiently for Thy *lila.*

The following is the most powerful Lord Vishnu mantra:-

Om Shanta-akaram, Bhujang-shaynam,
Padam-nabham, Suresham;
Vishv-adharam, Gagan-sadrisham,
Megh-Varnam, Shubhangam.
Lakshmi-Kantam, Kamal-Nayanam,
Yogirbhe-Dhyain-Gamiam;
Vande Vishnu, Bhav-Bhaya-Haranam,
Sarve-Lokiak-Natham.

This is an important *Mantra* in the worship of Lord Vishnu from *Shastras.* As per the Shastras Lord Vishnu is an *Adi-Purusha* (The first manifestation of Brahman in the human form and is one of the lord of the Trinity (*Brahma, Vishnu and Mahesh*). Its meaning is:-

Shanta: Peaceful	Akaram : Form	Bhujang: Snake
Shayanam: Sleeping	Padam : Lotus	Nabham: Naval
Suresham: Lord of the gods.	Vishve: World	Adharam: Base
Gagan: Sky	Sadrisham: Equivalent	Megh: Cloud
Varnam: Form & color	Shubhngam: Auspisious	Laxmi: Goddess of wealth
Kantam: Glorified	Kantam: Glorified	Kamal: Lotus
Nayanam: Eyes	Yogir: Yogi	Dhyan: Meditation
Gamiam: Come in	Vande: I prey/ Worship	Bhav: World
Bhaya: Fear	Haranam: who removes	Sarave: All
Lokiak Austral worlds	Natham: Lord God	

The following is the famous *Sloka* from Geeta, in which Lord Krishna has assured the humanity for His reincarnation to re-establish *Dharma* at the right needed time.

Yada Yada Hi Dharmasiya Glanir-bhavati Bharata !
Abhyuthanam Aharmasiya Tadaatmanam Srijamyaham !!
Paritranaya Sadhunam Vinashaya cha Dushkritam !
Dharam Sansthapunarthaya Sambhavami Yuge Yuge!!

... Bhagwad Geeta: IV: 7 & 8

O Bharat (Arjuna), whenever there is a fall (decline) of *Dharma* (God's religion) and rise (increase) of *Adharma* (non-religion), I used to manifest a human form for Myself. I help the s*hadhu-purusha* (persons with good deeds and devoted to know God), protect the virtuous and punish the guilty & bad persons, who are busy in mis-deeds (*dush-karmas*) and are against God, and I used to manifest in human form as an *Avatar* to reestablish the religion (*Dharma*) in different *Yugas.*

If God has to come on earth in human or other form with all His mysterious powers unmasked, which He could very well do, all will follow Him, without any doubt. Sometimes He does come as an *Avatar*, in whom He keeps His powers partially hidden, so that he might play His *lila* for the benefit of mankind. God re-incarnate from age to age. When the spiritual aspirants pray He comes. The main tasks of an Avatara are to reestablish Vedas and fostering the devotees. Generally Avatara behaves in a human way so that the humanity can feel kinship with Him. Every Leela of the Avatara is pre-determined.

When God decides to descend from Godhood to manhood and assume a human-form, appear or take birth on earth, play His divine *Leela* along with His super miraculous powers is known as *Avatar* of God. It is an intentional mischief of some human to put any kind of restriction on Almighty God such as God cannot assume human form, cannot perform miracles or cannot take birth as an *Avatar* on Earth. When the lord created the universe, both the good and evil forces co-existed. Whenever the evil forces gained an upper hand, the lord assumed various forms of *Avatar* (descend from Godhood to manhood), to protect the virtuous and punish the wicked and guilty. Only Almighty God and no one else can accomplish the creation, preservation and dissolution of universe. An Avatara is naturally accomplished by the power to perform miracles to create in humanity an unshakable faith in God and His miraculous omnipotent powers.

Shastras are full of the detailed descriptions of *Avatars.* But in this chapter we will discuss only few human personalities, who were *avatars* of God and took human form to re-establish religion (*Dharma*) on earth. There have been so many *avatars* of God on this earth, but I will deal with only Lord Rama, Lord Krishna, Yogiraj Mahavatar Babaji, Sri Sathya Sai Baba and few others. Rama was a paragon of *Sathya* (Truth) and *Dharma* (Religion), Krishna was epitomized *Shanti* (peace) and *Prema* (love). These days in *Kali-yuga* all these four basic human values are in constant danger and disintegration. Now Sri Sathya Sai Baba an avatar has taken the responsibility of upholding all these values to re-establish.

God is omnipotent, omnipresent and omniscient. There is nothing wrong if, God takes a human form (as an avatar) with all His super powers and come to earth to play lila with His children to establish religion. From the very first breath an avatar has all the powers of God and He know that He is God and He is not under delusion or Maya. He need not meditate on God to remove His ignorance or *Maya* like a saint. Avatar means descend from higher level to lower level. An incarnation of God descends from higher Godly level to lower manly level, is known as Avatar.

Lord Rama and Lord Krishna are well known *Avatars* throughout the world and are the finest example of God's avatars and their lila on earth. Lord Rama took birth in *Treta Yug* nearly one million years ago. Lord Krishna took birth in *Dwapara Yug nearly 5230 years ago.* Remember that the existence of an *Avatara* does not end completely like ordinary human beings and saints, at the end of leaving His physical body. Lords Rama, Krishna and other Avatars still exist and can be seen and realized during samadhi.

Lord Rama

Lord Rama is an incarnation of Lord Vishnu, and He took birth nearly a ***million*** years ago, in Treta-Yug. He was a full avatar with all the miraculous powers of God. Rama came to fed the roots of truth and right conduct on earth. His life history (*Lila*) is known, through two famous *Shastras*, known as *the Balmik-Ramayana and Tulsi Das: Ram-Charit Manas. Balmik-Ramayana* was written before the birth of Rama nearly one million years ago. The Ram Lila is known by all-most, all the persons of the world and need not be repeated here. The most of the events of Lord Rama's period are miraculous and un-believable as compared in the present context of *Kali-Yuga.*

But one must not doubt upon its truth for even an iota on the Holy *Shastras.* ***Ramayana is not a myth but a reality.*** Lord Rama is a historical reality and he actually took birth on our planet. Ramayana is not a novel of imagination. It has been wrongly misinterpreted as ***myth*** by some of the western historians who had no knowledge of Hindu *Shastras* and were non-believers of God. They had also some hidden, selfish and biased motive to harm the Hindu *Shastras.*

The life in *Treta-Yuga* was much different then the present *Kali-Yuga.* The age of man in *Treta-Yuga* was nearly 10,000 years. Rama ruled over the earth in *Ayodhiyia* for nearly 11,000 years. The animals like monkeys, bears and vultures were educated and cultured like man, and used to speak human languages. They had their own kingdoms and kings like men. Some of the men, *Rakshasas,* animals and birds were having the miraculous divine powers, achieved through yoga. Some had the ability to fly at a tremendous speed with or without vehicles. Some had the power to create their divine destructive weapons used in the battlefields as per their simple desire and need. They had the power to magnify and to diminish their physical bodies at their will. They had great healing powers to recover from the injuries and diseases spontaneously.

Hanuman, Sugreev, Angad, Bali and many others were monkeys and great warriors during Rama's period. But Hanuman was an Avatara of Lord Shiva. He is still alive in his physical body and thousand of His disciples have seen Him throughout the ages. So many saints have seen Lord Rama and Lord Hanuman during their Samadhies. Hindus are celebrating *Deepawali* and *Dussraha* festivals every year without fail and billions of disciples of Lord Rama have seen and experienced Lord Rama in their meditation, even after His demise. No doubt Vedas were created before Lord Rama, since in Vedas there is no description of Lord Rama, but in Balmik Ramayana there is description of *Vedas* at so many places.

Although Lord Rama was the full Avatara of Lord Vishnu, even than Lord Rama did never declared it openly, to the humanity that He is God. His *Lila* was of an ideal example of a noble man life. It is to be followed by all human beings in their life. He did not emphasized much on preaching, but His ideal life to be followed by everyone, itself is His preaching to humanity. The following are some of the great miracles performed during Lord Rama's period:

- Hanuman, Ravana and many others could fly in the air.
- Hanuman, Ravana, Kumbhkaran (brother of Ravana) and many others could magnify or diminish their bodies to any size at their will.
- Although there was not much of physical science, many persons like Ravana and so many gods had their airplanes to fly. Ravana had his *Puspak Viman (airoplane)*.

- By the spiritual miraculous power of Rama, a stone bridge was constructed on the surface of sea to connect India with Sri Lanka. By simply writing the name of Lord Rama on the stones they floated and arranged themselves into a huge bridge on the sea surface and liked *Bharata* (India) with Lanka. How this could happen without the omnipotent power of God?
- The monkeys, bears and birds were intelligent, educated and cultured. They could talk, meditate and behave like men. They also had the knowledge of language, religion and God.
- The average age of man was 10,000 years. The yogis used to seek God for 1000's of years of yoga practice, sitting inside forests.
- Man had the knowledge of miraculous herbs like the *sanjeevni booti* and others. These had miraculous effects and power to heal and cure the injuries overnight.
- Some of the men and animals had the power to transform their bodies from man to animal form or vice versa. Even from male to female or female to male. How they were able to do such changes in their physical bodies?
- The divine destructive weapons used to appear or disappear at the will of the warrior in the battlefields and had the miraculous powers to destroy the enemy

The life of Lord Rama is a finest example of an ideal man and it teaches everything the human should behave in their life. If the humanity follows Ramayana, the sufferings will be minimized.

Lord Krishna

The life (Lila) of Lord Krishna was also as miraculous as of Lord Rama, described above. He was full incarnation of Lord Vishnu with all the miraculous powers of God.

Krishna came to foster love and peace on earth. The main difference is that Lord Krishna was born at the end of *Dwapara-Yuga* and Lord Rama in *Treta-yuga.* Due to the change of Yuga the age of man was reduced from 10,000 yrs to few hundred years at the end of Dwapara Yuga. Some of the persons in this Yuga had the miraculous divine powers. The divine powers of men were further reduced in this Yuga. Kali-Yuga was started after the death of Lord Krishna. The age of the man was further reduced to 100 yrs.

As per Hindu *Shastras* Krishna was born 3228 years B.C. on 20th July. As this is 2002 A.D., Today He will be 5230 years old. The *Mahabharata, Bhagwat Geeta, Srimad Bhagwat are the main Holy Shastras,* which describes the Lila of Lord Krishna. These *Shastras* and Lord Krishna are not Myths as described mischievously by some of the historians. Lord Krishna is a historical reality. All the *Shastras* mentioned above have description of the Holy *Vedas* at many places, but there is no description of Lord Krishna, or Lord Rama in *Vedas.* This proves that Vedas were created, much earlier than Lords Krishna and Rama.

Lord Krishna was the full *avatar* of God. He came to the earth with all His full powers. He declared openly to the humanity, that ***He is God***. His *Lila* was not a *manav* (human) *lila.* His *Lila* was a *Brahman* (Godly) *Lila.* Whatever lord Krishna did in his life is not to be fully followed or copied blindly by men. Whatever Lord Krishna did in His life, only the Lord had the right to do it, not the man. Lord Krishan preached the world (mainly through Bhagwad Geeta). All the men should follow His teachings and not His Lila. Lord Krishna is known as the *Yog-raj* (Lord of Yoga) and Lord Shiva is known as the *Yogi-raj* (Lord of yogis) among the yogis.

The following are some of the few miracles performed during Lord Krishna's period:

- During Krishna's period some of the miraculous powers of living beings were reduced or lost. Still some of the *Rakshasas* and men had the miraculous powers and they could magnify and diminish their bodies. They could fly also.
- The man had miraculous war weapons, which frequently used during the Mahabharata. The miraculous war weapons were used to appear and disappear at the will of the warriors. Krishna's *Sudershan Chakra, Gandeev Dhanush etc.* were supreme divine weapons. Such weapons were frequently used during the *Kurukchetra* war.
- The life of the man was reduced to few hundred years. *Bhisma* (great grandfather of Arjuna) was 300 yrs old at the time of Mahabharata war.
- Some of the yogis had the divine visual power to know every thing happening in the world, sitting at one place. e.g. *Bhagwan* Ved-Vyas and Sanjay. It is not correct to say that there were televisions like instruments at that time. *Bhagwan* Ved-Vyas himself has written most of the *Shastras* and such a huge literature of supreme quality, cannot be written by ordinary human intelligence, without the grace of God.
- Krishna created a huge magnificent town known as Dwarika just by His Will and transmigrated 1000's of people from Brindavan and Mathura to Dwarika in no time.
- Krishna had the miraculous power to multiply 100's of his duplicates at a time and danced with 100's of Gopies (milkmaids) during the *Maha-rash-Lila (Maha means great).* One Krishna danced with each Gopi

separately. What more science needs for God to do, to accept the existence of God in the universe?

- Lord Krishna declared openly before 1,000's of warriors just before the Kurukchetra war that He is God. To His dear disciple Arjuna, He provided the divine eyes to observe and comprehend His Cosmic Form (the universe is a part of it) of God. Remember only in Bhagwad Geeta God has opened His own secret, through His own mouth openly for the benefit of the humanity.

Yogiraj Sri Mahavatar Babaji

Sri Mahavatar Baba Ji is an incarnation of Lord *Shiva* and he is the great deathless eternal, yogi Guru of India. He lives in the Himalayas. He is the most revered, miraculous and spiritually advanced Himalayan Yogi. He has earned a great respect among the yogis. He is the great grand Guru of Sri Paramhansa Yogananda (the author of the '*Autobiography of a Yogi*'). Sri Mahavtar Babaji came in textual context first time through the 'The Autobiography of a Yogi'. His age is said to be in ***millennium***. He is still a mystery. He has a very attractive look. *He looks like a yogi saint of 25 years only. He doesn't eat & drink anything, doesn't need sleep, doesn't get tired, and doesn't need rest. He appears and disappears at any place at any time as per his will. Whatever he says must happen.*

But he doesn't appear publicly before the masses. He doesn't publicize himself. As he doesn't have a time bound program, it is most difficult to find and meet him, without his grace. He has no ashram, no residence nor any address or any contact number. But he used to materialize many different bodies, out of his body (incarnations). Many times he used to disappear for months together from his disciples.

Even his close disciples remain without any information about him. But Babaji has assured his devoted disciples that he will appear before them whenever they really *need* him but not when they *want* to meet him.

Nobody knows about his next program and the place of availability. Without his permission and grace, no body can meet him. None of his actual photograph or picture is available. He has the divine powers to cure anybody and give life to dead persons.

Once, Mahavatar Babaji has said to His disciples, "*He is deathless. Death has nothing to do with Him. He is the death of the Death. He is the whole universe and the whole universe is inside Him. There is nothing in the universe other then Him. He is present everywhere. He can do whatever He wills. The whole universe is just an expanding bubble ready to burst before Him.*"

Yogiraj Swami Sri Amar Jyoti Babaji

Sri Amar Jyoti Babaji is said to be many hundred years old. Nobody knows about his early childhood and youth. Now a lady of 95 years old is a witness that Babaji used to visit their family since she was 3 years old. He looks like an ascetic saint of 50 years. He is a bachelor and lives a secluded life. He has long hairs (*jatas*), sound health, pleasant appearance, wears white clothes and do not uses specs. In appearance and in many other ways he looks like Sri Mahavtar Babaji. Sri Amar Jyoti Baba Ji also doesn't eats or drink, doesn't tires, doesn't need rest or sleep. He is always active & energetic with a pleasing attractive smile. He also possesses many kinds of divine miraculous powers.

His disciples narrate so many stories of personal miraculous experiences of their lives with Babaji.

Previously he had no ashram or any residence. But recently a beautiful ashram-cum-meditation centre has come into existence in the Himalayas under the name of "Mahavtar Babaji Meditation Centre" at Dhraman near Palampur, Himachal Pradesh, India.

This ashram is surrounded with the most beautiful, natural green mountainous scenery of the Himalayas in a pollution free environment. As he is very much mobile without any pre-plan program, it is difficult to meet and contact with Babaji. He has assured that he will be available at Palampur Ashram on Guru-Purnima-Day, which falls generally in July.

The less said is more than enough about him. I was lucky enough to meet him few times during the last few years. No word was spoken, no word was heard, but every doubt was cleared. Every question was answered and every prayer was heard. Man becomes wordless in his presence and a deep peace of bliss is experienced which lingers on for many days after his *Darshan* (meeting).

Sri Hedakhan Babaji

Ms Jai Shree is in contact with one of the ***American lady saint Marge Devivo.*** She is running a Cyber Ashram in USA and is a disciple of Sri Hedakhan Babaji who is in her close contact. Sri Hedakhan Babaji used to answer the quarries of his disciples all over the world, through a secret website and e-mail address known to her. She used to reply daily 150 to 200 quarries through her e-mail as answered by Hedakhan Babaji, e.g. to one of the question of Babaji's disciple Mr. Young Len Raja, Sri Hedakhan Baba has replied as follows. Please read it carefully. How wonderful the reply is?

"The Eternal Sprit can create a body. The Eternal Spirit can master a body. I have ***created many bodies***. The Transfigured have immortal bodies. But, few will keep a body. Few will master a body. Few will create another body. I taught you the techniques of mastering the body through Fire, through Water, through Breath, through Affirmation & through the *Maha-mantra.*

Form must change. Change is the law of the universe. But I am '*no thing'* (not nothing). I am no one. 'No thing' is changeless, eternal, behind manifestation. No thing is not in form. 'No thing' manifests form. Form does not manifest 'no thing'.

I have come to this body in this period to focus on the ***darkness*** that is descending on the planet. A darkness that creates division. A darkness that allows the corrupt few to control the many. A darkness that dissolves freedoms. A darkness that corrupts the land, sea and air. A darkness that creates the poverty, diseases, and war. A darkness where many have a little. A darkness that creates weapons of mass destruction. A darkness that will inevitably lead the misery and despair.

I have come to focus on the destruction of the Lower Self through Truth, Simplicity, Love and Service. I have come to seek Beacons of Light among the devotees so that they may serve as Lighthouse to those who desire to be guided through the sea of darkness.

I am not here for recognition. I am not a show, not an entertainment. I am only here to serve. I am not here in this body to create ashrams, build ashrams, or manage ashrams. That is the realm of the devotees. I am here to share the Teachings of Truth, Simplicity, Love and Service. I showed you the Infinite Being. I showed you the Infinite Intelligence. I showed you the Infinite Manifestation. I also showed you the foundation of all in the concept of Truth, Simplicity and Love. This is the foundation of the ground of Manifestation. This is my focus, here, now. I seek Beacons of Light. I seek to lift the burdens from the hearts of many of the devotees.

He further said, if you are happy, I am happy Young Len Raja. I am no one. I have come from no thing. Take as much as you need from me. I am only here to give. I am always with you.
Om, Namah Shivaya.
Babaji."
The following is another reply to a question of a devotee by Sri Hedakhan Babaji. How wonderful it is?

"I was in that body. I knew the name of my website years before you decided upon the name. Understand? I speak to many hearts in many ways. You will learn this. Many will say this and many will say that about Babaji. How can they know any thing about no body? How can they know about no thing? If the mind tries to put Babaji in one place, in one body, in one culture, in one time, in one form…how can that mind understand how to use the teachings of spiritual growth? Shall we live in the dead past or shall we move forward through the eternal now? Now what could I possibly add to that?
Om Namah Shivaya.
Love and Blessings.
Babaji."

Sri Hedakhan Babaji has predicted an encouraging development about the future world. Reply to one of the question of Dr. BOB is as follows:

Dr Bob: "And what can be wonderful after all of this destructive change you are predicting?"

Babaji: "After the Great Revolution, this world will enter a golden age. The environment will be in balance and mankind will have a change in its ways by living on the higher path. There will be tremendous technology. It will take you to the stars in this galaxy and beyond to other galaxies. You will become a great race creating life throughout universe. And you will meet up the sentient beings from other dimensions of space-time when your science breaks through the quantum backdrop, the ground of being from which everything comes, the ***Holofield***."

Dr. Bob: Wow. And where does this all lead?

Babaji: You are the eyes and the ears of the universe. You are the observers of creation and its myriad things. And eventually…this leads you back to your real self…the Creator…when you will start another universe…over and over in the dance of the Creator …Remember, by just calling my name, I will hear you. If you are open I will guide you…repeat my mantra…live in truth, simplicity and love...and remember your purpose in this body in this world is to serve…(silence)"

Sri Mahavatar Babaji and Sri Sathya Sai Baba both have a huge following of the world's top class scientists. But why the rest of the scientists of the world are silent? Why they are ignoring such a great world miraculous phenomenon and events? Why do they not accept the miracle as a possibility and as the reality in their scientific terms and investigations? It is not scientific to ignore something, a world miracle, a phenomenon or an event, which does not, suits or fits in our mind or philosophy.

Our mind is under delusion and *Maya.* Some of the non-believers of God simply criticize against the miracles of the great yogis, without spending even a second to understand them scientifically. They live in false paradise, think and criticize those scientists, who believe in such miracles and call them backward or un-scientific. In fact they themselves are un-scientific and under the delusion and *Maya.* Nobody has got any right to comment on something unless he has thoroughly understood it? The non-believers have neither proved that they are correct, nor proved that the believers in miracles are wrong.

The scientists usually presume, imagine and believe in certain imaginary hypothesis, to develop their theories, which suits them and which may not be even true, while doing their research work. But due to some unknown reasons, the scientists are always afraid of accepting the existence of God and His *Maya*, which controls every thing in the physical universe. This is a paradox.

A Miraculous Divine Personality of Sri Sathya Sai Baba of Puttaparthy

In the 20th Century, ***Sri Sathya Sai Baba*** is an Avatar (incarnation of God: Lord *Shiva* and *Shakti*), a divine miraculous personality, existing in our own times on our earth. The avatar of Sathya Sai Baba is the highest blessing of God that the humanity shall ever possess. His avatar is the most auspicious event of the history of mankind. He is considered as a full avatar, having all the divine powers of God by millions of people of almost all the countries. An avatar is an extremely rare and monumental event in the history of mankind. His teachings & discourses are universal. He represents the highest expression of divine potential: infinite consciousness without limit, universal love without boundary. We are fortunate enough to witness such a divine incarnation of God in our life.

He is now 76+ years old, lives almost in his ashram at Puttaparty near Banglore in south India. He is a miraculous divine man by birth. He is a man of highest spiritual order. He has seldom been outside India or to any foreign country. He visited only South Africa once long back. Among all the saints, he commands the highest respect as he has all the divine powers and a following of millions of disciples in India and almost in all the countries of the world. They respect him like God. His teaching is purely *Vedic*, *Puranic* and secular in nature. He gives equal respect to all the religions of the world. He performs frequent miracles before the gathering of thousands of disciples, without any trick.

His disciples include thousands of top class scientists, engineers, doctors, saints, psychiatrists, professors, politicians and eminent personalities from all over the world. Thousands of such people daily visit his ashram at Puttaparty to have a glimpse of the miraculous divine personality from a distance, as it is now very difficult to meet and talk to him personally. Nearly 50,000 disciples from all over the world generally live in his Puttaparthy Ashram, in a perfect self-discipline atmosphere and many thousand new disciples from all over the world daily visit his ashram.

As per the *Shastras & Bhagwad Geeta* the embodiment of Avatar in human form is a rare event. It happens only when the religious and cultural human conditions have extremely deteriorated to such an extant that nothing else can re-establish *Dharma* (Vedic-religion) again. We cannot deny that the present deteriorated situation of the world fully demands the Avatar's appearance.

Sri Sathya Sai is a world teacher with a great spiritual mission. He protects the right-doers and uplifts the evildoers instead of punishing, with His weapon of pure love. If we accept him as an incarnation of God, we will accept him, as the greatest being on this earth and indeed the greatest being that could possibly exist. No avatar in the past has commanded such a high respect, from such a huge followers, in his lifetime as Sri Sathya Sai Baba.

Most of his disciples have experienced many miracles of Baba all over the world. Each individual disciple has his own miraculous experiences of Baba in his life. For them Baba is an incarnation of God.

Many of his disciples are highly educated, even the scientists, doctors and professors. Most of them have grown up in a western life style and philosophy of non-believers in God. In their early life many of them were non-believer and had no faith in the existence of God and religion. But when they witnessed a miracle with the grace of Baba, their life, behavior, philosophy, thoughts and ideas were changed spontaneously. Baba's powerful miracles have shaken their dis-beliefs and mis-conceptions of God and holy *Shastras.* Sathya Sai Baba has transformed them into perfect faithful disciple of their own religions. He doesn't change the religion of any body. There is a miraculous transformation in their soul from non-believer to a highly devotional man. Although there are countless of miracles, some of the most common are:

1. On the pictures of Sri Sathya Sai Baba and other Gods including Jesus Christ, there is, materialization of

Vibhuti (sacred ash) at the homes of the disciples. It is miraculous that a sacred white-gray powder is deposited, all of a sudden on all the pictures of Gods of all the religions. Miracle is just as a witness of his divine love to his disciple. Some of the disciples have never met Baba personally. Out worldly most of his disciples never met him and Baba also does not know them. Even then the miracle happens in their lives. The materialization of anything out of nothing at any place in the world is beyond the known scientific laws till now.

2. Baba spontaneously materializes *Vibhuti* or a ring or a necklace or a *Shivling* (an egg shaped object representing Lord Shiva) or any other thing before a gathering of thousands of his disciples. Some times he simply changes the shape of the ring or necklace, which is already in possession with the disciple. All the materialized objects are immediately given to the disciple as a symbol of his divine love. Materialization of things by Baba is beyond the law of conservation of matter and energy and many other scientific laws. What science can say about it?

3. Sri Sathya Sai Baba renounced the world when he was a child in 7th class. After that he never joined any other school or college. After that he does not need to read any schoolbook. Even then he knows all the languages of the world without learning any. He is the master of all the holy books and the *Shastras* and has the knowledge of all the sciences of the world. How he got the knowledge of everything, without any learning? It clearly proves that all our thoughts are already existing and stored in ether and all the knowledge is coming from within not from outside?

4. Baba knows each and every thing about all the human beings and living beings of the world, whether they

have ever personally met him or not. He knows each and every thing even about our dreams, which we have forgotten. He knows about our past lives, which we have forgotten and our future too. To communicate with him we need not to talk him personally. He knows even our thoughts without even meeting him. How he is able to do all this? Is he not a Super-human?

5. There was a ***world-miracle*** in the year 1972 observed by USA based NASA. Through its Satellite, NASA took a photograph of Puttaparty, where Sathya Sai Baba has his ashram. NASA was surprised to note that a natural image of Sathya Sai Baba is clearly hidden in that photograph. NASA released the Photograph to the whole world through the media. But the world's scientist deliberately ignored the great miracle and this news. Why, it was ignored? For the scientists, it is not scientific and ethical to ignore a miraculous world phenomenon, which doesn't suit their philosophy, thinking and bring a transformation in their ideology.

On the other hand it has been noted that some of the religious elected heads are neither saint nor know God. They intentionally deny the miracles performed by the saints of other religions. The religious elected heads of an organization are simply social workers. They may not have done any *sadhana or tapasya and may not have* divine powers. They can't be categorized as saint in real terms without their actual experience and communion with God or unless God witness them as saint. The real saints are above and beyond delusion and *Maya*, while a religious elected head is an official officer of prestige and may be very well under delusion and *Maya.*

6. Some times Baba performs living miracles. One of the living miracles performed by Baba before Dr. Ajay Kumar Gupta, who was a doctor in WHO-UNDP and now a permanent resident in Canada. He was called by Baba as a hospital consultant for the designing and construction of His Super Specialty Hospital at Puttaparty. He got the opportunity to have a personal interview with Baba along with other doctors. In the group most of the doctors were non-believers of God and the miracles. One of the doctor in the group requested Baba to show a living miracle.

On his request Baba created a miniaturized small living monkey. Lo, the small monkey began to grow with a speed before every body. Within few minutes it was a full-grown adult monkey and began to play with others. Later one of the doctors requested Baba to send him back. The monkey sat silently at one place and began to reduce in his size. Ultimately monkey disappeared before their eyes.

This miracle was a big blow to the philosophy, ideas and thinking of the doctors and so many others who deny God. There was an instant transformation in their soul and consciousness. Strange, they were no more non-believer of God. Baba removed their doubts, created & established their firm & unshakable faith in God. Their life and philosophy after was completely changed. Only one miracle is enough to bring a change and transformation in their lives. Their later lives were peaceful with joy & bliss.

It is not clear what else the scientists and the world are waiting from God? What God should do for the humanity to create a firm faith in His existence? Should He go personally to each and every individual, to show and prove His existence and beg like a beggar standing before his door, till the non-believer believes in His existence? God does not expect any thing from anybody, except his love to Him. We all are His children and His creation. God is waiting impatiently for our love. He will never force us to love Him back.

When shall we stop our attachment to His creation (worldly things) i.e. *Maya,* delusion and ignorance? And when we shall began to think of Him and began to love Him back? Are the miracles performed by Baba on our earth not sufficient to prove the existence of God? Why inspite of millions of his miracles, the world is silent and has not changed much?

The above miracles are simply the witnesses and proofs that our universe is under the delusion and Maya of God. Our laws of science are not the absolute truths. Baba is beyond *Maya* or delusion. He is omnipotent, omniscient and omnipresent and has a control over all the living beings and the whole universe. All the miraculous powers are in his palm. The aim of Baba to show the miracles is not to extract or expect anything from his followers, but to express his divine love as a divine gift to his disciple. These miracles have a great impact in bringing a complete transformation in their soul and consciousness.

His disciples are convinced about his absolute powers of God and that the universe is not an absolute reality. But it is just visualization or a great thought or a great dream in the Mind of God. Our sense organs experience just the images, on the curtain of four-dimensional space-time continuum as defined by Albert Einstein.

Baba is a bachelor (never married), a *sanyasi* (left his home, wear saffron cloths), a desireless and a renounced saint. He has all these miraculous powers since his very childhood. By his miraculous actions to his disciples He wants to create a firm faith in Almighty God, irrespective of any religion. None of his teaching contradicts any religion of the world. He speaks perfectly secular. As per his teachings the ultimate aim of human life is self-realization and to know God. It is easier to get self-realization through a self-realized saint, known as *Guru.*

At his age of 10, when nobody in south India or Puttaparty, had known or heard about ***Shirdi Sai Baba***, he declared that he is an incarnation of Shirdi Sai Baba. But now after a short span of 66 years there are millions of disciples and thousand of temples of Shirdi Sai Baba. Millions of disciples have witnessed the existence of Shirdi Sai Baba after his death in 1918. The people of different religions worship him like God all over the world. Sri Shirdi Sai Baba had predicted His one more incarnation after 8 years of His leaving His body. That has come true by the incarnation of Sathya Sai Baba. Sri Sathya Sai Baba has also predicted that he will have one more incarnation in the name of *Prema Sai Baba.*

Sri Sathya Sai Baba is a brilliant orator and a great teacher. He uses simple examples to explain the most complex phenomenons. He is trouble-shooter par excellence and often surprises professionals with his versatility. Sri Sathya Sai Baba used to give His blessings of divine love to His devotees around the world through his appearance in dreams and visions. His surprise visits in physical form, appearance of *Vibhuti, kumkum, sandal* and nectar in many homes are the witness of his love to his disciples. I am writing the few pages below in Baba's own words, to enlighten the readers and to maintain the originality of the Baba's text.

Sri Sathya Baba has said, ¶"*The previous Avatar, Shirdi Baba, laid the base for secular integration and gave mankind the message of duty is work. The mission of the present avatar is to make every body realize that the same God or divinity resides in everyone. People should respect, love and help each other irrespective of color or creed. Thus all work can become a way of worship. Finally the Prema Sai, the third avatar, will promote the evangel news that not only God reside in everybody, but also everybody is God. That will be the final wisdom, which will enable every man and woman to go to God. His three avatars carry the triple message of work, worship and wisdom.*"

Baba has said, "*I am every thing, everywhere, omniscient, omnipresent and omnipotent: so whatever I* ***will***, *instantly happens. The qualities of truth, love and peace, are the things that generate the atmic (godly) or cosmic forces behind the universe.*" ¶

The following is the original discourse of Baba given to so many disciples and in the presence of professor Plum and Samuel H. Sandweiss both from USA, taken from his book "Sprit and the Mind" regarding the question asked, "***What is science? And what is a scientist?***

¶"*Science is the way of looking at the outer world through the mind. The mind's nature is duality. It divides reality into different names and forms -- it dissects, compares, contrast, separates, categorizes -- tries to define and bind reality in terms of words and concepts.*

All of the cosmos—the entire material universe, as vast an expense as it seems—is just a flake of froth, a bubble, on the ocean of reality. And the mind which views it through it senses and tries to grasp and comprehend it—this mind is even bigger than the cosmos; it can eventually encompass and understand it. But even this vast mind is like a little wavelet on the ocean of reality. You are the ocean. You are not the flake of froth and you are not the wavelet—you are beyond the separation. You are everything—you are the ocean.

The mind sees separateness, duality: but there is another way of experiencing reality—as unity. It is through the heart, by the process of love. Love reaches out to merge with others; two become one. Love sees unity. For the limited little wavelet self to know that it is the ocean, it must merge back in the ocean—through love.

The scientist says, 'What is this?'— 'this' lies in the outer world and is seen through the senses. The spiritual aspirant says, "What is that?'—'that' lies beyond the outer world and the senses, beyond duality and the mind as well. 'That' as the ocean from which all this arises."

Baba further asked, "*Why is that everybody says 'I'?"* And then pointing to some of the disciples in the room for emphasis, he continued, *"She says 'I', I say 'I', you say 'I'; we all look different but there is this common sense of 'I'-ness. What is the meaning behind this? We have to look beyond this constantly changing world of different names and forms in order to see the underlying, unchanging and immutable reality: the reality that always was and always will be, the underlying unity which gives rise to all this diversity. How can the scientists with his mind try to grasp unity? The mind sees separateness; love sees unity. The only way that the wavelet can know the ocean is to merge back into it—to become one with it. Love is the way; merge with love, through your devotion to God.*

My name is Sathya means Truth. I represent that which is beyond mind. I have come to show you who you are—the reality that lies beyond mind. How can a scientist comprehend me? I am at all places at all times—everything that aver was or will bè. I can transmute the earth into sky and the sky into earth. …But I don't do it often because it causes inconvenience to some people".¶

¶The disciples laughed and Baba was immensely joyful with our happiness. He continued, "*How can the scientist understand my reality? See, how can you understand this?*" And with that Baba became even more animated and began to move his hand in a large circle in the air. In a startling, electrifying instant he was holding a beautiful silver ring. It had come as if in a flash of light—and at such a moving point in the spiritual discourse that the disciples were left stunned and gasping. It was a miracle as if one is sitting in front of the creative force that gave birth to all matter.

¶At that moment, Baba beamed with happiness. He showed the beautiful ring to everyone and then looking at the professor Plum, " How can you understand this?" He took the professor's hand in his own and Plum turned into a little child. Baba slipped the ring on Plum's right hand ring finger and it was a perfect fit. ¶

--- The paragraphs marked ¶ have been originally taken from the book: "Sprit and the Mind" by Samuel H. Sandweiss.

Shirdi Sai Baba an Avatar

Shirdi Sai Baba is an incarnation of God (Lord Shiva). Sri Sathya Sai Baba is an incarnation (rebirth) of Shirdi Sai Baba as declared by him. The people of all the religions worship Shirdi Sai Baba all over the world. His teachings are universal, all for Hindus, Muslims & others. He never said, "I am God," but used to say, "Allah sabka Malik hai" i.e. "Allah is the Lord of all". He lived like a Muslim saint in a Mosque of village Shirdi, but his followers were from all the religions mostly Hindus. A part of his life history has already been explained above.

He has been one of the most miraculous saints in his life and even after his death. How the science can ignore him?

Remember:
"Sooner or later a time will come to everyone when this dream of God will vanish. We will find that the whole universe surrounding us as a condensed dream-drama of God, and our soul is separated from God due to His Maya. In this struggle of Maya and our journey back to God, a time will come for our self-realization. This is only a question of time, which is negligible in cosmic infinite time. We can afford to wait and be calm."

"A yogi who follows the yogic principles such as honesty, forgiveness, integrity, endurance and devotion to God, gets the piece of mind, pleasure, joy and bliss."

7

Who is Guru? How to get Self-Realization?

Who is Guru? &
How to get Self-Realization?

Prayer

O God, O Lord, I may never forget Thee. May I always devote myself to Thy service? Help me to control my naughty mind and minimize my desires. Make me free from all worldly temptations and desires. I surrender myself at Thy lotus feet. Make me free from the immense pains of births and deaths, life after life. I am no more interested in Thy enchanting worldly pleasures. Since long due to my own ignorance I might have forgotten Thee. But now I am interested only in knowing Thee. Thou art just behind the curtains of the powerful delusion and *Maya.* Thou art smiling just behind the sun, stars and other heavenly bodies. Remove my ignorance. One glimpse of Thy grace can destroy my ignorance and the enchanting desires. In comparison of Thy greatness, I am a little child. I do not want to be a preacher, but Thy little babe. O beloved Mother, reveal Thy-Self.

Famous Guru-Mantras

Om

Gurur Brahma, Gurur Vishnu,
Guru Devo Mahashwara!
Gurur Sakchahat Parambrahamaha,
Tasmaii Sri Gurve Namaha!!

A real Guru represents all the three deities of *Brahma, Vishnu and Maheshwara* (Shiva). A Guru is really *Param Brahman* (Supreme God); I bow my head to such a Guru.

Om

Brahamahanandam, Param Shukhdam,
Kevalam Gyan Moortim!
Dwanda-teetam, Gagan Sadrisham,
Tatvam-asi-adi Lakshanam!
Ekam, Nityam, Vimalam, Achalam,
Sarv-adhi-Sakashi Bhutam!
Bhavateetam, Tri-guna Rahitam,
Sadgurum Tam Namami!!

Brahamahandam: Permanent Ananda (Bliss) of Brahman (God), Param: (Supreme), Sukhdam: giver of the pleasures, Kevalam: only, Gyan: knowledge, Moortim: an idol of worship. Dwanda-teetam: away form all kinds of dualities, Gagan: sky/space, Sadrisham: equivalent, Tatvamasi: God like, Adi-Lakshanam: qualities of God. Ekam: only one, Nityam: who is permanent & eternal, Vimalam: totally pure, Achalam: immovable, Sarvadhi: present everywhere, saakshi; witness, Bhutam: atma or soul, Bhawateetam: away from all kinds of emotions, Tri: three, Guna: qualities or properties, Rahitam: devoid off, Sadgurum: self-realized guru, Tam: you, Namami: I bow my head at thy feet.

In fact a self-realized Guru is God and the God is Guru. Both are same. There is not much difference between a Guru and God, except one. God is the creator of Universe and *Maya* (Satan or Devil). Maya creates ignorance and is the cause of duality in the universe. God is the Divine Father of all living beings including the Guru. In the beginning we all were one with God. God created us and has separated us from Him with the help of His Maya. God has given a freedom to human beings to seek Him or not. God neither helps nor hinders in our search for God. We are free whether to love Him or not. But a Guru helps his disciples to seek and realizing God.

Guru uses so many methods and ways to mould his disciples in seeking God. So as far as a seeker of God is concerned, a Guru is more important. It is the Guru, who provides a searchlight or the knowledge of God and creates love for God in his disciples. Without Guru, God is difficult to realize. But without God, there cannot be any Guru.

Difference between Guru, Teacher and Instructor

We have come across so many teachers during our schools and colleges. ***Teachers*** are the individuals who teach us and from whom we learn some thing. The teachers simply supply information, about their different subjects, to their students. Generally they do not have any philosophical and ideological background and linking of their subjects. They cannot claim themselves as true teachers. A teacher without any philosophical thinking and ideology, while teaching, is simply an ***instructor.*** In schools and colleges we have so many instructors these days, but have very few teachers.

In the beginning we may have many good teachers, who help us, in our search for God. But our spiritual-Guru is only one in our life. There is a teacher-student relationship between a teacher and a student. But there is a Guru-disciple relation between a Guru and his disciple. Generally the job of a teacher is a paid one and a student or organization pays for his services. Generally a teacher is not concerned with the spiritual developments and progress of his students, but only of his subject contents. The teacher may be believer or non-believer of God.

A teacher who is also a self-realized soul and looks after the spiritual development of his disciples is called a ***Guru***. A Guru is a searchlight in the inner spiritual path to know God, for his disciples. A Guru is send to a deserving seeker of God, by God alone, at the right time. The Guru must not be changed throughout the life. But the seeker of God can have the consultation, guidance and blessings from other spiritually advance saints. There is no ban or harm in this.

Who is a Guru?

A Guru is a living embodiment of scriptural truth. He is an agent of salvation appointed by God in response to the devotee's deep devotion to seek God. No man can find a Guru, unless the God has drawn that disciple to a Guru. A *Guru* is not an ordinary teacher. A *Guru* is a spiritual guide and a teacher of Holy *Shastras* in the inner path of yoga. Guru must have already realized God. Only a self-realized Guru who knows God and has a victory over the delusion and *Maya* can lead others to know God. As a blind man cannot lead others to show the path similarly the un-realized guru cannot realize God to others.

Generally a self-declared guru is not a self-realized Guru. He may be a highly educated spiritual preacher but not an enlightened real Guru. Such a guru may be expert in so many holy books or *Shastras,* but spiritually he is as blind as the other seekers. He cannot lead others on the path of self-realization. Such a Guru also needs an enlightened Guru to get self-realization. Before accepting some one as a Guru, one must be sure about his spiritual enlightenment.

Somebody may write his thesis for Ph.D. in swimming after lots of his studies for many years without learning the art of swimming practically. Such a learned man in swimming will be drowned in deep water in his first attempt of swimming. So it is quite clear that a Guru must have experience of self-realization rather than the bookish knowledge. A Guru is fixed and sent by God to the seeker of God and Truth at the right time, when he really deserves and needs a guru or whenever God is pleased with his devotion.

Beware of Self-declared and Un-realized Gurus

These days in the world there are so many self-declared spiritual gurus, who themselves have not realized God. They may be well known in the world, have big ashrams and a mass following of disciples. ***Beware of them***. They may be great spiritual scholars or teachers and have learnt many spiritual holy books, but if they are not self-realized, they cannot be the real Gurus. Some of them also make their frequent publicity through the Newspapers & posters on the street-walls, T.V. channels and other communication media to increase their followers and to increase their earning too. Due to the advancement of publicity and media technology they might have been very successful to establish big ashrams.

At the initial stage for a seeker of God or for a spiritual layman, these so-called gurus are useful to a great extant. But at the later advance stage they are of no use to get success on the path of self-realization. Such gurus are generally money minded. They extract money from their disciples and they live worldly luxurious lives.

A real self-realized Guru does not need to publicize himself, as a beautiful rose flower does not need publicity to attract the viewers. He has left with no worldly desire. He does not expect any thing from his disciples, except their love and regard. He is a *sidhpurusha* and has the divine powers to perform miracles. Generally he avoids performing a miracle, but rarely the real Guru does so, to create a firm faith of his disciples in God and in him. A real Guru is authorized by God to lead others and his disciples to realize and seek God. Some time even a self-realized saint is also not authorized to function as Guru by Almighty God.

A Guru must be chosen, only after thorough search and tests to measure his spiritual advancements and achievements. He should not be chosen simply due to his scholastic achievements. Remember wisdom is better sought from a self-realized Guru than from the inert mountains, without knowledge of God.

A Famous Historical Event In Search of Guru

The ***Alexander the Great*** was the king of Greek. He went to his Guru ***Aristotle***, to get his blessings, before his departure for the victory of the world. He bent with reverence and asked to his Guru," *What should I bring for you, when I return after my victory of the world*?" His Guru said, "Bring the following five spiritual things for me, from *Bharata* (the pre-historical name of India).

1. *Ganga Jal* (sacred water of river Ganges).
2. *Bansuri (flute or wind-pipe)* like that of Lord Krishna.
3. A cow like that of Lord Krishna.
4. A *Srimad Bhagwad Geeta* and
5. A *Self-realized Guru* for myself."

After the victory of *Bharata,* when Alexander was willing to return to his motherland Greek, he asked his solders to find out and collect the five things required by his revered Guru. His soldiers easily collected the first four things, but the last 5th i.e. a ***self-realized Guru*** was not available and traceable any where. They had no concept of the self-realized Guru. There was a thorough search to find such a self-realized Guru everywhere, by every body. At last they came to know about such a Guru, at a far away place at the bank of the Ganges. Soldiers were sent to bring him, but the saint Guru refused to accompany with them.

Then the Alexander himself went along with his soldiers and high officials to meet and bring the Guru. When the Alexander reached, the saint was relaxing, enjoying and lying in the sun naked, on the sand along the banks of the Ganges. Alexander ordered him to accompany with him to the Greek.

But the saint politely refused to go with him. Then the Alexander offered him so many attractive & enchanting worldly temptations like huge wealth, gold, jewelry, beautiful women, wine and also the kingdom of many places in his country Greek.

But the saint said," I do not need any of the thing from you. I have already got every thing I need. I do not have any desire or the temptation of anything. I am the king of the universe. I am the king of the kings. He said the whole universe is inside me just a tiny bubble. The sun, the moon and the stars all obey my command. The sun and the moon rise & set with my permission and I am the brightness inside them. I am the ultimate cause of the brightness in all the stars, sun and the moon. I am desireless and have no desire left to be fulfilled.

I am always one with God. I am always in permanent Bliss and Joy. What pleasures and joy, your kingdom, jewelry, gold, women, wealth and worldly things can give me? Are you now satisfied and happy with all the things you possess and have acquired in your life? You have almost conquered the whole world. Still you have so many desires left to be fulfilled, even after your victory of the world and killing millions of innocent people. Even after getting so much of wealth why are you not satisfied? Why are you not happy with your victory? Now, first of all you must go away from me, as you have stopped coming of the pleasant sun-rays to me."

But Alexander was under *Maya* and could not understand his teachings. After this Alexander lost his temper and mental balance. Out of his anger he was ready to kill the saint with his sword. But some of his elderly wise men stopped him doing so. They requested him not to kill the saint. After that the Alexander left India desperately and went to his motherland Greece without accompanying with him a self-realized guru needed for his dearest guru Aristotle.

Note that his victory of the world after killing millions of innocent men and his accumulated whole wealth and power could not get him a self-realized Guru. When he died, he left this world alone, without even a single penny with him. We come alone in this world and go alone from this world without our asking, not even our body accompanies with us. Only our *Samskaras* (fruits of past actions) goes with us. Whatever we get in the next life is according to our fruits of past actions, in this and other previous lives. Even we shall born as a human being or not depend on the fruits of our past *karmas* (actions).

When a disciple, who is a seeker of God, really needs a guru, God sends him a guru. And when one is able to find a guru, there should be unconditional devotion and surrender to the guru, because he is a vehicle of God. The sole purpose of guru is to help his disciple, to show the inner spiritual path of seeking God and self-realization. God receives the love of a devotee through the love he offers to his guru. So we must love both God and Guru.

An average devotee cannot seek God without a guru. The devotee requires 25% of his regular devoted practice of meditation on God, 25% grace of guru and 50% grace of God to achieve self-realization. In fact there are no exact mathematical rules and calculations. There is guarantee that by doing constant effort for a long time, one will get self-realization. It differs from an individual to individual, depending upon his practice, intensity of seeking God, his love for God and the fruits of his past actions (*karamphals*). But the disciples must obey his Guru perfectly, in every thing, because the guru is a man of wisdom, purity and is a representative of God. A true guru is a servant of God. He carries out the plan of God, to liberate his disciple. The obedience to guru is not slavery because a Guru does not need any thing from his disciples except their love and devotion.

Never Make Calculations for the Reward of Your Sadhana (Yoga-practice)

To explain it I would like to tell you an interesting story. Once there was a yogi in *Sat-yuga,* who was proud of his long *tapasia or sadhana* in a forest for thousands of years. At last God was pleased with his yoga-practice & appeared before him. As usual due to His divine mercy, God offered him to demand any thing to fulfill any his desire.

But the yogi was much proud of his thousands of years of long *sadhana* & yoga-practice. Yogi was in the impression that no body else has done so much yoga-practice for such a long time. He was expecting something extraordinary from God, which no other yogi had ever achieved. So he requested God to give him only that much reward which he really deserve as per his long period of yoga-practice. God again advised and offered him to demand anything he needs and assured him to fulfill the same immediately. But the yogi did not agreed and left the decision of reward on God. Then God promised the yogi to reappear before him after seven days.

To teach him a good lesson and to remove the false proud of the yogi, God disappears all the water resources from everywhere around the yogi, through His *Maya*. The yogi couldn't find water anywhere and became extremely thirsty after many days. On the seventh day he reached at the point of his death. Then he saw a man passing nearby having a jug of water with him. The yogi requested him to give him the water, as he was just going to die due to his thirst. But the man refused to give him the water as he was having only a little water to survive himself. At last the yogi offered him the half of the fruits of his rewards of thousands of years of his yoga-practice, in exchange of half of the jug of water. The man agreed and gave him half jug of water in exchange of half of his fruits of *Sadhana*.

Later God reappeared before the yogi at the right time and again offered him to demand anything to fulfill his desires. But the yogi again repeated the same that God may be pleased to give him whatever he deserved against his long *sadhana*. Then God told him that he has already exchanged half of his sadhana for a half jug of water. Then God offered him half jug of water for the rest of his half *sadhana*. Immediately the yogi realized his blunder but God disappeared.

This story teaches us a good lesson. Remember that whatever we have in this life is all due to the mercy of God upon us. It is not due to our own efforts or our matter of right to have it. During our *yoga-sadhana* for seeking God we should never make our calculations of time and efforts devoted and about the return of the fruits of *sadhana* from God. We have to perfectly surrender ourselves to God and it is the mercy of God that He may give us anything whatever best God decides it for us. One may get self-realization very soon and the other may not get it in his whole life inspite of his best efforts. All our actions should be fruitless, without any desire for reward. A yogi should never forget his ultimate aim to seek and to know God, to merge with God and to get Moksha. A yogi should avoid demanding from God anything but there is no harm to demand above things, as we are God's loving children.

Difference Between Ignorance, Information and Knowledge

Information is the data that the scientists, the educationists, the teachers and other agencies are supplying to us about their studies of ***creation*** around us and is mostly transferred to the students, through their teachers in our universities, colleges and schools. The media is also a good source of supplying the information. But the data that remove our ignorance due to Maya and lead us more and more nearer to God or to understand God and our ownself is called ***knowledge***. While the data, which creates more confusion, and lead us away from God i.e. to deny the existence of God, is called ***ignorance***. Most of the times the same data is interpreted in different ways by different people. It may become ***knowledge*** or ***ignorance*** as per their interpretations.

Bhagwad Geeta, Shastras and Bible are the good source of knowledge of God and our soul. So these are the ocean of knowledge and not mare information. The events stated about a war in newspapers and the contents given in general knowledge books or tests are only information. There is Ministry of Information or education in most of the Governments, but there is no Ministry of Knowledge in any Government.

As fog disappears before the Sun, ignorance melts away before knowledge. Divine Knowledge is acquired by constant meditation upon God. We can remove all our doubts by consulting the self-realized saints and our Guru. When our ignorance due to delusion disappears, our true Self (*Atma)* shines in its own splendor.

Difference Between Self-Realized Saint & Avatar

A saint is a person who seeks God, do his spiritual *sadhana* and practice yoga. He has no attachment with worldly things and has no material desire. He has renounced the physical pleasures of the world. He has no desire other then to know God. He has a full control over his desires, body and mind. But a saint may also be under the delusion and *Maya*, till he attains self-realization.

When a saint achieves self-realization in his lifetime, he becomes a self-realized saint. Then he becomes one with God. After that there is no ignorance or *Maya* between his soul and the God. The ultimate Truth of God is revealed to him. He then possesses all the qualities of God. A self-realized saint when took birth, is as ignorant of God as any other human being. Before his self-realization he is also under *Maya* and lives under the *karmic*-law. Every human being has been given a power of discrimination to discriminate between good and bad *karmas* (actions) and he is bound to get the reward of his *karmas*: good or bad. Due to his consistent s*adhana, tapasia* and his devotion for God he achieves self-realization in his later life.

Although a self-realized saint is not allowed by God to perform, frequent miracles before the masses for his fame, livelihood and earning, but rarely he is allowed to perform a miracle to his disciples to promote their faith in God and himself. After self-realization a saint becomes just like God, but not God. He cannot be called an *Avatar* of God. There will be no temple for him like an *avatar* (like Rama or Krishna) and he is not worshiped in the temples after his s*amadhi* (death). Some of the self-realized yogis also merge themselves in God after their *samadhi* as a water drop merges in the ocean. They get *Moksha.* But some of the self-realized gurus retain their existence even after their *samadhi or death to uplift their disciples back to God.* They continue to serve God for long time.

An ***Avatar*** is an incarnation of God, when God assumes a human form. *Avatar* is a *Sanskrit* word means *avataran (descend).* An A*vatar* descend form Godly level to manly level. When an avatar appears, takes human form and his first breath in this world, He knows that He is God and has all the super powers and qualities of God like omnipotence, omnipresence and omniscient. Contrarily a saint does not know that he is God at the time of his birth, but an avatar knows that He is God. An avatar is empowered to perform frequent miracles, without any fruits of his actions. The actions of an Avatar without any reward are known as *lila of God.*

An avatar is not under the karmic-law (law of action & reward). An avatar does his *lila* (actions without any reward) only. He need not do his *sadhana, tapasia* or meditations to know God, as He already knows that He is

God. An avatar generally comes along with the incarnation of many other saints and gods, to play his big *lila* jointly in this world. The actions of avatar are unique. He becomes a well known renowned personality soon in the world. After leaving the world there will be temples of Avatar, where he is worshiped. Generally there is existence of an avatar after leaving his body in the world, as of Rama, Krishna and Shirdi Sai Baba. Sri Sathya Sai Baba is also an avatar and not simply a self realized saint.

There Should Not be Contradictions Between the Self-realized Saints

If God is one, then the Absolute Reality or Truth is also one. Truth cannot be many and there can't be self-contradiction in Truth. It is interesting and important to note that all the self-realized saints and avatars have said exactly the same thing, about the religion and the absolute reality of God. There may be different ways of worshipping and seeking God. But should not be any kind of contradiction between the religions. A contradiction means two opposite kind of statements: such as some religions believe in the existence and rebirth of soul and somc does not. Some religions believe that God appears in human form as an Avatar, play His lila in the world, some says He can't. Some religions are silent about the existence of God and soul. These are examples of contradictions.

If there is any contradiction between any two saints or any two religions, then at least one of them is not correct and also the founder of one of the religion may not be self-realized and may be under *Maya*. Transcendental knowledge may be the same in different religions, but in one it may come through an angel or a prophet, and in another through a deity or God Himself.

A true religion of God must have also the Holy *Shastras* to support its views and as its basis of authenticity, for the benefits of its followers. The *Shastras* are written by the self-realized divine personalities and not written by ordinary worldly writers. As done by many writers, a mere collection and interpretations of writings or sayings of different saints, at different times cannot be of the standard of ***Shastras*** or the Holy Books I am talking about. Some of the so-called holy books have been written by some learned men but not by self realized saint. The writers might have charged some payment for their written work with the profit motto. Some of the writers have written the religious literature under the orders of a king on payment. Such literary books cannot be called *Shastras.* The book I am writing is also not a *Shastra as per the definition.*

Most of the religious heads these days are the elected ones and are not self-realized saints. A person who has a majority of votes in the election is selected as head and a person having lesser votes is rejected. The real or self-realized saints are no more interested, in worldly fame or to be elected for powers for an official post or chair. So it is not necessary and a rare possibility that the religious heads of the religions have achieved self-realization. He may be a powerful, learned, respectable and a social man but not a self-realized man. You may generally search or find a self-realized saint only in the remote areas, meditating in caves, away from the crowd, noise and the politics of the world. But there may also be some self-realized saints in the crowd of the society, unknown to the world.

Many religions do not have any *Shastras* or any philosophical base to support their religions. The followers of these religions are governed by the rules framed by a group of their elected heads from time to time instead of the *Shastras.* Since their foundation and base of religion is weak and man based, their faith could shake very easily.

Misconception Between The Asanas and Yoga

Asanas are different kind of postures to be practiced by the yogis, to send the life force, forcibly to different parts of the body. Asanas are the stretching and relaxing different parts of the body slowly without any jerk. All the organs of our body are functioning, due to the life force flowing in them. The lack of the life force in the body organ due to our inactivity and wrong sitting posture, during the day causes some diseases or illness in our body. By regular *asanas* the life force begins to flow properly and body is cured from the diseases. But the curing of the body from diseases is not the ultimate aim of yoga. There is much more to achieve in Yoga. Asanas are only one of the eighth parts of yoga to be practiced regularly.

Some of the individuals or the organization all over the world are busy in providing training for a*sanas* to cure some of the diseases. There is no doubt that the asanas keeps the physical body healthy and sound, fit for yoga. Asanas are only the preliminary third-part out of the total eight-parts in the hierarchy of *Patanjali* yoga. *Asanas* does not mean Yoga. In India most of the schools and colleges have appointed a yoga-teacher to teach Yoga to their students. The yoga teachers generally provide the practice of some of the asanas to their students like a mass PT exercise. They never tell them that the asanas are not the yoga and they never bother about the devotion to God and other seven parts of yoga defined by Patanjali. What type of yoga the yoga teachers are teaching to the students?

It is strange that to talk about devotion to God in educational institution in India, is prohibited in the name of so called ***secularism***. Secularism does not mean not to talk about God or Yoga. Yoga is a universal science of seeking God or the Creator, as other natural sciences are busy to know the creation. Secularism means equal importance and respect to all the religions. No religion is to be criticized. But it does not mean to ignore God.

Most of the students have acquired a misconception in their minds that the asanas are the complete yoga. It is a misconception we are installing in the minds of our young students. Even the educational authorities are ignorant of what yoga really is? Yoga means communion of soul with God. Without love & devotion for God, what kind of Yoga we are teaching. Asanas have nothing to do with God. We should call such teachers as Asana Teachers and not the Yoga Teachers. It should be clearly understood that the asana teachers are not the Yoga Gurus I am talking about in my book. Even outside India so many persons & organizations are providing the training for asanas privately and claiming it yoga. They are minting money from the ignorant people.

There is nothing substantial to achieve in this world except the God-realization. No body has ever achieved any thing nor he will achieve, nor can he achieve except God-realization. It's mere our foolishness, ignorance, delusion and waste of time in achieving wealth, health, honor, prestige, victory and comforts etc. It is nothing but our sheer deception of our ownself. None of these things will accompany with us at the time of our death and none of these things accompany with us even during our daily sleep. To acquire any of the above things, we will unnecessarily indulge in sins, and will have to suffer for our sins as per the *karmic-law. Remember it is always better to minimize our worldly needs and physical pleasures.*

"Our time is distinguished by wonderful achievements in the fields of scientific understanding and the technical application of those insights. Whom this would not cheer? But let us not forget that the knowledge and skills alone cannot lead humanity to a happy and dignified life. Humanity has every reason to place the proclaimers of high moral standards and values above the discoverers of objective truth. What humanity owes to personalities like Buddha, Moses, and Jesus ranks for me higher than all the achievements of the enquiring and constructive mind?"

...Albert Einstein

"Remember, a lazy and irregular seeker of God, can never find God. The idle mind is a devil's workshop. But a constant regular practice of deep meditation with firm faith & devotion helps in early self-realization."

8

Spirit and Self-Realization

Spirit & Self-Realization

Prayer

O Heavenly Spirit, O Ocean of Knowledge, Thou art the dearest of the dear, nearest of the near, and the closest of the closest. Thou art just behind the curtain of my ignorance, vision and enchanting senses. Thou art the beauty of the flowers, forest, mountains and the miraculous beauty of the vast sky. Whenever, I look in my heart, thou art inside. Thou art the greatest Lover in universe and our souls are Thou beloved. But the worldly loves are not permanent. I am always crying for Thy Supreme Love, which is pure, loving and eternal. When Thou will have a mercy on us and play a divine romance with Thy beloveds? Thou beloveds are waiting; to have a romance with Thee, since thousands of our past lives. Thou art also waiting for our love too but playing the game of hide & seek. O Lover of disciples now reveals Thee.

How to get Self-Realization?

For the seekers of God & self-realization, I may suggest a few holy books that are most useful as their holy Bibles, in their divine path of Yoga. Some of them are:

1. ***Bhagwad Geeta*** (*The Song of the Lord & Bible of yogis*) is the most important sacred and authentic holy book for the seekers of God all over the world. This is the only Holy Book, in which the God Himself has opened His own secrets. It is one of the greatest philosophical and yogic dialogues known to man. Through Bhagwad Geeta, Lord Krishna gives the Knowledge of God in most condensed form and also to the whole world through His dearest & closest friend and disciple Arjuna. It is the Bible for the

yogis and seekers of God. It is a guide for the inner path of self-realization. All the *Puranas* support the truth of Bhagwad Geeta. The *Puranas* are the records of great historical spiritual events with a great teaching motto and philosophy. But Bhagwat Geeta is a pure spiritual Knowledge and Truth about God revealed by Lord Krishna Himself for the benefit of the world through Arjuna. Knowledge is that which removes ignorance or Maya and brings us nearer to God. Maya keeps us away from God. Bhagwad Geeta informs us briefly what God is, and what are the different paths of seeking God? Every one of us is full of anxieties and tensions, because of Maya. Our existence is in the atmosphere of non-existence. Bhagwad Gita is a search light for our intelligence to take the righteous decision in life and overcome the anxiety.

There are in all 18 chapters and 700 *slokas* in it, which covers different topics of yoga (the science of seeking God). Bhagwad Geeta has been translated in most of the languages of the world. Bhagwad Geeta provides a brief but condensed knowledge of many different paths of Yoga like *Sankhyia* (Knowledge) *Yoga, Karam* (Action) *Yoga, Bhakti (Devotional) Yoga, Hath Yoga* and the most important the ***Kriya Yoga*** etc.

2. ***The Lessons on Self-Realization***, by Sri Paramhansa Yogananda is a set of sacred literature on seeking God. These lessons provide us, *step-by-step practical detailed instructions on science of Kriya Yoga and Meditational Techniques.* Sri Yogananda himself has written all these lessons, in most systematic and scientific manner for the benefit of God seekers. These lessons are very useful and convenient to yogis, as these are practical in nature and can be studied and practiced, sitting at home at our convenient time. If someone read these lessons, then

there is no need for him to leave his sweet family and home, to leave his job and to live in Guru's ashram in his physical presence. All these may disturb the life of God seeker and his family. A true God seeker should do his duties to God, to family and to the society also.

At present these lessons are available only in English. There are nearly 200 lessons, but not available in book-form, from any bookshop. Before getting these lessons one has to the member of YOGDA or SRF. These are either available from Self Realization Fellowship Centre, San Rafael Avenue, Los-Angeles, California- 90065, USA or Yogoda Satsanga Society of India, Paramhansa Yogananda Marg, Ranchi-834001, India.

3. ***The Autobiography of a Yogi*:**
by Sri Paramhansa Yogananda

This is the rare autobiography of a self-realized yogi available in the world. Most of others books are biographies of yogis not written by themselves. It is Yogananda's life story with an absorbing account of his singular search for Guru, Truth and God. It is skillfully interwoven with scientific explanations of the subtle but definite laws, by which yogis perform miracles and attain self-realization. It has been translated into more then 14 languages of the world and is used as an authentic textbook and a reference book in most of the colleges and universities throughout the world. It gives us the glimpses of the great miraculous gurus & saints of the world, mainly the Jesus Christ and Mahavtar Babaji.

The main aim of this book is to understand the real aim of life of a yogi and how to achieve it? After reading this book, you will be convinced that the main aim of life is self-realization to know God and nothing else. Why do the saints and yogis renounce their families and worldly pleasures, because they are hankering after seeking God.

Some Useful Points to achieve Self-Realization

All of us dislike any kind of bondage. But we all expect honor, prestige, praise and favor from others. How strange it is? All these expectations lead us to bondages. He, who expects anything from others, is bound to be a slave of expectation. All kinds of such bondages are great hindrance in God-realization. Remember that God is free from all kinds of bondages. So long we aspire worldly things, we cannot aspire to God-realization. So we must give up our desires for aspiring the worldly things. We should not expect any kind of favor, benefit or praise from others.

If we have any desire, it is a weakness in us. It is an indication of spiritual poverty. Why do we invite poverty for nothing? We should not expect anything from others. It leads us to bondages. We should not demand or expect any worldly thing from God also. One should not depend upon such things, which are subject to change or destruction. Our real self is eternal, immortal and does not subject to decay or death. One who expects benefits from others is not a rightful claimant. One who wants honor or prestige from others does not really deserve it. On the other hand one who deserve honor and prestige does not hanker after it.

Running after material things produces discontent. The desires have no end. If we become the slave of our senses, the desires will not leave us till our death. The desires are unquenchable thirst. Only the intense love for God and deep meditation can make you desireless, while doing all your duties in this world.

He who hankers after honor and prestige is slave of these and is not worthy of it. Even if a saint hankers after a disciple or wealth, is a slave of his disciple or wealth. He who has no desires and no craving for any kind of thing is the king of kings. Even the kings have so many desires to be fulfilled and are not free from bondages.

We want a thing only until we have it. When we get the thing the pleasure diminishes. We find that after some time our joy from getting it is gone or lost. Very soon we will forget that it was once our desire. The joy of fulfilling any desire is short lived. But the joy or bliss of communing with God is everlasting. So we must seek God for everlasting joy and not a temporary joy or entertainment from worldly things.

"*The human soul is a spark of the Divine Fire. It is immortal, ever conscious, free from impurities, and is blissful.*" *(Manas—7/116/1)*

"*Brahman is one, all pervading, omnipotent, and immortal. It is ever-present, conscious and blissful.*"

(Manas—1/22/3)

In fact both the soul and *Brahman* are same. The only difference is that soul is separated from *Brahman* by the ignorance of the soul due to *Maya.* Try to get rid of the *Maya.*

We take delight in eating, drinking, sleeping, talking, watching TVs, and idle rest on bed. But we do not have any time and the same delight to love, pray and worship God. We have been given only one mind and one brain. We may devote it to any thing we like. God has given us freedom whether we devote it to God or to worldly pleasures. Only the right decision, the extreme love and devotion to God, can help us to distract our senses from the worldly pleasures and desires.

A seeker of God must exclusively devote some of his daily time to the pursuit of God-communion. He should not get himself entangled much in the favorable or the adverse circumstances of his life in the world. Otherwise it will become a great hindrance in seeking God. We must give us our deepest love and true devotion to God. We should totally surrender our heart, mind and soul to God Almighty. We must seek Him in our actions and in meditation. In Bhagwad Gita (VI: 30) Lord Krishna has said: "*He who perceives Me everywhere all around and behold Me in everything. He never loses My sight, nor do I ever lose sight of him.*" So always seek God.

There is nothing more substantial to achieve in the perishable world except God-realization. It is our mere delusion to feel satisfied in achieving wealth, health, honor, prestige, victory and comforts etc. in the world. It is nothing but deception of our ownself. If we die nothing will accompany with us except the fruits of our past actions and the achievements of God-realization.

To achieve or acquire wealth, honor and prestige, we have to indulge ourselves in dishonesty, cunning cheating and deceiving others. For indulging ourselves in sins committed, we have to suffer from the fruits of our past actions (*karmas*). Without experiencing the fruits of all our past karmas (actions), no self-realization or salvation is possible.

None of our worldly wealth or achievements will come to our rescue, when we breathe our last. We are simply wasting our precious time in trying to acquire huge worldly things. Rather we should devote our lifetime to seek and to know God. Remember we should not always think of the comforts and entertainment of this life, but think of your life afterward.

From all above, I do not mean to say that you should stop working at all and do nothing for your livelihood and life achievements. But there should be a proper balance of time for all the activities of your life. You should devote your time to worldly things, which are absolutely necessary for an honorable and pleasurable life. But side-by-side you must devote some of your time daily exclusively to seeking of God.

There is a great difference between *what we need, and what we desire*? Needs are those worldly things, without which we cannot survive in the world, like good food, air, water, clothes, shelter, education, medicines and a little money to lead a comfortable life. We should have that much of money so that we need not to beg anything for our livelihood from any body.

Desires are innumerable and endless and the creation of our own mind, and causes bad habits. One may have a lot of un-necessary desires, which are not necessary for the sustenance of his life. A yogi should not have any desire except to know God. Remember that the desires can be controlled and minimized by regular Satsanga, meditation, reading good spiritual literature and intense devotion to God.

A yogi should not worry about future. *Future is unknown.* It is in the hands of God. We do not know, what is the best for our future and for present. Only God knows what is the best and what we shall need for our future. We should surrender completely all our desires and needs to God. *God will take care for all our needs, only if, we completely surrender to Him.* Always remember: *"When every thing is lost, our future still remains."* So never be discouraged or disheartened, if the things are not according to our plans. Whether we are under pleasurable or miserable circumstances, we should have no feeling of pride or aversion for them. We should be indifferent to pleasure and pain. We have already been entangled in this duality of pleasure and pain. This is the grievous error due to Maya. We should keep on realizing this error.

By complete surrender, I do not mean to sit idle and do nothing in your life. You should do all your duties assigned by God in this world, but do not have any desire to have the reward of your actions. You have only the freedom of action, but the reward is in the hands of almighty God.

"*He, whose mind is untroubled in the midst of sorrow and is free from eager and desires amid pleasures…is called a yogi or sage of settled intelligence."*
"Whatever pleasures are born of contacts with worldly objects are only the sources of sorrow."
… … (Bhagwad Geeta: 2/56 & 5/22)
Due to the development of Tele-communication and Electronic-media human beings are now exposed to great events & happening daily throughout the world. Naturally the viewer is excited and is un-necessarily involved in such events. The seeker of God should avoid such involvements. He should observe the events in such a way, as an observer of a movie keeps him away from his indulgence in the movie. While you are awake, be detached (not inactive) from all worldly activities, things and happenings. This will help you to maintain equanimity in the midst of sorrows and sufferings.

"*He who neither loathes nor desires, should be known as one, who has ever the spirit of renunciation; free from dualities he is released easily from bondage, O mighty armed Arjuna.*" ... (Bhagwad Gita 5/3)

Constant *Japa* is very useful in seeking of God. *Japa* is a Sanskrit word. It means to utter the name of the Lord repeatedly either mentally or in a very low voice. *Japa* means the adoration by repeating reverently God's name as a sacred mantra. God is adored by His innumerable names symbolizing His positive and negative qualities. *Japa* reveals both the positive and negative aspects of God. *Japa* insists on the ultimate truth of oneness of Supreme Being with the soul. Remember that the Supreme God may manifest itself in various forms, shapes, and colors, but ultimately it is one.

God manifests Himself as many, yet one. He is both Beauty and Truth. He is the all the Creator, Savior and Destroyer, Chastiser and Merciful. He is the inner light and essence of all the prophets, kings, saints, messengers and all the gods. He strikes fear in no one, yet He is always fearless. He is manifested in everything still He is unmanifested. He is both Knowledge and *Maya* (Ignorance), the darkness and the light; the quarrel and the peace. These may look contradictory to us but God is above these contradictions.

After the realization of God, there shall remain nothing more to do anything. Once we are awakened in God, we are awakened forever in God. As we have to do nothing to learn to awake from our sleep or to sleep from awakening, similarly we have to do nothing to enter *the kingdom of God* from the material perishable world after self-realization.

Understand that God didn't create this world just for the people to indulge in human emotions. God created the

Maya or the devil (*Satan*) too. Devil has further created the temptations and ignorance. God is watching and testing every one of us, every moment, whether we are tempted with his creation or to love and seek the Creator God. To convince us about the non-reality and the delusion of the physical universe, God is giving us daily experience of the dreams to attract us towards Him. God always knows that He is throwing us into the worldly troubles, but remember He also suffers too, due to our troubles. God has imposed the same rules on Himself as on us. God also seeks our love too & suffers if we ignore Him.

Do not think too seriously about the reality of the world and this life. This life is short and will end very soon, before we know it. All the wonderful past dreams of our childhood & youth have already forgotten. In the remaining part of our life we must always remember Him. If we seek God earnestly, how can He remain away from us and ignore our love? We should constantly and inwardly remember & whisper with Him always. Give your soul call, and then He cannot remain away from you.

Our Pride and Ego are our Greatest Enemy and Barrier to Wisdom

Our Ego 'I' (*Ahankar*) is the *cause of our pride,* which is *our greatest enemy in the world.* Due to our pride generally we think that we are correct and others are wrong. We do not want to understand and learn from others and their useful experiences. It is great hindrance in getting knowledge. It is due to our Ego 'I', *Maya* and ignorance that we think that we are the sole doer, in the Cosmic Drama of God. Our successes in worldly affairs & achievement make our ego stronger. We often say that my house, my father, my mother, my property, my children, my bank-balance, my intelligence and my mind etc. All these leads to our false conclusion that whatever we possess in this world is due to our own efforts and intelligence. God has nothing to do with these achievements. Due to delusion we also think that only we are correct and others are wrong. In fact the *truth is just opposite to it.*

The universe around us is the great Cosmic Drama played by God and we are just the actors or images in this universal *movie house.* We do not know, what shall be our role tomorrow and what was our role in our past lives and when we shall leave this temporary hotel on this earth? We shall be deprived to take any thing with us, even our next breath, a penny, our dear ones and even our own physical body, which are our dearest. *Remember, we have to leave every thing all of a sudden against our will.* We don't know our next journey after our death. We do not know what will happen to us at the time of our death. We daily see others dying and leaving the earth all of a sudden. But due to our ego and *Maya,* we do not want to accept the reality that we will also have to leave this earth very soon.

In our past lives we have already experienced so many births and deaths, but we have forgotten them due to our ignorance and *Maya.* Even if we come to know that some of the persons are able to remember the past lives, we intentionally ignore them and do not believe them for no valid reasons. It is most unscientific.

All Thoughts Are Coming From God

Realize that, all our thoughts are coming from the Cosmic Ocean of Knowledge of God. All the streams of thoughts are flowing to our mind from the great reservoir of *Ocean of Thoughts in ether.* Due to *Maya* thoughts distract our mind away from God. To know and realize God we have to stop this stream of thoughts coming to our mind and become thoughtless. God listens to the language of our heart in the depth of our silence of mind and need no other human language. Our mind is like a peaceful lake. Thoughts make our mind turbulent and restless. Then we cannot see the bottom of the lake and our reflection in the lake. But when our mind becomes thoughtless and peaceful, the lake of mind becomes silent. Then the reflection of our ego 'I' is visible clearly in the lake.

Do not believe that God is far away from us and doesn't respond to our prayers. Rather, God is closest to our soul and the ego 'I'. God listen to our deep prayers everywhere at all times, but some-times He answers differently than our expectations. He answers our prayers, but we are unable to receive it, as we have not tuned our mind properly to God. If we first commune our mind properly with God in deep meditation, and then pray, we will be able to listen God's response. We should not doubt on it.

Love and Devotion to God are Must for Self-Realization

It is said that Education without Character, Commerce without Morality, Science without Humanity, Politics without Principles and ***Yoga without Devotion is not only useless*** but also dangerous to society.

If you want, you can practice, all the teachings and instructions of yoga without any love & devotion to God. It may also benefit most you in your life, like sound health and sound mind. But if you do not have love and devotion to God, you may misuse your achievement against others and you will never be able to seek God. Unless and until you have an intense fire of devotion to God, God will not reveal Himself to you. He loves us all. He is waiting and standing at the door of our consciousness, to enter our heart, but we do not allow Him to let in our heart. Remember *God is also suffering too, to seek our love.*

It is a big question, why should we suffer *disappointments* in our lives? It is noticed that we get so much comforts, love, prestige, children and wealth etc. in our life from God. But all of a sudden all these are taken away from us as in case of sudden deaths, accidents, diseases and business losses. The cause is, we have also betrayed God in our life. In the similar way we have disappointed God, because He loves us, waiting for us and we have denied our love to Him. Remember, ***God is suffering too, caused by the separation of our soul from Him and due to our indifferent attitude to Him. Why we have denied our to Him?***

"All things betray thee, who betrayest Me."
...The Hounds of Heaven, by Francis Thompson

Science has informed that all object are inflammable, but a minimum ***ignition temperature*** is required to ignite an object. A minimum amount of velocity or ***escape energy*** is needed to escape an object from earth or to escape an electron out from its orbital. Similarly a *minimum intensity of meditation fire*, love and devotion is needed to contact with God. God is not indifferent to any body. All our prayers are recorded in the heart of Supreme God. He will definitely answer to you at the right time. If you are not able to listen to His answer, do not doubt upon Him and don't be discouraged also. Try to introspect and find out your *own shortcomings, if any* and do your efforts with stronger will, devotion and more energy.

Stop doubting and questioning God. These will never end. But once you experience God, all your questions and doubts will vanish immediately. The ignorance or your darkness on soul cannot stand before Knowledge of God. Some may argue, how can I feel love for an unknown God? Let us eat, drink and marry now. Such a philosophy is a waste of precious life. Doubt without any base is our biggest enemy. If God offers a glass of *Amrita* (the divine drink which makes soul immortal) out of His love and grace upon us, and if some one creates a false doubt in our mind that the glass contains poison, then we will be deprived of drinking the *Amrita.* Isn't it?

Do Not Be Afraid of God

God is the most *beautiful and lovable entity* in the universe. God is not an embodiment of fear as generally presumed. Many think that God is like a man sitting on a thorn in the heaven and God must punish the guilty immediately one does any thing wrong. But God waits, watches, and punish the guilty once when many of his guilts are accumulated. If God respond and punish the guilty immediately after his sin, He would have become an embodiment of fear like a devil and not the embodiment of love and worship.

But don't think any body can escape from the punishment of his sins and His omni-watching eyes. It is a fool's paradise to think of escape. So you must always talk and whisper to Him. He is always with you and you should never afraid of Him. A newly born child always feels safe in the lap of his mother. Similarly you will not be afraid of anybody, if you are really convinced that God is always with you. If you are afraid of the past misdeeds, t*ry to repent for your sins with your inner heart. Pray God to forgive you for your sins and you should not commit more sins in your life.*

We have ***come alone*** temporarily on this earth and will go alone without your asking. We are ***living alone in the big crowd*** of people around us. The crowd includes even our wife, children, family members and friends. None else on this earth will be responsible for our past misdeeds, not even your wife and children, for whose comforts we have been doing misdeeds in the world. God is not far away from His creation. He is always with all of us. He is present in everything, as ether is omnipresent throughout the universe. God does not need a physical body or a vehicle to be with us.

Do not be Afraid of Death

Every body including a king, a V.I.P., a wealthy man or a healthy man is afraid of death *Death is inevitable to all.* There is only one reality i.e. God. But d*on't be afraid of death* if God and Guru are with you. If you are awakened in God now, both will be with you at the time of your death. We shouldn't worry anything, if God is with us. Fear of death is due to our ignorance and inexperience of death. If someone once gets the experience of death, and keep it remembering, the fear of death will go automatically. We are not afraid of sleep as we have a daily experience of sleep. *Death is just as good as permanent sleep, but we have forgotten the experience of our past deaths.*

Our ***birth and death*** are the two most important events in our life. They are the two faces of the same coin i.e. life. We make all kinds of efforts, preparation, planning, timetable and management for all the important events of our life like: first joining of the school or job, examinations, our marriage, birth of our child, marriage of our children etc. But do we ever bother and thought, about the preparation, management and planning of the most

important event of our life i.e. death which is certain one day?
You should always think: what will happen to me at the time of my death and what will happen after my death? Where shall I go after the death? Will I take any rebirth? If so, in what form and where I will take birth? Will I take birth as a man or an animal or some other creature? What after that? Is any thing more important for us, than the answers of these questions? Will science help us to answer these important questions?

A yogi gets the answers to these questions, in this life during samadhi and then he is not afraid of his death. Many advance yogis gets the experiences of death of his physical body and again coming back to his physical body. Then he is not afraid of death. For such a yogi the death is just a sweet sleep and to replace the old diseased body with a new physical body.

If you are *not awakened in God* and are given the, whole wealth and kingdom of the world and the universe, very soon you will be bored of it. You will not remain happy forever with that kind of achievement. Contrarily, if you have nothing, but are in communion with God, you are always ever blissful, happy and need nothing else.

Don't think that *I am not fit for the spiritual yogic life. Do not believe that to seek God or to know God is impossible* for you. This is the greatest impact of *Satan* or *Maya* on you. The greatest *weapon of Maya is to separate or keep the man away from God. Maya* creates a false reasoning in our mind and makes us believe that we are not ready to commune with God. To keep *Satan* away from us, try to have the company of God seekers and the Holy *Shastras.* A yogi should never sleep without meditation at night. He should feel the presence of God everywhere in all the things. Throughout the day and night in each of your breath talk and whisper with God. ***"O my Father, Thou art always with me in my heart. Do not play the game of hide & seek with me any more. Reveal Thyself."***

Remember:
"Self-control, tolerance & cheerfulness create mental harmony and peace. If we reform ourself, the world will be reformed itself."

"During the meditation one should visualize that the cosmic life-energy is entering his body through the medulla oblongata at the centre of the skull and he should try to direct the flow of this energy by his will power to each and every part of his body through the Chakras in his spine."

"Almighty God is the eternal source of all our happiness & joy. Seek God and feel Him within. To get success one should completely surrender to God without any pre-condition. God is the driving chariot of our life & body carefully and avoiding our pitfalls in life (like Lord Krishna driving the chariot of Arjuna). If you have unshakable faith in God, he will surely take us out of the great Ocean of Maya."

"We should stop finding fault & criticizing others. Rather we should try to introspect and search our faults within ourself. Only then we can reform ourself and we can expect to reform others. Our fault finding & criticism of others develops enmity, bad relations & violence. So try to avoid it. Instead of other's criticism, develops your own peace of mind and friendship with others. Try it."

9

The Nature of Our Dreams and Death

What are Dreams?

Dreams are Materialization of Thoughts

To Create an Object First a Thought is Required

Various Illusions of Dreaming Men

What is Death? Is Death a Dream?

The Universe is a Condensation &
Materialization of the Dream of God

Desires are Causes of Suffering in the World

A Story of Contented Shepherd from USA

Dream Nature of the World

The Nature of our Dreams & Death

Prayer

O Director of Dream-Worlds, O Creator of thoughts and the Lord of Dream-Universe, teach me to understand Thy great mystery of my sweet and horrible dreams. Teach me to understand Thy great Dream-Movie of the wondrous universe around me. How my thoughts, past memories and future events are combined and converted into dreams during my sleep? How to interpret the dreams we experience? Since my birth, I am not only curious to know Thy creation, but also curious to know my mysterious dreams. I am forced to experience unwillingly the horrible dreams during my sleep just as a puppet. Virtually I do not have any control over my dreams and I experience helplessly the horrible, fearful & unreasonable dreams. My little mind is not able to understand their cause, meaning and the purpose behind them.

I am standing on the brink of eternity, ready to jump from the world of delusion into Thee. Make me to realize my oneness with Thee. Awaken me permanently from my false awakened dream of Thy delusive universe, so that I am able to remember Thee forever. The nightmare of death, rebirth and delusion always dances around me. I do not know what happens at the time of death and after death? How my soul takes rebirth again and again? Do humans take rebirth as lower creatures also?

O, Beloved One, O Spirit Divine, Thou have created the *Satan* (*Maya*) to separate us from Thee. Let the *Satan* not delude those who are seeking Thee. The *Satan* is very strong and powerful, but Thy love is far greater and potent. One touch of Thy grace and love can drive away the *Satan* controlling my mind, intelligence, senses, heart, body and my fate.

O Father, I don't want anything except Thee. I can't live without Thee. I don't want to teach anyone, but discipline my ownself. What is there in anything, O Lord of dreams?

I am convinced that everything in this world is false and a dream. Even my body is a dream in the awakened world. My desires are also dreams. Thou art the only reality behind this dream-drama world. Make me free from this delusive dream of *Maya.* O, Eternal Omniscient Light, awake me from the dark dream world, and take me to the Eternal Ocean of Thy Infinite Light.

What are Dreams?

In this chapter we will try to understand about the mystery of our dreams. All of us are experiencing the dreams helplessly, during our sleep and we have no control over our mind and on our dreams. During the sleep state of consciousness, our physical body lies uncared and unbothered by ourself. During sleep state we are not aware of our physical body at all and also not aware of any thing of this universe.

The universe, which exists during our awakening state, does not exist during our sleep or dream state of consciousness. The dream universe is a creation of our mind and is different from the awakened-universe. Our mind is like a *TV tuner* and is tuned to different cosmic frequency of dream world, during our sleep. During awakening the frequency of tuning is different. This should be clearly understood that "*no dream can come to us without any cause behind it*'. The cause may be anything, even the fruits of our past *karmas*. But can we predict by any scientific way about the dream we are going to experience in the following night? Is it possible?

The ***thought-films*** of all our past experiences of this life and previous lives are stored in the memory of our mind. It is like the storage of memory in the hard disk of a computer. *The dreams are the mental motion pictures projected by our unconscious mind. The dreams are the creation of God and not always purposeless as generally thought. Dreams have a great purpose of God to realize men about the dream nature of this false world.* The creation of the dreams for man is to provide the proof that this universe, which looks real, is false and is also like a dream.

We create and possess a *subtle body (made from ethereal matter and* not from physical matter) for ourself during he drcam world and we have a power to create a new dream universe for us. The subtle body possesses all the five sense organs, five organs for actions, mind, intelligence and ego 'I' etc. During our dream we are forced to experiencc all kinds of emotions like joy, pleasures, happiness and grief, sorrows and pains, fear, laugh and weeping etc. We may also experience our death.

Generally when we see our dead relations during our dreams we forget that they are already dead. Some times the old man experiences that he is a young child and forgets all his past history. How it is all? It appears that nothing is in our hands during our dreams. Our helplessness of experiencing the dream which are not of our own choice clearly proves that we are just puppet in the hands of Almighty God in the Dream-Drama of the world.

Dreams are the Materialization of Thoughts

All the ancient *Shastras* are the creation of God. They are universally true forever. It is a misconception that *Shastras* are exclusively for Hindus. Before millennium BC there was hardly any other religion except Sanatan Dharma in the world.

There are evidences of human skulls nearly seven million years old found in Botswana, South Africa (A News in H.T. dated 12-7-2002). Will the historians tell us the human history of this last seven million years? In fact the *Shastras* and the *Puranas* are for whole humanity belonging to the people of all the religions. All human beings have equal right on the *Shastras* created by God for the benefit of all the men. The *Shastras* have explained that our universe is a materialization of the great *Thought of God and it is a Cosmic Dream of God.* This may be little difficult for us to realize, to understand and to accept the truth in it.

Our dreams are the materialization of our thoughts in combination with our stored memories and the fruits of past actions of the present and previous lives. It is true that some times the dreams give the glimpses of our future. Thoughts are invisible, but can be made visible as dreams by the cosmic life energy. When thoughts are further condensed and materialized they take the form of dream, like the water vapors when condensed change into liquid. When dream is further condensed it takes the form of material things as the liquid water when solidified changes into ice.

It can easily be understood by the example of making a film. First the invisible thoughts come in the mind of a director of a movie film. The invisible thoughts are further visualized or dreamed in the mind of the director in so many different ways. Then the he further picturize or materialize his dream thought into a motion film through the acting by the actors. The motion film when played on a screen gives the illusion of reality to the viewers of the film.

The viewers and observers of the movie film think that every thing shown on the screen is real. But a little logical thinking convinces the viewers that the film is a combination of series of millions of pictures fitted together and projected on a screen. The cosmic universe is merely a dream projected by God on the 4-dimensional space-time screen of the universe as told by the self-realized saints. The God's projector and His created films are far better then the man created ones. That is why the universe looks just real to us.

As per the Bhagwad Gita, we are the ***immortal souls*** and have taken birth on this earth to enjoy the fruits of our past actions (*karmas*) and to fulfill our unfulfilled desires. We should see the entire happening around us, simply as an observer of three or four dimensional movie film, projected around us by God. Every thing around us is a false image and not the reality as our image in a plane mirror also looks like the real one. But remember our soul is immortal, unchangeable and unaffected by anything from this dream.

As we have the power to materialize our thoughts in dreams, God has the omnipotent power to materialize or dematerialize any of His thought in the universe. So a man when achieves self-realization becomes one with God, he attains all the powers of God. He can then materialize or dematerialize any thing at his will. Jesus Christ who was the 'Son of God', demonstrated this truth, so many times in his life by performing so many miracles. He was able to cure so many persons from incurable diseases and gave life to even dead persons.

"It is rightly said that if you want to *know an atom completely*, you have to become atom yourself, if you want to *know Albert Einstein completely* you have to become Einstein yourself and if you want to *know God completely*, you have to become God yourself."

To Create or Materialize any Object First a Thought is required

We know that everything on earth is, either man-made or God-made or made by some living creatures. It is universally accepted that nothing can be made without any cause. Whenever a thing is manufactured in a factory, first ***a thought or an idea*** comes in the mind of the engineer. And then the thought is visualized and materialized to manufacture the thing. There cannot be any thing without first having an idea or a thought about it.

Similarly whatever is in the universe or on the earth is not just by accident and it is just not possible without any initial cause or a thought or an idea. There must be a cause for everything existing in the universe (Law of Cause & Effect). First the idea or thought of the universe came to the mind of God and then it was materialized into physical form in exactly the pre-decided design. A single thought was enough for God, to design the whole universe from the beginning till the end of the universe. Remember as water (liquid) is a condensation of steam (gas), and ice (solid) is a condensation of water, similarly *dreams are condensation of thoughts and materials are the condensations of dreams.*

Various Illusions of Dreaming Man

The dreams are generally seem to be ***irrational, puzzling*** and stray in nature and not much connected with our daily life experiences. During the dream the existence of our awakened universe is completely lost. We totally forget the existence of universe and the body we live in. If we are suffering with a sever pain and sorrow due to an accident before sleep, these are lost and forgotten during the dreams.

Reciprocally, you may experience during dream that you have murdered some one and for that you are going to be crucified soon. Little after you watch that you are crucfied and have died also. After that, your horrible dream is broken and you are awakened from your dream. You are wondered to realize that your horrible dream was totally false, and you are still alive. Nothing has happened to your body and it is safe. After this you have realized and convinced that it was all ***illusion motion film*** and you were forced to dream it.

Conversely you may experience the similar false nature of our real life universal dream in which you are living. One day you may have a sudden accident and have broken most of your bones. Then you suffer with severe pain and suddenly you die. But immediately you again *wake up in an astral world* after your death. You may find that you have another *astral* body to act and experience. You may realize that you were dreaming in the false physical universe and have awakened in another astral universe. You realize that your present new astral body is perfectly O.K. Your bones are also O.K. You are not dead, but still alive. You also find some mysterious things that your new body does not feel hunger and need no food or water and so many other things to survive. You may laugh at your past dream of fetal accident in the awakened-world. This is what generally happens to most of the ordinary men at the time of death and after death. Has science done anything on these important subjects?

What is Death?
Is Death also a Dream?

Birth and death are the two face of the same coin i.e. life. These are the two most important events through which everybody pass from one dream to another dream. Our lives, which looks so real are just nightmares and dream pleasures. Death is simply the dream matter, which sends us back into the consciousness of God or in some other worlds. Death releases the soul from the bondages of the physical body, and to precede soul back to God.

So d*eath is not a punishment* to us as it is generally presumed. But it is a *gift of God* and is a part of the process of salvation and *Moksha* of our soul. It is a fundamental law that whoever has taken birth has to die one day, even the inert matter, the universe, any literature or religion, if taken birth will vanish one day. But our soul is immortal and a spark of God. It was always there before our birth and will remain after our death. It will never die, but will merge with God again after salvation.

It is notable that only human beings have been given the right of salvation and self-realization of God. If the souls and even the deities want to free themselves from the pangs of births, deaths and the miseries of life, they have to take a birth in human form and seek God for salvation or *Moksha*. Only the human soul will merge in the Ocean of God.

Our reincarnations are a series of dreams within the great cosmic dream. When we daily see every body dieing and suffering at death, we feel that God is cruel to the world, by creating horrible death. In fact it is not so. *God is merciful even at our death.* Remember that the world is not real; it is a dream in the mind of God. God make us free from the bondages of the world and give us either salvation (*Mukti*) or another astral body after our death.

Our new astral body go to an astral world after our death, where we realize that we do not feel hunger, need no food, no fire can burn us, no water can drawn us, no need of any transport and so many necessities of life. In the astral world we are free from all kinds of bondages, diseases, troubles and fears due to the perishable physical body. But if some of desires had been left unfulfilled in our life, then after some time we would like to come back to earth to fulfill our unfulfilled desires. *So the unfulfilled desires are the cause of our rebirths.* If we have no desire and we remember God, at the time of death, then there will be no rebirth and we will merge in the Ocean of God forever.

The reincarnation of a soul can be in any part of the world. You may take birth in a country, which you hate and do not like. You may take birth in the family of your enemy or in the religion you do not like. You must have to account for all your past actions. Will you continue helplessly to take births and rebirths and experience all the horrible troubles of the delusive world? Or will you like to follow the path of salvation for no more births and rebirths? It depends entirely upon you.

If you identify your soul with your body or with the unreal world, you will be facing lots of troubles and sufferings. Our life is not real and we are under a great delusion due to

Maya. The world is a Great Drama. Remember w*e are dreaming this world inside the Dream of God.* We are experiencing so many pleasure and sorrows in the dream delusion world.

The Universe is a Condensation and Materialization of the Dream of God

Whatever dream we experience, it must have a ***cause.*** Almighty God must have designed that dream for us. No dream can occur randomly, without any purpose and without any cause. In order to understand the process of materializing thoughts into dreams, we must be able to concentrate on our thoughts and by our strong will power, till they are converted into visible manifestations or dreams. This is known as visualization of thoughts i.e. thoughts are condensed into dreams. By learning further concentration on our dreams, we can learn to materialize dreams into material objects. The material objects around us are condensation of the dreams of God by the great will of God.

The yogis who achieve this power can materialize and dematerialize any object at their sweet will. Such yogis have already realized their unity with God as Jesus Christ. By regular practice the yogis achieve the great power of concentration on thought and the power of visualization and they are able to demonstrate any miracle to their disciples. I do not deny that there may be some cheaters, who may use some magical tricks to show a miracle to lure the innocent people. But it is not scientific to conclude and declare that all the persons having the power of miracles are simply magicians and cheaters and nobody can perform any miracle.

Our pains and aches disappear from the screen of our consciousness during our sleep. If life was not a dream, you couldn't get away from your pains and aches even during the sleep or dream. We should look at this world as a great dream or a ***movie film observer*** and should not indulge in. We should not take everything in the film very seriously. In the world we may observe the great disparity like poor and rich, healthy and sick, pain and pleasure, powerful and weak etc. All living beings are playing their roles assigned to them (by God) and enjoying the fruits of their past-karmas (actions). Take it as such. It is a truth.

Every thing is coming to us from a great factory of God. Don't you agree with this? To criticize God for everything is most un-scientific. As per the plan of God, God is not supposed to solve all the problems of the world, which have been created by us. To solve the problems of the world, God has given us the power of discrimination and intelligence. If God decides to solve all our problems, then the world drama will become no more interesting for man. Our life will become dull and purposeless like an animal life. But once we realize fully that the universe is a condensation of the dream of God, all our desires and sufferings will vanish. We shall become peaceful and calm. Realize it, it is possible.

Desires are the Cause of Sufferings in the World

This is again a false thinking due to *Maya* that if your desires are fulfilled you shall be happier. Truth is opposite to it. Generally your desires are the cause of your problems and your sufferings in the world. No doubt you may have a desire to have a good house of your own to live in. To fulfill this desire, you start working very hard. You may ask all the members of your family for the same. You may sacrifice the most of pleasurable time of your youth, in earning money from different sources. It may take 20-30 yrs of your youth, to collect the huge amount of money required to construct the dreamed house.

But when your desire is going to be complete, you find that you are old. You may be asked to leave this world soon. Your house may become the bone of contention and quarrel between your children. They may even kill each other There are instances that the children asked the parents to leave the house constructed by the parents and live in a simple small rented room, separately in the old age. You may feel that it would have been better, if you had not constructed that house.

By this example *I do not mean* that you should stop doing your efforts for any noble cause. What I mean is to say that the happiness of your life does not lie in the fulfilling of your desire. The source of your happiness is within your ownself and not in the outer material things and fulfilling of your desires. You may have a *desireless desire* to have a good house of your own, but do not think that your life will be a hell or a waist, if your desire is not fulfilled. You should maintain a proper balance of your mind, in both the circumstances that the desire is fulfilled or not.

The Thought Provoking Story of Contented Shepherd from USA

This is one of the *interesting and impressive stories* (not the real one) to explain my above point of view. Once, one of the states in USA was found economically backward, as compared to other developed states. The Federal Govt. of USA appointed a commission of experts to find the causes of its backwardness. One day the learned members of the Commission started their journey for the state in their luxury cars. On the highway in the mountains, they noted that the people of the state were not hardworking and were idle. On one side of the road at a lonely place, they found an aged poor man sitting idle on a big stone under a tree. He was sitting peacefully and doing nothing. His cattle were grazing in the field nearby.

The old man ignored the cars coming toward him. It was an abnormal behavior of the old man. The head decided to stop their cars and went to interact with him. It was further astonishing to the learned members that the old man was ignoring them as they were approaching nearer to him. The members analyzed that the old man was a lazy and idle. And it is one of the big causes of his backwardness and also of state. They conclude that if he works hard and makes himself busy in doing some extra profitable work, his life would be more happy and comfortable. They decided to educate the old man and approached to him.

They asked the old man, "Why are you sitting idle? Why don't you utilize your precious time to do some profitable extra work?"

The poor man asked, "*If I do some extra work, what will happen? What will it give to me?*"

They said, "You will have more income and more money."

He asked, "*What shall I do with that money*?"

They advised, "By your extra income you can purchase a radio, a T.V. a bicycle etc."

He asked, "*What after that*?"

They said, " You can have a car, a good house to live in and many other comforts of life."

He asked, " *What after that*?"

The members were little puzzled and irritated by his continuous enquiry. Then in the last they said, "***After that you relax and enjoy***."

The man smiled and said politely, "*That is what exactly I am doing right now and you learned people are disturbing me.*" He further said: "*I do not know, whether I shall be able to relax and enjoy myself later, after sacrificing my present state of bliss and joy in life? The bliss and joy that I am enjoying right now is absolutely free, without spending even a penny. How can I be sure that I shall be alive later to enjoy the extra money I earned, by sacrificing my present bliss and joy? I may die before that.*"

The learned commission members learned a new lesson on that day. They were convinced that the bliss and joy of life is not necessarily be achieved by making the life more and more hard and busy like a machine. The bliss and joy is inside our ownself. We have to explore and discover to achieve it.

Again by this story *I do not mean* that we should stop doing our efforts for the development and progress of our ownself and our family. But we should not forget to spare some of our valuable time daily to commune with God, which is the source of all bliss and joy of life and is absolutely free.

In the past India or the East has been busy more with God, and ignored the development of physical science and technology for the development of its people to provide physical comforts and pleasures. Hindus and Buddhist do not believe in violence and the forcible conversion of people to their religion. Their non-violence has been the one of the big reason for the slavery of India by other countries for thousand of years.

On the other side the west has been busier in science and technology for the outward physical development of its people to provide more comforts and pleasures. But they have been ignoring the spiritual science for the development of their self and the spirit. That is why, inspite of all kind of comforts and facilities, the people of advance countries in west are not fully satisfied with their lives. They feel something specially is lacking in their lives and they have now started to look and find out that specially missing in their lives. That is God. *Without God their life has become purposeless, aimless and devoid of bliss.*

There is an old self-realized American *Sanyiasi* saint, who lives in India since long. He is the head of a spiritual mission in India. He is a highly educated architect engineer from US, but remains always in peace, bliss and joy. He spent his childhood and youth in luxurious life in USA. For an Indian it is not surprising and difficult to renounce the world and become a *sanyiasi*, but for an American it is most difficult and surprising to become a *sanyiasi.* With reverence someone asked him, about his reasons to become a *sanyiasi*?

The saint smiled and said, "I was one of the greatest Architect of America. I had earned a lot of money, fame and respect in my country. I was leading a happy married life with my family. My aim of life was to become the greatest Architect of the world. Luckily, once I got an invitation to attend a World Conference of Architects in Switzerland, where the greatest Architect of the world was also supposed to attend it. I thought it as a great opportunity to meet such a great personality, during the conference, as he had already achieved the motto of my life.

But when I met him, I was surprised to found that he was the most frustrated & unhappy man in his life. He was frustrated with his wife, children and every body in the world. Inspite of the huge wealth & fame he had acquired, he had a complaint about every thing in the world. He was suffering from psychological depression and to complain unnecessary about others. He was not happy at all with what he had achieved in his life. I was shocked to see his pitiable condition.

At once I reconsidered and re-analyzed the aim of my life. I enquired myself. Is that what I wanted to achieve in my life? The other fellow has already achieved that. And even after achieving that motto, his condition is so pitiable and sad. He is not happy with his achievement of life at all. So I, at once realized that to become the greatest Architect of the world is not the real aim of my life. I realized that I have wasted my precious time of my life till now. I renounced the world immediately and became a *sanyiasi* (seeker of God, who renounce the world & wears saffron cloths) and after that I never went back to my family or my home."

What a strong will, a correct analysis of the purpose of life and a firm determination, the American saint had. All these qualities later greatly helped him to realize God easily. Now he is the one of the most happiest, respectful, joyful and blissful man in the world.

So, there should be a proper balance in both the physical and spiritual developments and our knowledge of both the continents of East & West should be exchanged for the all-round development of the world.

Dream Nature of the World

The past experiences of the world have trained our mind in so many different ways. Our mind is attuned with so many baseless and needless desires. We have begun to think that we couldn't be happy, if our desires are not fulfilled. This is false. We should always try to make our life as simple as possible by minimizing all our desires and needs. Otherwise the bitter experiences of life will lead us to sorrows and sufferings.

In our dream we may met with a fetal accident and experience that we have lost our body limbs. But when we wake up, we find everything O.K. We laugh and say, "Oh, what a fool I am. It was only a false dream and not a reality." It is exactly the same, during *samadhi*, when we wake up in God; we realize the truth that the world is a dream in God. We all are simply images in the dream of God. Nothing is real in the world. Death is also a dream or nightmare. We are only dreaming the suffering from death.

We should not be afraid of anything in the world, as it is all a big dream. Nothing can harm our immortal soul the observer of dream. The dreams created by God are not to harm us, but to educate and to realize us that there is no reality in the world. Even our death is also a dream and we are awakened in the astral world after our death with a new astral body to act.

Now we may be convinced intellectually that life is a dream thought of God, but it is not sufficient, unless we realize it completely. We all are already trapped in the great ocean of delusion due to Maya and it is our sad state of mind and consciousness. We must do our best efforts to escape this trap of Maya and try to realize God at the earliest in this life. Do not postpone your efforts, as we do not know when the death will come and which shall be our last breath to leave this temporary world?

"We should have a firm and unshakable faith in God & in ourself. We are the dear children of Loving God-Father.

We have been sent to this world with the aim to spread the Knowledge, Salvation, Peace, Love, Happiness, Joy and Bliss. It is our divine duty to make this world spiritual, pleasant, peaceful, beautiful and free from fear & violence. Feel the divine presence within all. If we do all our duty with love and devotion to God, we will never feel tired."

Om Peace, Peace, Peace!
Om Shanti, Shanti, Shanti!

10

Are the Miracles Really Miracles?

Are the Miracles Really Miracles?

Prayer

O, Divine Creator, I am exclaimed by the wonder, to see Thy great miracles of Superpowers which have created trillion of mysteries in the universe, I live in. O Divine Dynamo, producing all the currents of life forces, it is due to Thy hidden power that all living beings breathe, eat, walk, talk, love and the life force flow in their bodies to keep them alive. Thou art the cause of life in all-living beings. I am Thy little tiny bulb and Thou art the light within it.

Divine Father, my little mind and intelligence are unable to comprehend and fully understand the great miracles performed by Thy saints, throughout the world in all the times. I understand and believe that, Thou art just behind all these miracles. These miracles are just a little spark of Thy great wonder of creating the huge universe. The universe is a condensed thought or a dream in Thy Infinite Mind. Have a pity on me. Reveal Thyself. Remove my delusion and *Maya.* Provide me Thy power of mind and intelligence to understand Thy great miracles, which seems to defy the laws of science in my little mind. Though art omnipresent, omniscient and omnipotent. *Nothing is impossible for Thee.*

In this chapter we will try to understand the miracles performed by saints through the latest scientific laws and researches. Are the laws of science compatible and in consonance to the spiritual knowledge given by our *Shastras* and the self-realized saints? Is there any contradiction between them? We will find that both the systems are ultimately approaching the same absolute truth. We will also conclude that the miracles performed by the yogis and saints are *really not miracles* but are within the *broader sense of scientific laws*, which the scientists have still to discover from the Mother Nature. The yogis and saints are really the Masters of physical matter and all the scientific laws. The science is still in its childhood stage. There are limitations of science for limited resources and it needs further research work to find more comprehensive laws.

What is a Scientific Law?

We should first understand what a scientific law is? A scientific law is a statement on which the scientists believe that it is true, but it can neither be proved nor be derivable mathematically or logically, from the already existing laws of science, on which we believe them to be true. But a law can be tested or verified once or so many times in the laboratory. Whenever an experiment fails to verify a scientific law, then it is discarded or modified. A scientific theory is generally based upon certain assumptions, axioms many hypothesis and the scientific laws already discovered.

All the creation in the universe is governed by natural laws discoverable by the scientists. But there are so many undiscovered subtler laws, which rules the consciousness and the spiritual planes are also knowable only through the science of seeking God, known as Yoga. Till now science has ignored this field. The self-realized saints and yogis perform their miracles by mastering and using these laws. For yogis these miracles are not miracles, but very much scientific and within the natural laws of God. Miracles are nothing but the operation of the super-mind and super-consciousness laws.

No Law can be derived From Any Other Law

If a law can be proved or derived from other existing laws, it does not remain a law any more. It becomes just a corollary or a theorem or a derivation from which it has been derived. Further all the laws are independent of each other. Remember no law can be derived from any other law.

Newton defined three laws of motion instead of one, because none of his three laws can be derived from any other law. There was a need of three separate laws instead of one. It is wrong to say that Newton's 2nd law is the only law of motion and the 1st and 3rd law can be derived from the 2nd law of motion. Those who say the above do not understand Newton's Laws of motion exactly.

A scientific law cannot be proved practically in the laboratory. It can only be verified practically. It is wrong to say, "Prove the Newton's 2nd law of motion in the laboratory". You cannot prove a law but can only verify a law in the laboratory 100 times or 1,000 times. The law will be verified 100 or 1,000 times accordingly, but it will still remain unproved even if you verify 1,00,000 times. On the contrary a law can be proved wrong, if only once you fails to verify it in the laboratory. *So to prove a law even millions times verification is not sufficient, but to disprove a law only one experiment where it fails is sufficient.*

Do the Scientists Create the Laws of Sciences?

No. It is also a wrong notion that scientists are the creator of the laws of science. No scientists have ever made any scientific law. They have simply discovered or explored some of the scientific laws, which already existed in the universe. Scientists may discover the innumerable more scientific laws in future, which at present has still not been discovered and are unknown to the humanity. God alone and nobody else have created all the laws of science. No existing law of science can come to existence, without any creator. There can be no doubt in it.

Did Newton created the Laws of Motion & the Law of Gravitation?

No, not at all. These laws were already there before Newton or before the origin of man on earth or since the origin of the universe. Newton simply became an instrument, to get the privilege of discovering these laws, first time on the earth. Was there no gravitational force or gravitational law before Newton? Will it not be there, if Newton had not been born or discovered it?

This is not in the hands of the scientists to design scientific laws of their own. If the scientists would have the power to create the laws, then there would have been in-numerable laws for the same physical entity as per the choice and sweet will of the scientists. Can the scientists create the atomic particles of their own choice of size, mass, charge, color and other properties? No. Can they create new bacterias and viruses of their own choice? No, the scientists can simply study ***how*** the existing phenomenons are happening, but cannot tell ***why*** the phenomenons are happening as such?

All the scientists have wondered to know that the same laws of science are holding true throughout the universe and space, which extremely large. How the same laws are holding true continuously since the beginning of the universe is a wonder? How the same laws will remain valid till the end of the universe? These laws must have been created only by one super-power and not by two or more individuals. That super power *must be omnipresent throughout the universe, from its beginning till the end of the universe.*

It is true that science and technology can invent new machines or create more new things of utility like radio, television, computer, airplane or a satellite etc. But on the other side the entire God created things like the gravitation, electromagnetic waves, matter and fields etc. were already there before the creation of radio or television and other things. For an illiterate man in a jungle, who has never seen or heard of a radio or a television, all these inventions seems to be miracles, just like the miracles performed by saints before us. They can never understand, how the music can come out of a radio or a man can speak from inside a small box? He cannot understand how the living movie pictures can be generated on small T.V. screen? Also the functioning of a computer is beyond their comprehension.

But for educated scientists or engineers the scientific inventions are not at all miracles. But the scientists and engineers have utterly failed to make the illiterates and uneducated persons to make them understand the secret of the science and technology behind these creations.

Scientists have informed us there are billions of invisible infinitesimal living ***viruses and bacterias*** of so many diseases present around us in the air and everywhere. Most of the viruses and bacterias are our enemies, but some of them are our friends too. Does an illiterate uneducated person can believe on it? No. To understand the viruses and bacterias is beyond their comprehension. Due to the delusion and *Maya* they cannot see these viruses and bacterias through their naked eyes. The existence of bacterias or viruses is a miracle for them.

So as the illiterates and uneducated persons cannot comprehend the discoveries of modern science and technology, similarly the scientists, technologists and the ordinary human beings cannot comprehend the miracles performed by the great self-realized saints, yogis and avatars. For an ordinary person (including scientists) who is under delusion and *Maya* a *miracle is a miracle*, since the miracles are beyond the ordinary laws of physical science. But for a self-realized saint a *miracle is not a miracle*, as he is not under delusion or Maya and can comprehends the cosmic laws beyond ordinary consciousness.

Remember that the physical science cannot formulate laws outside the power of *Maya,* which gives the structure, planning and fabric to creation. Believe that the Mother Nature itself is *Maya* and it is present through out the universe. It is eternal and inexhaustible. Even during our sleep we are under the influence of Maya. The future scientists cannot do more then one probe after another probe to discover scientific laws, out of the infinite probes of *Maya.* They can discover one law after another law. Know that the old scientific laws may become ***obsolete***, after finding more comprehensive new laws of nature.

We are ignoring the Innumerable Miracles Around Us

If we introspect deeply and scientifically, we will find each and every event happening around us is a miracle. But if an event is happening repeatedly in a normal and routine way daily, we never bother about its mystery. Normally we presume that the event has to happen in the same routine way as it is happening and nothing is miraculous about it.

We ignore such a routine miraculous event. On the other side if any event does not happen in normal way, we began to worry and wonder about it. For example:

1. Is it not miraculous that every thing is falling on earth and earth is attracting every thing with a gravitational force? Till Newton, nobody bothered about this force of attraction. Before that every body assumed that it is just a natural and normal happening. Every thing should fall on earth and if something does not fall on earth it is miraculous. Why every thing should attracts the other with a gravitational force? Have we ever thought of it? Does science knows it? When everything falls on earth, why stars do not fall on earth? Did any body ever thought before Newton?

2. Is it not miraculous that our *heart is palpitating continuously* since our birth and will go on palpitating till our death? Who is palpitating our heart? *Can it palpitate itself without any external force? No.* Heart is like a compressor of a fridge and requires a huge amount of energy to palpitate. The work done by our heart each day is equivalent to the work done in lifting 200 barrels of water, of 200 liters each, to a 15 feet height. By which energy the heart is palpitating? Science has no answer. The energy used in palpitating is none of the known physical energy by the science. This energy is not supplied by the food we eat. We can neither stop nor run our heart faster or slower as per our sweet will. Our heart is not under our control or under our sweet will. Who is controlling our heart's palpitation? And who is palpitating our heart? But due to *Maya* every body presumes that the heart should palpitate as it is palpitating and there is nothing miraculous in it's palpitating.

3. The functioning of retina inside our eyeballs and of the living beings is one of the most miraculous creations of God. Our retina is made up of complex arrangement of billions of photosensitive bio-cells. Each image formed on the retina is changed into billions of optical impulses by each bio-optic cell in retina and then it is transmitted to the brain through billions of optic nerves instantaneously. The human brain then interprets the billions of optic signals immediately as it observes it. The brain further reports it to the observer ego 'I' in our body. And then we see the view of the picture, as the almighty God wants us to see.

4. Similarly the other examples are: *a seed in which the future of the whole plant is hidden*, digestion of food by our digestive system, excretion of waist material from our body, reflex action of our body, growing of our body in a perfect ratio, cause of sexual pleasures, formation of baby in the womb of mother, different faculties of our brain and their functioning etc. All these complex phenomenons are difficult to understand. Scientists are busy in discovering only the *how part* of these phenomenons happening in the world. But they are not able to answer the *why part* of these phenomenons happening? ***Why*** of the phenomenon is beyond the scope of science.

The Declaration of Vedas about Duality of Creation & Creator

Our Vedas have declared that our physical universe operates under delusion and *Maya* and it is governed under the principle of relativity and *Maya. Maya separates creation from Creator and creates duality.* The dual things are relative to each other like attraction and repulsion, positive & negative, high & low, good & bad, beautiful & ugly, pain & pleasure, birth & death and rich & poor etc. The dualities are just the two faces of the same coin.

Electric field has a phenomenon of both attraction and repulsion. Similarly magnet has both the attraction and repulsion and a magnetic field around it. An electric object has both positive and negative charges and an electrostatic field around it. A magnet has also both north and south poles and a magnetic field around it. But the gravitation has only attraction force and no repulsive force. What are these electric, magnetic and gravitational fields exactly? We are unable to understand them till now. We simply know the mathematical formulas by which these forces are governed. An anti-particle might have negative mass i.e. mass less then zero, and may have antigravity i.e. repulsive gravitational force.

All these ***fields*** are present even in the space and in the *ether* all over the universe. How two charges or two magnetic poles are able to attract or repel from a distance? What exactly transpires in the space (ether) around electric, magnetic and gravitational objects, which causes attraction and repulsion? Science is still unable to explain it correctly? The influence of electric and magnetic fields, from huge distances shows that the space around us is not vacuum but filled with some finest material called *ether.*

We know that the scientific laws for electric, magnetic and the gravitational fields are exactly same. But in case of gravitational field we have observed only *one force of attraction, not the force of repulsion. Why?* How the two heavenly bodies placed at billions of light years away influence gravitationally each other through the space? Is the influence instantaneous or travel with a finite speed in space is a big question?

Light travels with a vast speed of nearly 3,00,000 kms/sec. The distance traveled by light in one year is known as one ***light year***. The span of a galaxy is nearly 10,000 light years. The distance between two nearest galaxies is about million light years. The question arises: does the gravitational field travel with the speed of light or with an infinite speed? In any electric, magnetic or gravitational field some thing (disturbance) must travel from one object to another on which it is influencing. What is that which travels from one object to another at infinite distances? It is said that something like infinitesimal small particles called ***gravitons*** (much smaller then sub-atomic particles) may be emitted and travel in a gravitational field. What are these gravitons? We have no answer till now? Similarly there must be infinitesimal particles of electric and magnetic fields. You may call them ***electrotones*** and ***magnetotones*** or anything you like.

The miracles are miracles only to a person suffering from delusion and *Maya*. The delusion and *Maya* manifests ignorance and *avidya* (non-knowledge) on the viewer. Scientific thinking, analysis and intellectual convictions cannot remove *Maya* and delusion.

The physical matter in the universe is made up of molecules, atoms and elementary particles. The atoms are further made up of electrons, protons and neutrons. In the atom the protons and neutrons reside at its centre known as nucleus. The electrons revolve around the nucleus in different orbits, at different energy levels. None of the particle is at rest. All are vibrating and revolving with tremendous speeds closer to speed of light.

A Limitation of Quantum Theory

As per the Quantum Theory of Physics: matter and energy are discrete. That is, no energy can be less then a quanta or a photon. As per this theory, minimum one quanta of energy is required or released, to change the position of an electron to its adjacent orbit. According to this theory no electron can exist in between two adjacent orbits, because a fraction of photon is required to have the in-between position of the orbit. It is true that a photon changes their position of adjacent orbit by absorbing or releasing one quantum of energy. Since electron cannot have in-between position between the two adjacent orbits, hence it cannot jump from one orbit to another. Then question arises how an electron changes its orbit? Science has no answer to this phenomenon. The answer to this phenomenon is that *the electron disappears (vanishes) in one orbit and appears (reborn) in another orbit.*

So we are observing that matter can disappear at one place and reappear at another place in space or ether. Science has still to discover it. If it is so, than why we do not believe that an advanced Yogi who has mastery over the physical matter and its laws can make *his body appear or disappear at different places at his will?*

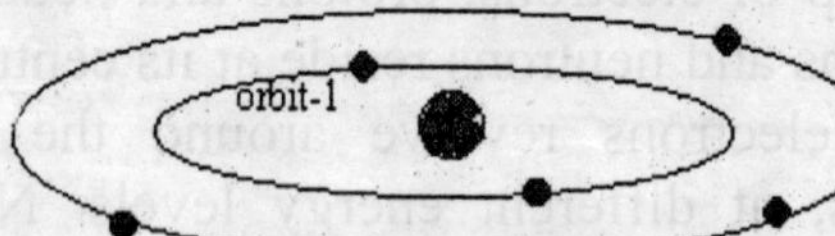

By taking one quanta of energy, the electron in orbot-1 first disappears and again reappears in orbit-2 and cannot take any position in between the orbits

The Einstein's Theory of Relativity Proves that there is only One Thing in the Universe

The Einstein's Theory of Relativity has proved the equivalence of the matter and energy by the famous mathematical formula: $E = mc^2$, where ***E*** is the energy produced, ***m*** is the mass of the body and ***c*** is the velocity of light. This equation shows that matter can be converted into energy and energy can be converted into matter. It means both matter and energy are inter-convertible. They are the different form of one thing in two different states. As water, ice, water vapor and steam are the different forms of one material i.e. H_2O, similarly the matter and energy are made from the same thing. This proves that *there is only one thing in the universe, and not two or more things as appears to common sense.*

We already know that the matter is made up of molecules, which consist of atoms. Atoms consist of subatomic particles, electrons protons and neutrons etc. In a nuclear reaction subatomic particles are interchangeable and atoms of one element is changed into another. This proves that all particles and matter are made up of one thing not from two or more. Science has rightly proved that the whole universe is made up of one thing and not two or more. It is exactly the same as already explained by the *Vedas.* So the whole universe is the manifestation of only one thing i.e. God Himself. This is what Vedas says *"Eko Brahman, Dittio Nahi".* (There is only one thing i.e. God and nothing else in the universe or the universe is the manifestation of one God and nothing else).

The Movies are Due to the Optical Illusion Created by Maya

The optical images, photos, pictures or films are built by the combination of trillions of tiny dots known as pixels.

But the naked eye is not able to detect these pixels or tiny dots separately and gives our eyes a delusion of an image through the inner-eyes in the mind. Each dot projects an image on the retina of the eye, which consists of billions of photosensitive optical cells and which further transmit each impulse in optical cell, through optical nerves to the brain. Our mind further analyzes instantly billions of information as an original picture as a whole and not as billions of separate dots of colors. Is it not a super-scientific miracle?

Similarly, in a motion TV picture or in a movie the images are seems to move continuously. In fact the image does not moves continuously. The secret is, more than sixteen photos per second are taken by the video or film movie camera for a continuous moving object. The sequence of images is then projected on a screen to replay, and then our eyes are not able to see the different images of the moving object separately on the screen. But due to the delusion our eyes see the images moving continuously in the motion film.

In a colored picture there are infinite different colors and shades. But we know that when a color picture is printed only four colors are sufficient to produce infinite colors. Due to delusion our naked eye is unable to see the dots and pixels of different four colors separately. Our brain and mind, which are under delusion, gives the false impression (as desired by Maya) that there are infinite colors.

Similarly we see daily in TV ads and the cartoon films, that the art of motion pictures and computer animation can produce any kind of miraculous effects in their pictures. We see multiple images of one actor to act differently. By special visual effect, an image can be miniaturized or magnified and manipulated, which can produce a very large or very small unbelievable image of an average actor. Computer animation with their lifelike images is creating new things, doing optical miracles or wonders these days. *If some one knows how to manipulate and control the creative light rays or beams, he can perform miracles. A realized-yogi knows this art.*

Just as the TV or films images appear to be real, but in fact the images are the combination of light and shadow only. Similar is the nature of the universe. The space around us is three or four-dimensional screen in which the universal three-dimensional picture of the universe is projected by the universal camera of God. We are not the reality we think but just images in His projection. Nothing is real in this illusion except our ownself (ego 'I') who is experiencing the Universal-Drama. Even the heavenly bodies like our earth, planets, sun, moon, stars and galaxies are just projected colorful cosmic motion pictures. Believe it.

Our Senses are not able to Perceive The Absolute Reality

The science and technology has given us powerful Electron Microscope, Radio and Optical Telescopes etc. which have revealed us, by scientific investigations that matter is not just as it looks to our naked eyes. If our eyes were able to see what an electron microscope and a powerful telescope can see, the world would have been looked totally different to us. *Whatever is visible or sensible to our eyes or senses is not an absolute reality, but it is what Almighty God wants us to observe.*

Whatever the senses receive and further transmit the observation to our brain or mind it is interpreted by our intelligence, which is under Maya. The interpretation by mind and intelligence ***differ*** from person to person and is also different in all living beings. So the final reception or interpretation by our ego 'I' or self is not the same for everybody. Hence this universe looks different to different individuals and different living beings. Therefore the universe cannot be real. A real thing must appear same to every body.

Sir James Jeans has written in his book 'The stream of knowledge': "*The Mysterious universe is heading towards a non mechanical reality, the universe begins to look like a great thought than like a great machine.*" It is exactly what the *Vedas* affirms.

A miracle is generally said to be an effect or an event, which is beyond the common human-sense and beyond the existing scientific laws. Generally all the events in the physical universe obey the scientific laws perfectly. But to convince their disciples about their super powers or the super powers of Almighty God and for a higher spiritual mission, the realized saints used to perform some miracles. They create a material object, transport their physical body instantaneously with speed of light, multiply many bodies out of their physical body, walk on water or on fire, cure patients from incurable diseases and give life even to a dead person etc.

To a person under delusion and *Maya* (Satan or Devil) the miracles seems to be as miracles. But to a realized saint who has mastered the super-mantle (above science) laws, the miracles are not miracles but most scientific. In any miracle nothing is contradictory and it obeys all the laws of the universe. When a person is not under *Maya* and becomes one with God, he also becomes omnipresent, omniscient and omnipotent and is able to perform any miracle.

We affirm that:

"We should seek and know God with the full strength of our will & soul. God belongs to all humans & is not the monopoly of any specific religion or any individual. God doesn't need anything from anybody except our devotion & love. God cannot be bribed by anyone by any means. God does not need our praise, gift or material thing. God wants only our unconditional love, devotion, surrender and nothing else."

"All know that the drop merges into the ocean but very few know that the ocean also merges into the drop, as ***'the action and reaction are equal and opposite'****. We all are the images of God and inside His Mind. Other way God is also within us sitting in our heart. When we watch the wave, we don't see the ocean beneath the waves; but when you watch the whole ocean, we see only one ocean beneath all the innumcrable waves. In fact the ocean & the waves are one only the turbulent Maya (ignorance) has separated both. During deep meditation one can realize this truth after seeing the ocean of Spirit beneath all the waves of lives."*

" Our love to enchanting world is perishable, but our love to God is more enchanting, pure, eternal and everlasting."

Om Peace! Peace! Peace!

11

Techniques of Meditation

Maharishi Patanjali Yoga-Sutras, Yama, Niyama, Asanas, Pranayam, Pratyahara, Dharana, Dhyana, Samadhi

Kundalini Shakti the Spiritual Energy for Involution

Types of Samadhies

Relation of Yogi with God

What Happens During the Meditation?

When and How to Meditate?

Concentration is Different from Meditation

Devotion & Love are Must for Seeker of God

Never Forget God

Techniques of Meditation

Prayer

O Divine Father, O Guru of all the gurus, O Creator of the delusion and *Maya,* teach me to practice the easiest and fastest scientific techniques of meditation. My naughty mind is always flooded with wavering unwanted thoughts. Teach me to control the unwanted thoughts of my mind in the depth of the silence during meditation. Teach me to control at my will the reception and flow of Thy cosmic life energy in my body. Teach me to cut off my five sense telephones from my body and naughty mind, at my will.

From the time immemorial I was separated from Thee, through my ignorance and have forgotten Thee. But now I have realized that Thou art my ownself, Mother, and my goal of life. O, Mother I can wait for unlimited time for any worldly petty thing, but not without knowing Thee. I have left with no worldly desire except to know Thee at the earliest in this life.

Divine Mother, pity on me, reveal Thee in the temple of my silence, remove the curtains of my ignorance to see Thy beautiful face. I know that Thou art hidden just behind my ego 'I' and *Ahankar.* Make me free from the bondage of repeated birth, death and rebirth. I am now tired of all these. Put me in Thy lap of infinite Ocean of Joy, Bliss and Peace forever.

Yog-Sutras of Maharishi Patanjali

This chapter deals with the scientific techniques of yoga and meditation. About four hundred years A.D. of Jesus Christ, ***Maharishi Patanjali*** has given the ***eight*** necessary steps of *Yog-Sutras* or Aphorisms of Yoga. He has defined Yoga as: ***Yogash-Chitvirti-Nirodha***. It means in yoga, c*hitvirtis* are to be stopped. *Chitvirtis* are the stream of thoughts in our mind. When the mind becomes thoughtless and peaceful and cut its connection with the five senses and become unaware of the physical body, then it is said to be in the state of ***Meditation***. In this state of consciousness, only the observer or ego 'I' or the self is remained, and everything else vanishes. The observer is situated in its ownself and observes its ownself without using any sense organs. It is a wonderful state of consciousness with ananda, bliss and joy.

... (*Patanjali Yogdarshan: Samadhipad*-I: 2,3,4)

To achieve self-realization faster & without any problem all the *Yog-sutras* are to be followed in an ordered sequence as follows. And no sutra is to be ignored.

1. Yama: A yogi should observe his moral code of conduct and restraint himself from its violation. This is known as *Yama.* A yogi must observe the rules like: non-violence, truthfulness, honesty, chastity, non-covetousness, non-acceptance of others possessions. He should love all, help the poor, never over-eat, observe regular fasting and should have the sympathy to sorrowful etc.

2. Niyama: The personal virtue and disciplining himself by a yogi is known as *Niyama.* The yogi should develop the good habits like: contentment, purity of thoughts in speech and action; study of scriptures and *Shastras.* self-denial and above all devotion to God. A yogi should attend *Satsanga* and serve the poor and needy people.

3. Asanas: A yogi should practice regularly different kinds of *yog-asanas* (postures) and some light exercises daily.

These asanas promotes and facilitates the flow of life energy in different parts and the body organs. Asanas keeps our body free from diseases, healthy and fit to meditate for a long time. Only a healthy body and healthy mind free from all kinds of diseases can go to a state of long meditation. A sick body and sick mind is unable to co-operate with the strain and stress of long meditation.

The cause of sickness and malfunctioning of some of the organs of the body is due to the lack of life force in some body organ. The distribution of life force is disturbed due to the wrong postures and idleness of the body. But by different kinds of *asanas*, postures and light exercises we try to send the life force, forcefully in every part of the body.

There is a great misconception about yoga-asanas among most of the beginners, who think that these *asanas* alone is yoga. It is true that asanas are very important, to keep our body and mind healthy and free from diseases. But the simple practice of different postures or asanas alone has nothing to do with the communion with God, which is the ultimate aim of Yoga. The *asanas* are enough to most of the persons in the world, who are only concerned to keep their physical body healthy and sound. But *asanas* alone are not enough for seekers of God. Many persons practice *asanas* regularly, and think themselves as a great yogi. It is a great misconception. *Asanas* are only the third step in the eightfold path of Patanjali *Yog-Sutras*.

Lord Krishna is known as the ***Lord of Yoga*** and the Lord Shiva is known as the ***Lord of Yogis***. Yoga and Yogis are different words. There cannot be any Yoga without devotion to God. To illustrate this I would like to tell you the following. In India there are many Yoga organizations in the name of Yoga. Some are providing a free training of *asanas* and *pranayam* to every body, in the open parks every morning. They are doing a great service to look after the health of people. You will find that they provide a beautiful show of group *asanas* and are useful to keep our body healthy. But most of them ignore God and talk about only the fitness of the physical body to make it free from all kinds of diseases. It is strange that none talk about the devotion and communion with God. The entire activity of their classes is concentrated on various asanas. None speaks to create devotion to God. What kind of yoga classes are these?

Once some body questioned pointed them for their missing devotion to God. Their reply was strange: "Most of the people are interested only in curing their diseases. They do not come here to seek and commune with God. The members of the organization belong to all the different religions. Some of the members dislike any talk about God. They do not like to prey to God, different from their own religion. So to avoid the confrontation, we have better ***shunted out God*** from our classes and we do not talk, seek and bother about God for the shake of increasing and pleasing our members."

It is similar in other countries also. In some countries the asana teachers are minting money in the name of Yoga. What type of yoga classes they are teaching, without any talk & devotion to God? *For a seeker of God it is better to be alone, than to mix with a crowd without any devotion and concern to God.*

You will appreciate the theme of the following interesting but imaginary story: "Once a black red-Indian Christian, who was very faithful and devoted to Jesus Christ was forcibly asked to get out from a Catholic Church, by some of the white Christians. The poor black Christian was mentally hurt and suffered with deep sorrow. He was weeping sitting alone outside the Church for a long time. After some time, a strange handsome bearded man came to console him. He was very much loving and sympathetic to him. He asked him the reasons for his sorrows to console him. The black man told him the entire unpleasant incident happened with him. The strange man sympathetically consoled him, "Dear son, do not weep and do not worry any more. I am with you always and I have also been thrown out from this Church." The black-man requested him to tell, who he was? The strange man answered, "*I am the Jesus Christ my son.*"

What I want to convey here is, some times we give more importance to our organization and its organized activities but ignore God at the cost of organization. But a real yogi who is the seeker of God is not attached to any organization at the cost of ignoring God. He never forgets his main aim of life to seek God and to know God. He never continues to keep himself attached to an organization, which ignores God and where the devotion to God is missing.

4. Pranayam: The science of willful control of reception, expense and distribution of the cosmic life energy, through the control of breath is known as *Pranayam.* It purifies our body, blood, the nervous system, mind and the brain cells. It also purifies our *ethereal body.* By its regular practice life force begins to flow freely through our *Nadis (Ida, Pingla & Sushumana).* Our mind becomes free from distracting thoughts. A thoughtless and peaceful mind is must to achieve the deep state of meditation. This is a misconception that air contains prana or life energy. Air does not contain prana, but simply oxygen, Nitrogen and other gases.

Breathing exercises are also not the *pranayam.* The *Prana* is the omnipresent cosmic life energy of God and we receive it through the medulla oblongata. Through proper inhalation and exhalation we control our thoughts, which increase the reception and reduce the expense of prana energy. Through pranayam we send the life energy forcibly by our will to any part of our body. (For details read the Chapter: Life force doing infinite works for us)

5. Pratyahara: The withdrawal of our consciousness from the outer physical world and to cut off the connection of our five sense telephones from the mind and the sense organs of the physical body is known as *Pratyahara.* Pratyahara is the regular practice of interiorization of the mind and its withdrawal from the out worldly distracting things and thoughts. Slowly our mind becomes peaceful and turns from extrovert to introvert. Our awareness is turned inward, away from the distraction of the five enchanting senses. The mind turns toward higher inner spiritual states of consciousness. Such a state of higher consciousness is known as *Pratyahara.*

6. Dharana: *Dharana* means concentration on a single thought. Thousands of stray unwanted thoughts always distract our mind from our goal. We try to focus or concentrate our mind & awareness on a single thought or an object. It may be a part of our body, or a picture or a thought of God, or sound of Om, or a pure thought or an imagination. By regular practice a yogi is able to fix his mind for a long time on a single object or thought and turn away all other stray thoughts, which distract the mind.

Many yogis begin to learn the art of concentration, by focusing their mind on a candle flame or a small luminous object. After some time, the yogi closes softly his eyes and tries to visualize the same inside his inner vision. His mind just becomes a peaceful observer/ viewer and simply watches the thoughts coming in or going out to the mind. If any stray thought comes to his mind he should let it go away just ignored, without any struggle of his mind. This activity of mind is known as *Dharana.*

7. Dhyana (Meditation): If a yogi is in the continuous state of thoughtlessness with awareness for quite some time, he is under meditation. In the state of *Dharana* mind is fixed on a single thought or an object for quite a long time. By a constant practice the yogi tries to get away this single thought, then his *mind becomes peaceful free from all kinds of thoughts and distractions.* But even then the sense of ego 'I' remains in his mind. During the state of meditation (*Dhyana)* the yogi forgets his body, cut of the connection of his sense telephones and the mind awareness, but he knows that he still exists.

In this state of consciousness yogi does not have the awareness of any space, time and place, but only his ego 'I' remains, to watch & observe his wonderful state of bliss and joy. Everything else melts away. Breathing becomes dead slow. The heartbeat becomes slow. But the yogi is still aware of his ego 'I' or Ahankar. The yogi may listen so many *Anahat* sounds during the meditation state and he may try to concentrate upon them to achieve *samadhi.*

8. Samadhi: When the yogi's ego 'I' merges with God or the transcendence of his soul consciousness with Cosmic Consciousness, it is called *samadhi.* In this state of higher consciousness there are extraordinary subtle experiences of subtle worlds. This is the state of *Ananda* (eternal Bliss & Joy) and yogi is in communion with God. It is so joyful that the yogi wishes to remain in this state forever. He becomes free from all kinds of worldly sorrows & desires. The ignorance of the yogi melts away. The *Ahankar* or ego 'I' merges with God. By continuous practicing this state of meditation, *Kundalini-Shakti* is raised one day, which is sleeping in dormant state in the lowest part of spine known as *Muladhar Chakra.* After awakening of the *Kundalini-Shakti* our inner journey or the Divine Romance with God begins.

All the above eight aphorism of Yoga (*Yog-Sutras)* are to be strictly followed by regular practice. If one practice meditation without practicing *Yam, Niyama, Asanas and Pranayam* one may be in trouble and may not get success to achieve *samadhi.* One should not skip, some of the steps of aphorism (*sutras)* to achieve the goal faster. *Devotion and love for God are must for all & for an early success.* Those who practice yoga without any devotion for God may become healthy with some of the mystical powers, but can never commune with God. There are two kinds of *samadhis*: ***Sabhikalpa & Nirbhikalpa samadhis,*** which will be discussed later.

Kundalini Shakti

The *Kundalini Shakti* mentioned above is different from primary life force or *Prana Shakti.* It is sleeping in dormant form at *Muladhar chakra.* It is the Creative Intelligent Force of God. It is also known as the '*Voice of Silence'*. By regular practice of *Yog-Sutras* and intense devotion to God, one day *Kundalini Shakti* is awakened by the grace of God on yogi. It is generally experienced to yogis as a snake sleeping in two & half round at *Muladhar Chakra.*

It is the divine liquid fire that rushes up through the interior of spine known as *Sushumana* and crosses through the seven *Chakras* one by one. *Ida, Pingla and Sushumana* are the three main *Nadis* in our subtle body. Without the awakening of *Kundalini* no subtle or *Samadhi* experience is possible. *Kundalini Shakti* is said to be the cosmic force, power or energy of the divine that created the universe and it is constantly evolving and developing new materials, atomic and sub-atomic particles and their different forms.

Generally *Kundalini Shakti* is spontaneously awakened with the grace of God. If Kundalini is awakened without prior purifying of the body, mind and spirit, it may give a great trouble to most of the yogis. Some times its huge mysterious power is uncontrollable by the yogis, as the inner passage of *sushumana* in the spine is not prepared for it. The danger is less if it rushes upward without any blockade in *Sushumana* but more if it turns downwards or sideways.

A yogi should not be afraid of awakening of his *Kundalini*, if he is practicing and following all the *Yog-Shutras* properly. But before its awakening the must purify his body, mind and soul otherwise it may give him some trouble. The process of involution (the journey back to God) and spiritual unfoldment starts only after the awakening of the *Kundalini Shakti. Kundalini* is an initiation for entry into the ocean of divine knowledge. As the *Kundalini* crosses the *Chakras* one by one, there are some subtle inner experiences of other worlds to the yogi and he achieves many *siddhies* (divine miraculous powers and knowledge). No self-realization is possible without the awakening and rushing up all the seven *Chakras* by the *Kundalini Shakti and merging in Sahasrar.* Without awakening of his *Kundalini Shakti* and raising it upto *Sahasrar* there can't be any spiritual *Guru.*

Types of Samadhies:

Samadhi is the highest step explained in the eightfold step by Maharishi Patanjali in his *Yog-Sutras.* There are two types of *Samadhies. Sabhikalpa Samadhi* and *Nirvikalpa Samadhi.* A *samadhi* is attained when the meditator, the process of meditation and the object of meditation become one with God.

The ***Sabhikalpa Samadhi*** is the initial stage of God-communion. In this Samadhi the life force is withdrawn from the body and the senses. Mind becomes peaceful, thoughtless & interiorized, but with awareness of ego 'I'. The body just disappears or appears dead. The Yogi is fully aware of his body, which remains in the suspended animation state. The yogi's consciousness merges with the Absolute Cosmic Consciousness of God. Yogi is in the state of Bliss, Joy and Ananda. Yogi gets some subtle experiences.

The ***Nirvikalpa Samadhi*** is a higher achievement than the *Sabhikalpa Samadhi.* Nirvikalpa Samadhi gives us full knowledge of *Brahman,* which further gives us *Moksha* or Liberation of soul from birth and death. In this state the mind is attuned to the contemplation of *Brahman,* with *Brahman. Nirbhikalpa Samadhi* is difficult to achieve and can be experienced by only the advanced yogis.

Relationship of Yogi with God

It is important for a yogi to have clearly defined his relation with God. If yogi has no relation with God, his bond of love with God will be weak. A Yogi is not a physical body, but simply an *Atma* (soul) and God is *Paramatma* (supreme soul). Both do not posses any physical body and therefore have no sex concept. The sex is related with the physical body and not the characteristic of the soul. Our soul is neither a male nor a female.

Most of the yogis develop the following relations with God: Divine Father--son; Divine Mother--son; Supreme Lover--beloved; Lord—servant (das); *Paramatma--atma*; Swami--disciple; Friend—friend; God--*gopika*; God and ego 'I' are one and the same (*'So-Ham', 'Aham Brahmashmi', 'Tatvamasi'*) etc. The relation may not be fixed or permanent throughout the life of the yogi. Generally it changes from time to time.

What happens during Meditation?

Meditation is an effort of a yogi, by constant practice to realize and express that pure consciousness is the reflection, or the image of God within you. Meditation is the joyful state of mind, when it is perfectly tuned with God. After a fixed concentration of mind for a long duration, mind becomes thoughtless but with awareness of ego 'I'. In this state, mind is undisturbed by the five senses and distracting stray thoughts of the outer world. Mind is totally interiorized. Our body consciousness is forgotten. We forget about all the demands and the necessities of the physical body. But we are aware of our ownself. Meditation is the dieing of yogi to the world without dieing of the body. Remember we should not sleep during meditation. During meditation we are neither in this world nor in the sleep world.

In meditation we are able to stop our thoughts consciously, what we do unconsciously every night to sleep. One experiences oneness with God along with bliss and joy.

During meditation the heartbeats become slow and Bp is lowered. Distracting senses are cut off from the mind. The outer disturbances like noise, smell, touch, taste and vision does not disturb the yogi as in the sleeping state senses do not disturb. The yogi's mind becomes like an undisturbed peaceful pond of still water. Breathing becomes deep and slow. Pulse rate is decreased. Body organs start feeling like dead one by one. The digestive system is slowed down. The expense of life energy by different organs of the body becomes negligible. The reception of life energy by the medulla oblongata increases many folds. Tired body cells begin to recharge, by the life force. The life force begins to repair the diseased parts of the body.

When and How to Meditate?

Since the digestion becomes slow during the meditation, it should be done only when the stomach is empty. The best times are early morning, evening, just before lunch or dinner, and just before sleep. During meditation some electricity is generated in the body, so the yogi should sit, on an insulated, soft and comfortable cushion to cut off the body currents from earth. There should be regularity of practice and time everyday. During meditation one must have deep devotion for God. Without devotion the achievement is less and useless. Ask your family members not to disturb you by anybody and even by a radio, T.V., phone or doorbell etc. during your meditation time.

Select a remote, clean, airy and beautiful place in your house for daily meditation at fixed timings. Since the earth magnetic field and rotation has an effect on the mind, it is better to face towards North or East in meditating posture. Sit on a clean, soft and comfortable cushion placed on floor. The cushion helps to keeps the body cut-off from the heat and electric currents from earth, produced in the body during meditation. You may sit, crossed-legged in a comfortable posture (*sukh-asana*) or in *padmasana* posture. For short meditation simple crossed legged is sufficient, but for longer meditation *padmasana* is better, which prevents the body from falling.

First watch the inside & outside of body thoroughly. If there is any tension in any part of the body relax it. Next lightly close the eyes to cutoff the light distractions of the outer world. Again watch your body thoroughly. If still there is any tension in any part of the body relax it. Then watch your breathing-in and breathing-out. The breath must be deep, long and slow. You should fix your mind on inhale and exhale breaths with association of '*So-Ham*' mantra. Inhale with the mental sound of '*Ham*' and exhale with the mantle sound of '*So*'.

Next watch the thoughts in your mind. Thoughts may be coming in and going out. Your mind may be calm and peaceful. Just watch the thoughts coming in and going out as an un-interested film-observer. Do not indulge, struggle & attach yourself with your thoughts. Concentrate on the *Aggyia Chakra*, the point between the eyebrows. It is also known as *nasikagra* mentioned in Gita. *Nasikagra* is the point from where the nose starts, which is between the eyebrows. The other end of the nose is the end point of nose and not the starting point (*nasikagra).* It is a misconception among many yogis. They think just opposite.

Concentration is Different From Meditation

The word concentration has come from concentric circles, which have common centre. Fixing of mind on one object or one thought is known as concentration. It is the tendency of the naughty mind to switch over to different thoughts and objects. The yogi tries to tame & fix his mind on a single thought. If it distracts to other thoughts, bring it back to the original thought. If your mind is able to fix on one object or a single thought for long, you are in state of concentration. It is just like the poring of oil from one bottle to another. Remember; during concentration one should not sleep, but keep awaken continuously.

Now try to get away with the single thought or object of concentration and become thoughtless and objectless. Mind should become blank free from all kinds of thoughts. It is now the meditation state. Your mind becomes thoughtless but with awareness of ego 'I'. You are neither sleep nor awake, but in between the two states. It is known as '*Turia-avashatha*' (a state of pure consciousness).

There are only two things: The world and the God. Human beings are placed between the two. Other creatures have no concept of God. We feel pleasures by coming in contact with the enchanting worldly things through our senses and develop attachment with them. But Yogi realizes that the bliss and joy in meditation is much more enchanting than all the worldly pleasures. Due to impact of *Maya* we avoid doing experiment with God, because we have neither tasted nor have the knowledge of God. None has helped us in developing the devotion and love for God. *If only once we experience the eternal bliss and joy of God, we will hanker after it for the rest of our life.* One should not doubt on it.

During meditation visualize that the cosmic life-energy is entering our body through the medulla oblongata at the centre of the skull. This life energy is directed to the *Aggyia Chakra*, which distribute it to other *Chakras* in the

Sushumana, which further distribute it to different body organs.

Try to *interiorize your mind, look within yourself.* Presume that infinite God is everywhere around you. Try to merge your consciousness into super-consciousness. You can speed your mind through eternity and can go beyond the galaxies. Try to listen to God's voice. Whenever we make a mistake, God warns us. If we ignore Him, He becomes quite. But when we pay attention to listen to Him, He will guide us. By constantly following His voice, we will be transformed into a peaceful, truly moral person. We should not doubt upon this.

Remember that all the thoughts are coming from God and are stored in the ocean of ether. God knows the course of all our thoughts. Unless and until we *completely surrender* ourself to God, God will not like to reveal Himself to us. When we surrender all our worldly desires to God, God blesses us. You may be very busy throughout the day and much tired, even then never go to bed, without the deepest attention & meditation on God.

Due to the power of *Maya* we perceive ourself as a body consisting flesh, bones and nerves. This is the cause of our many troubles and sorrows in the world. If we meditate continuously and unceasingly, we can quickly realize that not the physical body but the infinite essence of God. We will be free from all our problem, misery, pain and sorrow. It will also make us free from the bondage of our physical body.

Devotion and Love for God is Must for the Seeker of God

During the meditation your devotion & love for God is essential. The spark of this love of God is expressed in all the living beings through us. Understand that the sexual love is different from the devotional love for God. Sexual love is an animal biological instinct, temporary, selfish and a lust for opposite sex. Without this sex instinct there cannot be a sexual love. So we must realize the eternal love for God. This is without any sex instinct, so great and so joyful but permanent.

The greatest romance that our soul can have is the romance with the Supreme Soul (God). We have no experience and the idea of this divine romance with Supreme-Lover. But once we commune with God, we will find God everywhere. We will realize that everything in the universe is nothing but the manifestation of God. In samadhi or deep meditation God comes, whispers, guides, plays, loves and communicate with us. We are the best creation in the universe and children of God. God loves us all good or bad.

Remember, God does not need any thing from us, except our devotion and love to Him. Since our creation, He is also seeking and waiting for our love too. God too suffers when we deprive Him from our devotion & love. We should always devote a little bit of our daily time, to sit alone, to meditate and have a romance with God. Sri Radha, Sri Meera, *Gopies,* Sri Chataniya Mahaprabhu, Sri Soor Dass and so many other saints are the finest examples of the great divine romance with Lord Krishna.

God is the nearest of the near and dearest of the dear in this crowded illusion-world. We must cry for the love of God as a kid cry for his mother and a miser loves his money. Not even a single breath should go without our devotion to God. Like the intrinsic or escape energy, when our love and devotion for God is of high intensity, God comes and reveal to us. Only our intense pure devotion & love can commune and imprison God, nothing else. A yogi should develop an intense fire of pure love for God in his heart. You should always affirm that the beloved God is always with you in your heart, while you are working, sleeping, dreaming, meditating or doing any other work or activity.

The perishable world is a stage of big stage of divine drama for God. God has given only to man (others not) the freedom to act (good or bad). But our love is the only thing that God does not possess. Only our love can bind God. Although God is also seeking for our love, but He will never force us to love Him back. We have the freedom to love God or not. But believe me that God is watching, observing and recording all our actions, even our thoughts every moment. *God enjoy all our good actions but also suffers due to our bad actions or bad karmas.* Feel the divine love of God in all human & other creatures, and carry forward the message of love, peace and service to all.

Never Forget God

In both your good and bad times, never forget God. If something happens against your desire or will, do not blame God for it. All the good or bad events, hardships, failures, successes, achievements, diseases, losses and accidents etc. are simply the fruit of our past actions as per *karmic-law* and have nothing to do with God. When your desires are fulfilled and you are enjoying all kinds of worldly pleasures, even then do not forget God. All the worldly wealth, we are getting and enjoying is coming from God, out of His divine love and mercy upon us. Remember, without His divine mercy we cannot take even our next breathe in this world. We should prove our worthiness of His Divine Love.

God's love is unbiased, eternal, universal and all embracing like a universal loving mother. We do not know that during our past and present lives we might have committed so many sins. Only the intense fire of our deep prayer, repentance and love for God can wipe out our fruits of past misdeeds and God can forgive us for our past mistakes. Since everything in the universe is the manifestation of God Himself, including all living-beings, we must love and appreciate His whole creation too.

Our heart, if pure is the best temple of God. In the depth of silence we can whisper, talk, communicate, and express our feelings & love to God who is sitting in our heart. To convey our feelings to Him and to get His blessings too, no language is needed. The hidden universal silent language of heart does everything.

"*The hearts of the people cry out the Lord…*
Let your tears flow like a river day and night; …
Arise, cry out in the night…Pour out your heart like
water in the presence of the Lord."

--- Lamentations 2:18-19

!***Om Anandam Om***!

"If you could feel once even a spark of divine love, so great would be your joy & bliss…overpowering you …that you will hanker after Him for the rest of your life. That is why the name of God is Hari (who deprives you of everything)."

"The greatest romance one can have is the romance with God…God is the Supreme-Lover and our souls are His beloved. During meditation, when our soul meets the greatest lover of the universe, then the eternal divine romance begins."

"We must have clear understanding and strong will power to control our mental emotions, discrimination between wrong or right, and good or bad actions. Only our right thoughts and feelings can bring us the greatest happiness and joy in life."

"God has given us only one mind & one brain. We may devote it to any thing, we like. It's entirely unto us to devote it to God or to worldly pleasures. God has given us total freedom to decide & act and will not help or interfere in this matter."

"If you don't invite God to be your summer Guest, He will come to you in the winter of your life."

"Seek divine eternal wealth & not the perishable paltry tinsel of earth."

12

Scientific View of The Universe

Logical Proofs of Existence of God

Our Earth has a Special Status in the Universe

The Old View of the Newtonian Universe

Latest Concepts of Science in Understanding the Universe

The Latest Concept of the Universe as per

Prof. ***Stephen W. Hawking***

Scientific View of Universe

Prayer

We thank Thee, O Creator Spirit, for creating the wonderful Earth, Planets, Satellites, Sun, Stars, Galaxies, Supernova, Quasars, White dwarf and Black-holes etc. and creating human and other living beings on Earth. Divine Father, everything in the Universe is obeying perfectly Thy laws of natural sciences, since the beginning of the creation, without fail. I am Thy little babe and unable to understand, how the same scientific laws are applicable throughout the vast universe of billions of light years span. Among the billions of galaxies and billions of stars and planets in each galaxy, our Earth has a special status, due to Thy mercy and universal plan. Otherwise the existence of life could not be possible on Earth. If there would have been a slightest change either in any physical law governing the universe or in any condition prevailing on earth, the life could not have been sustained on this Earth. O Beloved God, Thou art caring everything for all of us and all the creatures.

O Beloved God, Thou hast given to all living beings water, air, fire, many kinds of essential energies, life force, food, vegetables, cloths, mind, intelligence, languages, transport, communication and thousands of essential and non-essential elements to create life on earth. Without Thy infinite and continuous help, such an advance life cannot sustain even for a second on earth.

The life on Earth is the result of millions of physical favorable conditions satisfied together all at the same time. If we disturb slightly even one or a few conditions, the life on earth would not sustain and it will come to an end forever. Mathematically, the probability of meeting all such conditions favorably together is less then the trillionth part of unity. This cannot be just by chance or accident. So without the powerful will and imagination of an infinite intelligent God, the life on earth is not possible.

Logical Proofs of Existence of God

Since the beginning of the human life on earth, the man is always curious and interested to know God and to know the logical proof of its existence. The proof of God has been always the hottest topic of all the philosophical and religious discussions, all over the world. I am hereby giving you a few most promising logical proofs of God. There shall be a big transformation in your thinking after understanding these proofs.

Once upon a time a non-believer but an intelligent educated man approached a realized saint sitting in a boat, in the morning on the bank of a river. He requested the saint, to give him any proof of the existence of God. The saint smiled, and asked him to wait for a little time, on the same bank of the river till he comes back from other side of the bank after completing some of his important works. The man agreed to wait, but the saint did not returned till evening.

After a long wait, the saint returned at night. The man upset, but asked with reverence, the reasons for his late coming? The saint said that when he reached the bank on the other side of the river, all of a sudden he found that all the wooden planks of his boat separated themselves automatically and floated away along the river stream. Then he waited till all the floated planks of wood come back, joined together and took the form of the boat again. It happened again but took a long time that is why he is late.

The man lost his temper as he felt that the saint was making lame excuses. He asked using harsh words, how it is possible? How the wooden planks of the boat can separate themselves, without any external intelligent being? How they can come back against the stream? How the planks can meet together automatically and take the form of the boat again, without the help of an intelligent being? Mathematically the possibility of such an event is negligible or it is impossible. You are befooling me.

The saint smiled and asked the man, when a small event described by him, is not possible automatically without an external intelligent being, how it is that all the particles, atoms and molecules of the universe arranged themselves in a beautiful and systematic manner to create living, non-living, heavenly bodies like stars, planets, galaxies and micro-organism like bacterias and viruses etc. in the universe? How it is possible to store and hide the future growth of a tree or a plant in its seed without an infinite intelligent mind? Every microorganism is a result of a beautiful and systematic arrangement of trillions of atomic particles and complex molecules. How can the billion of complex particles are formed and arrange themselves to form a microorganism without infinite external intelligent mind?

Even the heavenly bodies are not just the collection of atomic particles in a haphazard manner. Our Earth consists of trillions of different types of objects. Each object is made up of a beautiful and systematic arrangement of atoms and molecules. Not the slightest of the matter of any kind is made up of atoms just scattered in a haphazard manner. The nature without intelligence cannot do all these fine works. Only God can do all this. God is not like a man sitting in a remote place and controlling us from Heaven. God is the totality of both the manifested (known physical universe) and the un-manifested (unknown remaining part of God) and nothing is beyond God.

To explain further the concept of God to the questioner, the saint further pointed towards a nearby tree asked the non-believer to tell him, where the tree is? The man pointed towards the braches of the tree. The saint said that these are only the branches of the tree and not the tree. The man then pointed towards the stem, then leaves, then roots etc. one after one. But the saint went on refusing to accept any of them as tree. He told him that all these are the different parts of the tree, and none is the tree. In this way the non-believer failed to tell, where the tree was?

The saint explained that when none of the parts of the tree can be considered as a tree, then how the collection or the union of all the parts of the tree can be called as tree? It is a Mathematical paradox. The man was puzzled. The saint further explained that in the similar way apparently we can say that none of the part of the universe is fully God, but in fact God is the union of the whole manifested universe and the unmanifested part of God. There is nothing other than God in this universe. Only God has manifested Himself, in all the variety of mysterious things in the universe. But God has hidden Himself, and separated Himself from His creation due to His *Maya* from our senses. This was a big dose to shake the philosophy and thinking of the man. The man was fully convinced and bowed his head with a great reverence at the feet of the saint.

The following are the few more logical proofs:

If the Universe had a beginning at all, the beginning cannot rest on nothingness. Without a definite starting point in time, the present state of the universe is just impossible as it is impossible to jump out of a bottomless pit. So it is necessary to admit a first efficient cause, to which every one gives the name of *Brahman.* This starting point cannot be anything but God. Brahman is an idea or a concept of God. *Brahman* does not have any form except as a source of effulgence.

The whole of creation including living and non-living is too much complicated to have arisen just by chance. The Universe definitely shows a purposeful direction and an extraordinary infinite intelligent design to achieve its aim. Therefore the universe must be a product of an infinite intelligent designer. When a man comes across an airplane for the first time, he has no prior knowledge of what an airplane is and how it works. And yet the man rationally concludes that someone has designed the airplane and the design must have a purpose. It is totally false, if he assumes that the airplane has come just by chance out of nothing without any creator and without any purpose.

God transcends or rises above the things in the world, and is beyond even the cosmos. God has given us the ways and methods to communicate with Him. To communicate with God we must look within ourself, and not to a secluded divine realm beyond the cosmos.

Our Earth Has a Special Status In The Universe

Our Earth and the Universe are not simply random accident or event. Both are precisely calculated and beautifully designed creations with some aim and purpose. Infinite parameters had been considered and extrapolated accurately over billions of years continuously. *A millions of (or infinite) rare favorable events and conditions are required, simultaneously to be true, all at a time for the creation, evolution and sustenance of life on Earth. A small change in any of the condition may cause the end of life on earth. Such a rare event cannot happen without the will of Almighty Intelligent God. As a perfect idiot monkey can never write a poem by simply pressing the keys of a type-writer of English characters on a piece of paper. The following are the few examples of the infinite intelligent Mind in the creation of life on earth.*

1. The distance of the Earth has been so adjusted & kept optimum from Sun by the intelligent creator so that there is a moderate temperature on earth, for the existence of life. The huge sphere of earth was also forced to rotate around its axis in 24 hours to keep its temperature moderate throughout day and night for all the living beings to exist, on earth. If the rotation time around its axis is decreased say an hour, nothing could remain attached with earth. On the other hand if the rotation time had been much more, the portion of earth facing Sun would have become very hot. And the portion of earth away from Sun would have been very cold. Both the cases were unfit for existence of life on earth. The rotation of earth on its axis creates day and night.

2. The mass, size, the temperature and the optimum distance of sun from earth is kept such that, the sun gives the exact required amount of the rays of all different frequencies needed for the existence of life on earth. Neither it is more nor it is less. Who bothered to design all these? Can it be done by nature without intelligence?

3. The moderate force of gravity on earth is due to the moderate size and mass of the earth. The weight of an object on a bigger planet like Jupiter is very high, and it is very less on a smaller satellite like Moon. In both the cases life would have been extremely difficult, but not on earth. Who fixed the size of the earth for moderate gravitation for the existence of life on earth?

4. There is plenty of water on earth. Without water no life of any kind is possible. Huge oceans and seas were created containing the saline water. The saline water keeps the sea unpolluted and fit for the millions of different variety of living beings inside sea. The saline water freezes below 0^0C, which keeps the life under the seawater alive below 0°C. The maximum density of water was kept at 4°C and not at 0°C. It keeps the water not to freeze at the bottom of the sea; otherwise all the living creatures inside the sea might have died. Who bothered for the survival of all the living beings inside sea? Who bothered to give the extra ordinary properties to water?

5. The cycle of water, air, oxygen and carbon dioxide were programmed and designed, to fix their availability for the vegetation, men, animals and all the living creatures. Trillions of tons of clouds were created out of the water through the sunrays falling on the sea. The air was created on earth and was made responsible to transport the trillions of tons of clouds to the far away-lands and the mountains, for the survival of the life on earth. The density of cloud was assigned such that it is less then the polluted air or the smoke but more then the thin pure air at certain height in the atmosphere. All the pollution comes below the clouds, so that during rain the most of the polluted air is cleaned, by dissolving the impurities, which comes back to the earth. If the pollutants had gone above the height of the

cloud, it would have remained suspended forever in the atmosphere and life would have extinct on earth.

6. Infinite intelligent God designed a plenty of air on earth with optimum composition of Oxygen, Nitrogen, Carbon Dioxide and water vapors. The properties of all the components were also decided to support life on earth. A little change in the percentage of Oxygen, Nitrogen and Carbon Dioxide and others will disturb life on earth. The air helps in maintaining the moderate temperature on Earth also. Air prohibits the loss of heat radiation during night; otherwise the night temperature might have gone down much below 0°C on the earth. Due to absence of air and water on moon, no life can exist on its surface.

7. The vast oceans of water were also created in such a way that these help in the formation of cloud and rain of pure water not the saline water. The water was given the extraordinary properties to support lives of the millions of living beings inside and outside the oceans. The vast Oceans were filled with saline water instead of pure water or some other poisonous chemical. The saline water keeps the Oceans clean and unpolluted and favorable to life.

8. Plants and animals were made interdependent on each other. Plants inhale carbon dioxide and exhale pure oxygen; animals inhale oxygen and exhale carbon dioxide. Both keeps the percentage of oxygen and carbon dioxide maintained in the air. Plants and vegetables are the food for animals and men. Without plants and vegetables animals and men cannot survive. It is not correct to say, "There is a struggle for existence among the living being." Rather *all the living beings are supporting the life of the other living beings.* The living beings are not the enemy of each other. The lives of all are made interdependent on each other.

Plants and animals can survive only together. Animals can't survive without plants and the plants also depend on man & animals for there survival.

9. All the men, animals and the plants have been provided five senses of touch, smell, listen, taste and seeing by the Great Architect. Without these five senses, the life of man, animals and plants on earth would have been a hell. The Darwin's theory of evolution fails to explain the evolution and need of these five sense organs by the living organisms. Why all the living beings have been provided five senses? Why not more or less?

10. Hot lava was provided at the centre and below the earth crust at a suitable depth. It keeps the surface of earth moderately hot. Without the hot lava the temperature of earth would have gone down below –100°C. Without this hot lava inside earth the life on its surface is not possible. Who thought of the need of this hot lava inside the earth? Is it just by chance?

11. Only the man among all the living beings has been provided with the thinking power of mind and intellect. The life of man would have been very difficult to live without the thinking power of mind and intellect; he would have been an animal. If this power would have been provided to other plants, animals and living beings, there would have been inter racial wars. The man was also provided the language to express his ideas and expressions to others. Without language there would have been no communication and progress.

12. The plenty of herbal medicinal plants have been provided to man to cure against his most of the diseases. Man has to simply search and find out which particular

herb can cure a particular disease? It is our ignorance that we have forgotten their use and we don't know the exact uses of the herbs available around us. This is not the fault of the creator, but man.

13. The man has been provided the power of entertainment, recreation, sports, humor and pleasure etc. Without these the life would have been extremely dull and boring. If the life had been evolved just by chance, there had been none of the above things.

14. The love and sex power has been provided to almost all living beings. Sex and love, not only gives pleasure but is a way of continuing life and producing offspring. The creation of sex power is one of the finest creations of the Great Architect.

15. The universe is designed beautifully and it was painted multicolored by some Super Great Architect. The nature without infinite intelligence of God can't design such a beautiful universe with wondrous multicolor. A thought of a black and white universe without any artistic beauty is a fearful and horrible object.

16. An Ozone layer surrounding the earth's atmosphere was provided to protect us from the harmful effects of some dangerous ultra-violet rays coming from sun? The hazardous rays & the ozone were discovered only a few years back while the layer is protecting the living beings since the origin of the life on earth. Who bothered for even such fine protections of lives from harmful effects of sunrays? There might be millions of other protections like this by someone, which the science does not know even today.

17. Fantastically our body has been given, few friendly symptoms of diseases like the pain, fever, swelling, vomiting, loose motions, constipation, itching, headache and so many others. All these symptoms are our friends and not the enemies as wrongly presumed. These symptoms warn and protect us against the attacks of the diseases, bacterias & viruses and against the injury & malfunctioning of the body organs. Think what would have happened to your body without these symptoms of diseases and malfunctioning of organs? Without pain we will not be aware of any body organ is damaged, cut or removed from our body. Who decided to provide these symptoms of diseases?

18. Body has been given the power to produce the toxins & anti-toxins automatically, if any thing wrong happens and unwanted poisonous material goes inside the body. The toxins & anti-toxins are the complex chemicals produced immediately by the body to save us from external enemies like poison, virus or bacteria of diseases. During AIDS, our physical body loses this power of protection. Who decided to protect us from such dangers?

19. Our face has been given the power to express our different psychological and emotional behaviors like smile, love, anger, fear, peaceful, disturbed and anxiety etc. Think of your life without these expressions on your face. You may be like a robot. Who bothered to give us these facial expressions?

20. Living beings have been provided the peaceful sleep to relax and to recharge their body after the fatigue and tiredness. Think of a man who has never been able to sleep, in his whole life to relax? The Creator has provided the pleasant sleep to all of us. But remember He Himself

never sleeps even for a second. If God sleeps & stops working even for a second the whole universe will be destroyed and vanish immediately.

21. We have been provided the *Shastras* before the creation of life on earth to lead a pure and religious life. To create these *Shastras* God Himself has taken so much pain of so many incarnations and played his divine lila on earth. In all the incarnations, God Himself has chosen to suffer Himself a lot to establish His religion for the benefit of the humanity. Why did God chosen to suffer for us? Because we are His children and He loves us.

22. God has given the knowledge of yoga and meditation techniques only to man, through which man can think of God and realize God. Only man can achieve salvation (*Moksha*) after becoming one with God. Through Maya God has separated us form Him and through yoga He would like us merge in Himself again.

23. Along with the continuous creation of matter, cloud dust, stars and galaxies in the universe the black wholes were also created to destroy the matter and creation. These black holes are nothing but the mouth of Almighty God, through which He digest His creation as expressed in Bhagwad Geeta Chapter XIII. The matter inside the black holes disappears and dissolved in God for forever and does not exist for the universe.

24. Only the man has been given the intelligence to think, read, study, linguistics, science, arts, music, technology, communication ability and to discriminate between good and bad actions etc. If this ability had been given to other living beings also, what would have been the fate of the man in the world? Think, who prohibited in

giving these abilities to other living beings? Why all other living beings have been deprived of these abilities?

25. All the living beings are inter-dependent on each other. No living being can survive alone without the help of the others. A single man alone on earth also cannot survive. One living being is help for one and food for the other living being. There is a perfect balance of the population of living beings, in the habitats and in the environment on earth. Any imbalance in the environment is due to the folly of the humans and not due to God.

26. All the diseases, difficulties and problems on earth are due to our own past *karmas* (actions). *Satan* (creation of God) continues to create, new diseases and problems, to keep the humanity always busy in finding their solutions. God keeps the humanity busy to find the new medicines and the cures to eradicate the diseases and the suffering of the humanity on earth. If *Satan* does not create such new problems, the man's life will become dull, idle, non-challenging, bored and aimless

28. All the organs of all the living organisms are functioning continuously & harmoniously without our effort, control and will. We need not run or bother to palpitate our heart, to give movement to our stomach to digest, to work our intestine, kidneys, liver, all the glands, all the senses and our brain functions etc. Millions of actions and reactions are continuously always going on inside our body without our knowledge.

Who keeps us free from all the burdens of these important works and functions of the body-organs? Who is doing all these millions of works in our body, even during our sleep, when we are not aware of our body? When we relax, enjoy sleep and forget our body, He does not sleep and take rest and continuously looks after all of our body functions. Why does He bothering about us and doing all our works? What does He want or expect from us? Is there something or nothing?

We are His children and His creation and His ownself. He loves us all, without any bias. That is why he is doing our works, without fail or any return from us. But He also wants our love too. He is always waiting and seeking for our love. He does not need any physical material thing from us. Every thing we possess has come from Him alone. He is the creator of every thing. We are always busy in our worldly engagements. Will we be ever free from our busy life to seek His love, to talk and to communicate with Him?

29. The Sun is emitting all kinds of rays essentially required for life on earth, neither less nor more. Through Chlorophyll the plants converts sun-light into their food. Even if there is a slightest disturbance, in the ratio of the amount of these thousands of different kinds of rays emitted by Sun, the life on earth will become impossible. Who is controlling the exact amount of the mixture of these rays required on earth? Is it without any intelligent body and without any cause?

30. All the living creatures are getting their required food daily. No creature including man can create even a grain of wheat or rice. Who created all the seeds of plants which supply food, vitamins, proteins, minerals and thousands of complex chemicals inside the food required by the creatures survival, so tasty, so nutritious and energetic and without any trace of any unwanted or poisonous chemical. How the plants are able to manufacture complex chemicals without any huge chemical

industry inside their body? It is beyond human understanding. Only almighty God does it out of his love, because all the creatures are his children. God convert Himself into the food we need for our survival.

31. Why all the fruits and vegetables and other eatables are so tasty and nutritious? What was the need of different types of tastes? Why all the living beings are co-operating others and also dependent on other living beings? Why not all should be enemy of each other, as per the Darwin's Law for the survival of the fittest and the struggle of existence? Does this law not hold true, in this regard?

32. If all the living things of the universe are just the random creation, arrangement of particles without any infinite intelligence of God, then why not the scientists are able to create the new particles and further arrange them to create new living and non-living things in the universe, even by using their intelligence and powerful laboratory equipments? They utterly fail. Why?

If we think logically and deeply we will come to know that every thing designed on earth requires infinite intelligence of God and is miraculous. Nothing is possible just by chance, without intelligence and a definite plan. God is always active and doing all our works but has hidden Himself behind every natural physical and biological phenomenon. God has knowingly decided to hide Himself by creating his *Maya* from the eyes, senses, mind and intelligence of man and living beings. If God had not decided to hide Himself, the dráma of the universe would have been totally different. We would have stopped doing all our works and actions and had left every thing on God to perform all our works. The world would have been a total idleness and charmless.

The Old View of The Newtonian Universe

The concept of the universe is continually changing with the new discoveries and researches in the world. As per the British scientist Newton the Universe was a three-dimensional and suspended in an absolute space at rest. And this space was unchangeable, absolute and frictionless. All the changes in physical world were described in terms of a separate dimension called time. The time again was absolute and independent entity. It had no connection with the material world and it was flowing smoothly from past through present to future. The atoms of elements of this Newtonian universe were material particles, which were small solid and indestructible objects out of which the whole matter was made. The gravitational, electrical and magnetic forces were further responsible to bind together all the particles of the universe with each other.

As per the Newtonian view: In the beginning God had created all the material particles, many types of forces between them and the fundamental laws of motion and gravitation. In this way the whole universe including microscopic particles were set in different motion and it has continued to run ever since, like a machine, governed by immutable laws. Mass, length and time are three fundamental absolute physical quantities.

But the modern physics specially *theory of relativity and quantum physics* have changed this old Newtonian view completely. Now the atoms are not the basic building blocks of the matter and are not the solid particles. Atoms are further made up of electrons, protons, and neutrons. There are hundreds of many other elementary particles. The elementary particles are no more solids, which revolve around the nucleus inside the atoms. Even the subatomic particles are not the absolute in their forms. Time and space are no more absolute but relative. Space is no more linear but is curved. Time may flow in opposite direction i.e. from future through present to past. At subatomic level, matter does not exist with certainty, but shows a tendency to exist. At subatomic levels, the solid material objects dissolve into wave like pattern of probabilities. The elementary particles behave both as a solid particles and waves at the same moment of the time. Scientific researches are continually changing our concepts and nothing is final about the concept of the Universe.

Latest Concepts of Sciences that Help us in the Understanding of the History of Creation of The Universe

The following are the bases on which our Modern concept of the Universe is based:

1. The universe consists of billions of galaxies like our milky way. Further each galaxy consists of billions of stars like our sun. Each star may have so many planets like our earth revolving around it. Each planet might have few satellites revolving around it as our moon. The sun is 13 million times bigger than our earth. The light from sun takes 8 minutes and 20 secs to reach our earth.

2. Our Universe is *expanding* regularly in all directions, as all the galaxies are *receding away* from each other, with a very high velocity comparable to the velocity of light. The galaxies far away from us are receding with more velocity then the galaxies nearer to us. The expansion of universe is just like the expanding rubber balloon, which has large number of printed dots on its surface. Each dot recedes away from the other dots similar to the galaxies in the universe.

3. As per theory of relativity, the matter and energy are the two different forms of one thing. Matter can be converted into energy and vice-versa according to the Einstein's famous equation $E = mc^2$. All the atomic and subatomic particles can be converted into each other and are made of the same material throughout the universe. So the whole universe is made up of only one thing and not from two or more things. The elementary particles behave like solid particles and also dissolve in wave like patterns of probabilities. Nothing is at rest. Everything is in motion or vibrating. (*There is only one Brahman nothing else in the universe)*

Till now science has discovered that matter and energy are one thing and made from one material. Very soon science will discover that three things: matter, energy and mind are one thing and made from one thing. The universe is a dream in the mind of God.

4. As per the G*eneral Theory of Relativity of Einstein*, the velocity of light is the only fundamental constant in the universe. Light always travel with the same fixed speed in the space irrespective of its strength of gravitational field. The mass of an object is not an absolute constant and increases with its speed. The mass of an object approaches to infinity as its speed approaches the velocity of light. No material thing can travel faster than the velocity of light i.e.3, 00,000 km/s nearly.

5. The length of an object also decreases with the increase of velocity of an object known as *Fitzgerald Contraction*. So the length is not a fundamental constant physical quantity. The length of the standard meter is measured with speed of light of a particular wavelength.

6. The flow of time from past to present and present to future is not same or a constant or absolute for the objects traveling with different speeds. If one of the two identical twins travel to a nearby star with a high speed close to the speed of light and takes 10 years in his journey in going and coming back. He will be still young. But then 100s of years might have passed for the second twin brother on the earth. He might have become very old or have died long back on earth.

7. The space around us is not linear as commonly understood, but it is curved, as the surface of the earth is not linear but curved. There are curvatures in space around a heavenly body due to its huge gravitation. The light does not travel exactly in straight line but follow the *geodesic* path of shortest time in the curved space around us. The shortest air path for an airplane from Delhi to New York is also not a straight line but a curved path known as geodesic. It was also confirmed by the astronomical experiments during total solar eclipse that the sum of the angles of a triangle formed by three stars having a huge star with strong gravitational field between them is not 180° (see figure). Which shows that space has a curvature. But there cannot be any curvature in *vacuum.* So the space around us is not a blank vacuum, but it is filled with something known as *ether.*

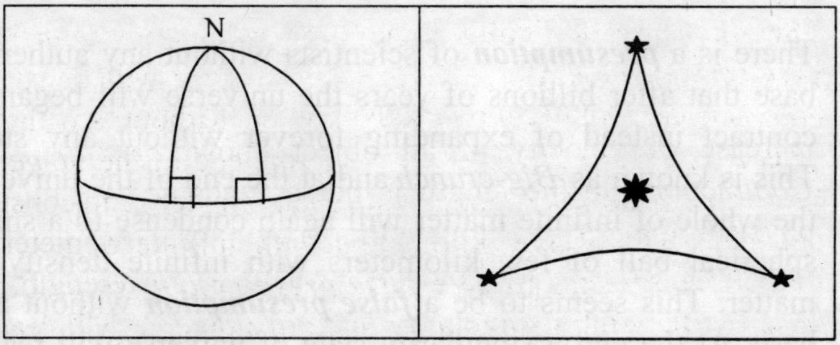

The sum of the angles of any triangle on the surface of the earth > 180°, because the surface of earth is spherical and curved.	The sum of the angles of triangles joining the three stars in space by the light path is < 180°, if there is a huge mass inside the triangle.

8. If space is vacuum (contains nothing), than there cannot be any *curvature in vacuum.* Hence the space throughout the universe is filled with a substance called *ether* (hypothetical finest material). It is present throughout even inside the atomic and subatomic particles. Ether is present every-where. (This *ether* is the first manifestation of God in the material form). Since ether is the finest material, finer than any kind of matter, no physical instrument can detect it. The whole universe is suspended in *ether.*

9. If the *2nd law of Thermodynamics is reversed*, or our universe begins to contract, the time will begin to flow in the *negative or opposite direction.* Then time will flow from *future → present → past.* In that case the happening of all the events will be reversed. That means we will die first and born later, i.e. we will grow from old to youth to childhood. Your old things will become new later. To understand the concept of negative time, run a video film in the reverse order.

There is a ***presumption*** of scientists without any authentic base that after billions of years the universe will began to contract instead of expanding forever without any stop. This is known as *Big-crunch* and at the end of the universe the whole of infinite matter will again condense to a small spherical ball of few kilometers with infinite density of matter. This seems to be a ***false presumption*** without any base. At the end a singularity state of universe will reach, where no laws of physical matter or science will hold. The time will also stop to flow at the singularity. This again seems to be a false presumption or an intentional lie without any authentic scientific base.

10. When a star bigger than double the size of our sun dies, it begins to contract under its own gravitation. But as it begins to contract the gravitation on its surface starts increasing more and more. Due to more gravitation it further goes on contracting more and more. Nothing seems to stop its contraction. The space inside and outside its intra-atomic particles is reduced to zero. The size of the star is reduced to a few kilometers and it is changed into a ***black-hole.***

In a black-hole the gravitation at its surface is increased so huge that even the light coming out of it cannot escape its surface. The light emitted out of its surface will again falls back inside the black-hole. Nothing can come out of a black-hole. Therefore we shall never be able to observe the inside of the black-hole as we can never get any information from its inside through any kind of waves or particles. There are billions of black-holes in the universe. A black-hole can digest the whole galaxy and will become more stronger.

11. The negative mass, anti-matter and anti-atomic particle of all the particles are also possible. Negative mass means the mass of a body less than zero. The particles of negative mass will not be attracted due to the gravity of the earth but will be repelled by ordinary matter. The anti-matter and anti-particles also exists in the universe. Each particle of ordinary matter has an exactly opposite anti-particle in the universe. When a particle of ordinary matter combines with an anti-particle of opposite kind both destroy each other completely, and are changed into a huge energy as per the Einstein's Equation $E = mc^2$. This shows that matter and anti-matter are made from the same material.

12. In the development of the *General Theory of Relativity* we have presumed the state of infinite density of matter known as singularity in the beginning of the universe. The big-bang would have been the effective beginning of time in the universe. This simply seems to be a presumption or a hypothesis. There are no scientific bases for this presumption, it may be wrong. If so, our present picture of universe will change. The age of the universe is more then 16 billions and less then 20 billions years has been confirmed by Hubble Telescope. Before the beginning of the universe, the whole matter of the universe was concentrated at a point, with infinite density seems to be impossible baseless presumption.

The scientists further presume that infinite matter of the universe was condensed in a small ball of few kilometers, without an intera-atomic space. In that state there were no actions and reactions of any kind. Every thing was stand still. There was an infinite gravitation and nothing can come out of it. There was no time, no space and no place, no natural or scientific laws. It was a singularity when all the laws of sciences failed.

Then there was a Big-Bang, a Big-Explosion of infinite power (*A biggest scientific lie, without any base. Who is the cause of this Big-bang & Big-crunch? Scientists doesn't know*). And the matter inside began to go away from its centre and formed Galaxies, Stars, Planets, star-dust and gases etc. It is believed (presumption) that the expansion of the universe cannot be forever. The space and volume of the universe is continually increasing. The scientists are unable to explain how the particles that are infinitely condensed with infinite gravitation, separate themselves and formed stardust-cloud, without any cause?

Again as per presumption, when Big-Crunch will start, the universe begins to contract, then a time will come when the entire matter in the universe will condense in a small ball of infinite density. And again it will be the end of the universe; the flow of time and all the laws of natural sciences will fail at infinite density of matter. (*Who will stop this Big-Crunch from further contraction, inspite of the infinite gravitation).*

Some of the scientists believe that the Big-Bang and Big-Crunch requires the infinite power of God to start with. Again the infinite power of God is needed to stop further contraction of the ball of infinitely condensed matter. There is no known physical energy or power, which can start Big-Bang and again stop its expansion and again to start with Big-Crunch. In the expansion state the atomic and sub-atomic particles are forming and creating so many new stars and galaxies. On the other side so many stars and even the whole galaxies are going inside the innumerable big black-holes.

So many other wonderful mysterious heavenly objects have also been observed in the universe, like neutron stars, quasars, red-giants, super-novas, dust-clouds, white-dwarfs, quarks, nebulas etc. There are so many kinds of electric, magnetic and gravitational fields in space. There are so many kinds of electromagnetic waves like light, heat, sound, radio waves, X-rays, cosmic rays & gamma rays of different wavelengths. But the scientists have still failed to detect *ether* and the life force (prana), which is present throughout the universe and constantly doing infinite works for the existence of life on earth.

13. The same scientific laws are applicable throughout the vast universe irrespective of its big size and long age. How the same scientific laws are true everywhere since the beginning, science has no answer. All the particles of one kind are 100% exactly same and are exact replica everywhere in the universe. On the other side any two things manufactured by the man or by the scientists are never 100% exactly same or exact replica. They have no answer, from where the original Big-ball of infinite mass & infinite density of matter came into existence before the creation of the universe? Who created that Big-ball? From where it came into existence. What was the need of Big-bang? Who started the big-bang? What was the aim of Big-bang? They have no answer.

14. What was the need of the living beings on the earth? Is there life in other parts of the universe? Why the universe is, as it is? Why the life came into existence at all? Why and how the sex instinct was needed and created in all the creatures? Why and how the sex instinct created pleasure? Why and how the bacterias, viruses, diseases, sleep and dreams etc. were created? Why and how the emotions and feelings of hunger, joys, happiness, sorrows, laughing, weeping and sadness etc. were created? Science has no answer.

Why our common senses are not able to observe the absolute reality of the matter? Why the bare eyes are not able to see the infinitely small things i.e. the motion and viberation of atomic & subatomic particles? Why the bare eyes are not able to see the infinitely distant objects. Why the ears are not able to listen the sounds beyond human range? Why the universe does not exist for us when we are unconscious or in sleep? Why the fruits of our actions are not according to our planning and desires? Why the diseases, weakening of senses in old age and death were needed? The phenomenon of re-births and remembering the memories of past lives by most of the men is still a mystery.

15. The science can simply answer the ***how*** (the history of events) of the things have happened. But the science has failed to answer ***why*** (cause of events) the things have happened as these are? Science has failed to answer why should the universe or the things should be as these are in the universe? Why the things should not be different from the present state in the universe?

Why the formula of Newton's law of Gravitation is:
$F = (G \times M_1 \times M_2) \div d^2$ and not some other formula different from above? Who decided this law of gravitation, to govern the whole universe under this law? Newton is neither the creator of this law nor his other three laws of motions etc. The formulae were already there in ether before Newton and since the beginning of the universe. Newton's mind simply captured these formulae already stored in ether. He tuned his mind to capture and discover these laws, which already existed in the ether. All other laws of natural science discovered by other scientists are also simply the discovery of the scientific laws. These laws were already existed in ether. There are still millions of scientific laws to be discovered that are unknown by the humanity at present.

16. Stars we see in the universe are not of the present time. The light from different galaxies and stars may take thousands millions or even billions of years to reach our earth. What we know at present about these galaxies is of

billions of years before. What has happened to these galaxies at present is unknown and we do not know?

17. As per the experiment conducted by the physicist Alain Aspect of France in 1982: An atom emitted two photons (subatomic elements of light). These photons were going in just opposite directions. It was strange to note that these photons affected one another's behavior from a great distance, without exchange of any signals through space, but instantaneously affecting each other.

According to Einstein, two objects can never affect each other instantly in space and time without any signal send by one and received by other. And every signal must travel through space in a finite time, and with the maximum speed of light. But these photons were doing it faster then the speed of light and without transmitting any signal to other. Therefore it is evident that the influence could not travel through space. Instead the influence must belong to the domain of reality that we must recognize as the transcendent domain or the domain of consciousness.

18. A ***hologram*** is a unique form of three-dimensional photographic image, every part of which, if seen in isolation, contains the full image. According to Bohm and Pribram, the world around us is nothing more then an illusion like a holographic image that our brains mathematically construct by interpreting frequencies from another dimension. It is a transcendent realm of meaningful and patterned reality. *We can say that a brain is an instantaneous hologram-interpreting machine, interpreting the holographic universe.*

The Latest Concept of Our Universe As per Prof. Stephen W. Hawking

The latest concept of the universe has been given by modern science mainly by Prof. Stephen Hawking. He is Lucasian Professor of Mathematics at Cambridge University, a post once held by Newton and later by Prof. P.M. Dirac. His book "*The Brief History of Time From the Big-Bang to Black-Holes*" has given the concept of universe as per the latest scientific researches.

The scientists like Einstein and Stephen Hawking are a rare phenomenon in the world. Whenever at the right time, the Almighty God feels the necessity of revealing His secrets of the universe, for the development of mankind, He transfer the required thoughts and the scientific laws governing the universe through the scientists of the world.

His book has described the various changing scientific concepts in the minds of our scientists and the evolution of various different theories, about the construction and the design of the universe from the time of Aristotle 340 B.C. He has also described some of the prevailing western religious concepts contradictory to the modern scientific laws and contradictory to the scientific concepts of the universe. It is true the Prof. Hawking has a little bit knowledge of most of the western religions, but he is silent and intentionally ignored the *Vedas* and other Hindu *Shastras,* which are an authority regarding the origin of the universe. The reasons for ignoring he might know better.

But there is no doubt that if he would have a little bit knowledge of *Vedas* and *Shastras,* his concept of the universe or God or the contents of his book would have been quite different. In fact there should not be any contradiction between the sciences and the *Shastras* about the absolute truth. Truth and God are ***one*** and are the two faces of the same coin. The sciences, *Shastras* and the spirituality should lead to the same truth.

As our information of science and technology is progressively increasing, with better and more exact scientific laws, the concept of the universe is also *changing continuously*. This proves that our scientific concept of the universe is *not final* and there is a much further scope in future, for the modification and change in its structure and design.

Stephen Hawking is of the view that the infinite power of God is necessary and responsible for certain big happening in the universe, such as Big-Bang and Big-Crunch and many others. By logical approach he has compared the difference between the scientific and western religious concepts of the universe and discarded most of the western religious concepts. But he is silent on the evolution and the purpose of life on earth and about so many other infinite factors relating to the development of life on earth. So his view of universe seems to be incomplete.

Moreover he has not compared the scientific concepts with the *Vedas*, which are the authority of revealed knowledge of creation of the universe direct from God to the humanity. Either he has no information/ knowledge of the *Vedas* and of the concept of self-realization or he has intentionally ignored them for the reasons better known to him. It is notable that each and every world of *Vedas* is an unchangeable Absolute Truth and verifiable through yoga. The Vedas gives us much better view of the universe then all the sciences has provided & informed us till now.

We should understand that all the scientific views of the universe are based upon the *union and combination of so many separate partial truths found in separate parts, by the different scientists at different times and at different places.* No scientist has ever been able to view the *whole universe at a time and could see all the events from its beginning till the end of the universe. Contrarily a self-realized yogi does so.* So the scientific view gives us only the ***glimpse*** of the partial truths of the universe based upon so many false presumptions and the observations reported by our sense organs under the influence of *Maya.* We are sure that the senses under *Maya* report only the illusions and the delusions.

Absolute Truth cannot be interpreted in parts in contradictory ways. God Himself created *Vedas* before the creation of life on earth. Vedas are the collection of absolute truths, which are unchangeable in the universal clock of time. You will not find much difference in the higher Natural Sciences and the *Vedas.*

All the self-realized saints, realize the *Vedas* through intuition and deep meditation. All the self-realized men have observed the same truth. It is notable that none of the statement of any two self-realized saints has ever been contradictory. A self-realized man becomes one with the Truth and God. They observe the Truth as a whole, directly face to face and not in parts like the natural scientists. The yogi becomes one with the Truth and God. To understand the *spiritual view* of the universe as per the ***Vedas*** and ***self-realized saints*** we will first try to understand, how the knowledge is coming to us?

The next chapter deals with the spiritual concept of the universe. After that you may compare the two and conclude your own conclusion.

13

Spiritual View of Universe

Spiritual View of Getting Knowledge by Us

Spiritual View of the Creation of the Universe

Some Unexplained Mysteries of the World

Spiritual View of Universe

Prayer

O Divine Spirit, Thou art the Creator of *Maya*, Universe & all the creatures on Earth. Divine Father, everything in the Universe is obeying perfectly Thy laws, since the beginning of the creation, without fail. But Thou hast given us freedom to act, as per the *Vedas* to decide right or wrong actions. Thou art not only the Creator & Organizer but also the Savior of all the lives & inert matter and the Destroyer of creation too.

O Cosmic Dreamer, The whole creation is Thy great Thought in Thy Mind, which has further condensed into a Thy Great Dream and a Thought Film projected on 3-4 dimensional great screen of space-time continuum. Thy universe is just an expanding bubble ready to burst on Thy surface of vast Ocean of Knowledge, Love, Bliss and Joy. Naughty or good, I am Thy child. I am just a tiny bubble on Thy huge wave of Infinite Ocean. Thou Maya have separated me from Thou since millenniums. I am Thy prodigal son. I am no more interested in Thy sweet toffees and dolls of *Maya*, in Thy enchanting ocean of creation to distract my mind from Thee. Have a pity on me. Start my journey of involution (back to God). Reveal Thee remove my ignorance & *Maya*. Merge my tiny bubble of ego in Thy Ocean.

How the Knowledge is Coming to Us?
(A Spiritual View)

All the knowledge and truth, known and unknown in all the branches of science, arts and music, the mystery of the physical matter, particles & energy and the history of the creation of the universe and development of human beings, *is already existing (recorded) in the ether throughout the universe, as the viberation of truth.* It is similar as the software programs are recorded in the active memory of the computer. To catch these vibrations of truth from ether, we have to use our all-knowing intuitive power of the soul through meditation and samadhi. By the constant inward concentration and meditation of our mind we catch few truths from the vast cosmic ocean of knowledge and truth.

By constant regular practice a yogi becomes one with God and Truth during his *Nirbhikalpa samadhi* and during which a vast cosmic sea of knowledge & truth is transferred to him in his mind. All his previous stored small water tanks of knowledge become redundant, when the infinite flood of the knowledge is pored to his mind. After this nothing more is remained to know further.

Spiritual View of the History of Creation of the Universe

In the spiritual view one has to keep in his mind the truth that God, the man and the universe are not separate entity. God is the Supreme Force itself and has transformed itself as the manifested universe we observe. As per the scientific view and the *Vedas* the age of the universe is less then 20 billions years. It is universally acceptable that before the creation of the universe there was nothing. Not even the infinite matter condensed into a small ball, at infinite density at a point.

The hypothesis of scientists regarding Big-Bang seems to be unreasonable. There cannot be any Big-Bang (big-explosion) in this small ball of infinite mass and density without the infinite power of God to start with the creation of the universe (It is a false childish assumption based upon false hypothesis of some of the scientists and is not a verifiable fact). How the subatomic particles of matter condensed to infinite density ball (a singularity) and bonded by infinite gravitation can separate themselves, when even the light cannot come out of a small compact black-whole, which is of much smaller size? A natural question arises from where the initial ball of infinite matter came into existence? Who created it, when and why?

It should be self-evident and acceptable by everybody that not even a single atomic or sub-atomic particle existed before the creation of the universe. As nothing can come out of nothing, there must be one thing and nothing else before the creation i.e. God alone in His un-manifested form. He was all-alone, in His changeless form and there was no place, nor space nor any time, nor any particle of matter or energy, nor any law of science. The time flows due to the physical changes around us. If there was nothing around, no change of any kind was possible hence there could not be any flow of time before the creation.

God was infinite, omnipotent, omniscient, omnipresent, all-powerful and ever lasting. He was in His absolute state of Bliss, Joy and Consciousness (Sat-Chit-Ananda). But there was non-else to share His infinite powers and His eternal Love. As Love can always be expressed with others and *one cannot love one's ownself. As sugar cannot taste the sugar itself,* God could not enjoy His infinite powers of love and creation, without the creation of others. The following are the translation from *Rig Veda* (one out of the four Vedas):

"Neither non being, nor being was as yet, neither was airy space nor heavens beyond." *Rig Veda 10, 129, 1:*

"Neither was there death nor immortality, nor was there any sign of day or night. Totally windless, alone, The One

breathed; beyond that, indeed, nothing whatever was."

Rig Veda 10, 129, 2:

"Darkness was concealed in darkness. In the womb of water the seeds of creation lay hidden. Then the formless, through the divine contemplation brought forth The One."

Rig Veda 10, 129, 3:

"Before the creation, in the beginning there was only the Absolute-Self (Brahman) and He was all-alone. Nothing else was there. Brahman willed, "Let me create the universe." *Aitareya Upanishad 1. I. 1:*

All of a sudden God said, "Let Me create a universe and divide *Myself* into many individual souls that may play with Me in My unfolding big drama." God also have the infinite mystical power of *Maya* (ignorance and duality). He changed into the dualities like the Spirit & Nature, male & female, positive & negative and the creation & the Creator etc. It should be remembered that although God created the universe out of His delusive power of Maya, He Himself is not deluded and affected by His *Maya*. Brahman Said, *"There was no one to know who I am…till I created this world at my pleasure for Me… with one word (Om). From Om the five elements of creation came (Space, Air, Fire, Water & Earth) into existence."*

"I am the ultimate source of everything, from Me all the creation of the universe emerges out. After the realization of this truth, the wise, awe-stricken yogis adore Me. They concentrate their thoughts fully upon Me. They totally surrender their being to Me. They enlighten one another, proclaiming Me always. My devotees are fully contended with joy."

From this sheer compassion, I the divine indweller, enlighten them with the radiant lamp of My wisdom which vanishes their mental darkness that is born out of the ignorance (Maya) in them." (Bhagwad Gita chapter X)

God created this dream universe of *Maya* for Himself and also for His own entertainment. It is true and acceptable by all that the universe was not created instantaneously, but it took billions of years of pre-planned evolution to reach the present state of the universe. God also designed a plan for the *involution* (opposite of evolution i.e. to merge back into God) of the universe.

Cosmic delusion or *Maya* is the mystical power of God by which God differentiate His infinite consciousness, created the finite dream images and gave them a dream reality. Both God and Maya are pulling man to themselves. God is pulling man and all his creation back to Him (involution). But *Maya* is pulling man and the creation away from God (evolution). There is a big tug of war between God and Maya. Man has been provided the knowledge of *Shastras* and the intelligence (intuition) to take his right decision to decide between good and bad.

According to Vedas, God first created the Anahat sound of Om and then the five gross Elements came into existence as follows:

Om → Space (Ether) → Air → Fire → Water → Earth

"Everything has come out from Om. The Past, present or the future, and anything beyond is also Om. The creation of galaxies and stars were effected by Om."

Mandukya Upanishad, 1.1:

All of a sudden, The Brahman (the unmanifested form of God) decided to manifest His supreme omnipotent powers to enjoy and share it with others. To achieve this God decided to become many out of Him.

Contrary to present sciences before creation there was no small compact ball of infinite matter, no energy, no fields, no rays, no materials, except Brahman. For a very long time (billions of years) He was asleep, peacefully dreaming of the vast space. He was infinite, blissful and permeated by His omniscient cosmic intelligence. He began to think, "*I have been all alone for long, let Me manifest My infinite powers, let Me become many instead of one and let Me dream of the cosmos and the universe*". So the God decided to covert Himself (as there was nothing else) into gross elements like light, rays, energies, fields, atomic and sub-atomic particles and so many things.

Also God didn't want matter or His creation to become something different from Him. First *Brahman* decided to design the whole universe. It was just a ***great Idea*** or a great Thought in His Mind. By further power of visualization of His thoughts and condensation of the ideas, the Bahaman manifested His thought into dream. First the universe came into existence only in a thought-form and then in the dream-form in the great Mind of Brahman. Then the cosmic light (life-force) was created. The life-force was empowered by transforming the dreams into more condensed, definite forms and shapes.

Thought → Dream → Cosmic Light → Physical Forms

This way of creation shows that it is the work of some great Intelligent Mind and it must have a great purpose to achieve. The senses have been provided with the physical sense organs to relate with this world. Feeling of hunger was provided to inform the need of food by the living being. To achieve this enough food has been provided to satisfy the hunger by the living beings. We have been given the ability to look after our physical body and its needs.

Every thing is obeying the scientific laws, which shows that there is a great Director of the universal Drama who has given different forms and ordered the things to have the characteristic, as they should be and as they are. God has set all the standards and the laws by which all the living beings and inert matter are governed.

Further the creation of universe was not instantaneous. It was in the following sequence as:

Word (Om) → Space → Air → Fire → Water → Earth
First the great Word (Om) the *Anahat* omni-sound was created. From Om a vast space (not vacuum) was created. Space does not mean vacuum (which contains nothing). The Space was throughout filled with a finest omnipresent material called *ether*. Inside the ether the life force or the lifetrons were created throughout. The omni-sound of Om (Om is the infinite vibratory intelligent sound or the vibrating sound of the universal creation motor) and the life force (lifetrons) worked intelligently on ether and created visual light and other electromagnetic waves, atomic & sub-atomic particles.

First the universe came into existence only in a dream form of the God and then the dream was further condensed and given the material form. Out of the ether the dark fluid matter evolved and it took billions of years to take the present form.

"Darkness was concealed in darkness. In the womb of water, the seed of living creation lay hidden. Then the formless Brahman through divine contemplation brought forth The One." ...Rig Veda 10, 129, 3:

By His intelligent will power, God gave these subatomic particles a further strength such as the spinning force, which created the magnetism and electrical fields. And due to these fields the particles arranged themselves into atoms and molecules. Gravitational, electrical and magnetic fields and forces were created by that infinite intelligence.

A very thin and huge cloud of hydrogen atoms was created. When it began to condense and collapse, Fire (heat) was generated. Then Bahaman dreamed of nebulas, galaxies, stars and planets etc. Then He began to dream of very strong forces in nebulas to condense its gases into solids, liquids and many condensed gases (plasma). Remember not even a single particle was created or can exist in the universe without the will of God. God took billion's of years, in the process of this creation.

"*From the heart of Om came truth and all the worlds in their majestic glory."* *Rig Veda, 10, 190, 1:*
"From this universal Ocean came Time, the lord of each moment. Ordaining nights and days."
...Rig Veda, 10, 190, 2:
"Then as before He did, the Creator (Brahman) fashioned the Sun, Earth, Moon and the Heaven."
...Rig Veda 10, 190, 3:

"When the stardust or the hot plasma of the planet like our earth further cooled. The particles further locked themselves in an intelligent manner. By millions of chemical actions and reactions, air, water and other millions of the minerals were formed as desired by God.

Maya (ignorance or the principle of duality) was also created by God to hide Himself from His creation. By this *Maya*, God separated the creation from Himself but still have the full control. The inert matter began to take shapes. The millions of objects like sea, water, air, environment, temperature and gravity etc. and so many other factors were so adjusted by the Intelligent God, so that these were just fit together for the desired creation and for the survival of life on earth.

"The Brahman created the sky and the heaven beyond the earth and the waters below." Aitareya Upanishad I. 2:

"And the Brahman, too, is all the creatures, large and small and that also move upon the earth or fly above."

Aitareya Upanishad I. III, I, 3:

After this the microorganism like living cells, virus, bacteria etc. came into existence. Later the plant and vegetation came into being to provide freer expression. A scum was formed on the sea and out of which, living creatures appeared in the water. Some of them evolved gradually the lungs to breath in air and also the capability to live on land. Five sense powers were created and accordingly all the creatures were provided with the five sense organs: Eyes (to see), Ears (to hear), Nose (to smell), Skin (to touch) and Tongue (to taste). Creatures were also provided with a digestive and excretion system, brain, mind, thoughts and intelligence etc. Creatures were also provided some of the instincts like hunger, sex, pleasure, sorrow, weep, anger, love, hatred, peace and fear etc. Sleep and dreams were also created and provided to the living beings to relax and recharge their bodies with life forces.

"The essence of all the creation is Cosmic Consciousness. The Cosmic Consciousness is Brahman. And Brahman, too

is all these creatures, large and small, that move upon the earth or fly above." Aitareya Upanishad III. I, 3:

The seed of cosmic consciousness was planted in the soil of all these activities by His will. This seed sprouted into a huge creation, just as a small seed of tree is sprouted into a huge tree. When the seed was put into soil; the seed germinated and grew into a big tree. A software program of the future development of the whole tree was stored and hidden inside the small seed. It is just like the computer softwares hidden in hard-disc. After few days even the seed is destroyed in the soil, but the software of the future development of the tree still exist throughout the life of the tree.

All the living beings were also provided the ability to produce the seeds of sperms and ova to further generate their offspring. An instinct of parental love for the offspring was also provided to the parents to look after their offspring. Otherwise the offspring would have been just the orphans. *But remember that all this was possible only due to the God's dreaming it all in a perfect-programmed way.*

Remember that the cosmic creation is nothing more than a dream condensation of the Thoughts of God. A thought in mind is finer and of less condensed than a dream. A dream is finer and less condensed than the manifested physical gross things. The thought of a car is only a concept in mind, while a dream of car is a perceptible vision and more gross. A physical car is more realistic and condensed than a dream of car.

"Man was an animal, until the divine knowledge and the thinking power was placed in his mind."

... *Narshima Puran*

God didn't want His creation to become different from Himself. So a dreaming power during sleep and some intellıgence was also provided to the living beings. But only man was provided the highest intelligence among all the living beings and the creatures. By yoga practice, gradual awakening and development of this dreaming intelligence man can realize that matter, energy, mind and soul are one. Till now we know that matter and energy are one (a childlike stage). Very soon a time will come for the science to realize and understand that the universe is also a condensed dream in the Mind of God.

And then the science will be able to understand that matter, energy and mind are one. We are not merely the ordinary creatures created by God but we are the part and parcel of God. We are children of God in His image. So, God has to listen to us. Since we are made in God's image, God has given us all His powers and characteristics, but alas we have forgotten them due to His Maya.

The ***Darwin's Law*** of the "*survival of the fittest*" doesn't seem to be fit and totally true. We observe that the fittest of the living beings, may die earlier and even extinct forever, while the weaker ones are survived for longer periods. Among the species of any living being, it is not possible to predict the fittest ones or the weaker ones with accuracy. We cannot say, which one will survive longer and which one will die earlier. It is generally observed that the fittest one may die earlier and the weaker ones may survive for longer period.

Darwin's Law of the "*Struggle for Existence among the living beings*" also does not seem to be true. The life on the earth seems to be inter-dependent on each other, rather then the struggle against each other. No man can exist on earth all-alone without the company of other living beings like, animals, plants, trees, vegetables, fruits, milk, eggs and meat etc. etc. Even there are both types of the useful and the harmful bacterias. We do not know much about the utility of the harmful bacterias till now. The harmful bacterias may also be useful to us in some way, we do not know. God has not created anything against the man to make his life miserable. But it is the ignorance of man, who does not know the utility of the harmful bacterias and many other harmful living beings. *Science has still to find out the uses of harmful creatures.*

The Darwin's Law of "*Adaptation to the Environment*" also does not seem to be fully true. Due to the environmental changes and requirement of the physical body, the living creatures may develop some changes in their physical organs and bodies, but it is impossible and unreasonable to say that the living beings changes itself into some different kind of species and also retain their original specific forms. If man has evolved from monkey, than how the species of monkeys still exist? Why all the monkeys have not changed themselves into man? There are thousand kinds of species of monkeys in the world. Darwin's theory is unable to tell, which specie of monkey has developed into human form? *Without any proper scientific base the real scientists should not propagate any false and imaginary theory. It creates misconceptions in human minds and is a hindrance in the development of human knowledge.*

It may be true that the universe may begin to contract one day again with the will of God. But it seems to be just impossible that it will contract to the infinite limit of a single small ball known as Big-Crunch. As predicted by the *Vedas,* why can't all the creation and matter again merges back into God? And not even a single created particle will remain in the existing universe except God alone in its

Absolute State of Rest? How and why the scientists have discarded it and have propagated Big-Crunch? The spiritual view seems to be most scientific, logical and reasonable then the baseless presumptions of the scientists.

We have observed that there are so many ***black-holes,*** which exist throughout the universe. As described in Bhagwad Geeta (Chapter XIII) black-holes are the mouths of Almighty God, through which the God digest His creation. At the end of the universe all the galaxies and the whole universe will be dissolved back again in God through these black-holes and nothing else will remain manifested (involution process-opposite to evolution). The universe can never contract to a single ball of the infinite density of matter at a point. It is the biggest lie the scientists have propagated to befool the mankind in their selfish interests. They should not have done so. After the dissolution of the whole universe in God, God will sleep alone in that state of ever Consciousncss, Bliss and Ananda for billions of years. Again after billions of years God will start manifesting the universe as before. Saint John also supports it.

¶"*At the end of the creative cycle God dissolves every thing within Himself, there remains only one principal Spirit, which is ever-existing, ever-lasting, ever-conscious, ever-new Bliss. But in each new creative cycle the Spirit again project Itself as the Trinity: Father, Son and Holy Ghost.*"¶

... John 1:18 (Bible)

Here the Spirit means Brahman and the Trinity means: Aum, Tat, Sat or (Brahman, Vishnu and Mahesh).

"*It is only through the knowledge of the divine and the removal of ignorance, that the liberation can be attained.*"

... *Adi Shankaracharaya*

"To prove His own existence, He became many to witness His supreme powers. Bra*hman* (God) transformed Himself into all forms in the universe such as: human beings ... mankind ... trees ...plants ... beasts ... and birds; flying ... speaking ... hearing ... and all powers bestowed upon them by His Will."

In His plan for the involution (merge back to God) of the universe, God created the sufferings in the world to remind us to seek our union with God. The sleep and the Dreams were also created to remind us daily about the non-reality and falseness of the physical universe. But due to our pride and ignorance we are ignoring to realize and understand Him. During our old age all our sense organs were also designed to make weaker. The aim was to weaken our attachment with the delusive enchanting universe and to weaken the bond of Maya. So the old age is the opportunity provided by God to seek His union and merge again with Him (involution).

Some of the Un-Explained Mysteries of the World

There are numerous unexplained mysteries in the world, about which the science is unable to explain correctly. These mysteries are miraculous in nature and do not fit in our existing knowledge of natural sciences. These mysterious also do not fit in the cultural and historical development of man, searched by the scientists. Some of these are here for your curiosity:

❑ The huge pre-historical *Pyramids of Egypt* including their mummies preserved inside, which are still fresh. How and when these pyramids were constructed and who supplied the advanced technology involved in the construction of Pyramids and preserving the dead bodies?

❑ The *Great Bermuda Triangle is still a mystery.* It is a triangular region inside the Pacific sea between North and South America. In this region there have been numerous accidents of ships in the past few hundred years. Most of the ships were missed mysteriously, after a short massage of SOS "We are in danger and there is no way out of it". NASA has observed from space through satellites some mysterious lights and some man made water canals, at the bottom of the sea, inside the Bermuda Triangle. The canals are made up of huge cubic solid stones of the size 15ftX15ftX15ft. Such huge stones require an advance technology to construct, which we do not possess till now. We are unable to explain, how, when and who constructed these canals and what is the source of mysterious lights inside the sea-bed? We do not know where are the ships after the accidents.

❑ There are some mysterious places on the surface of earth, especially in California and China, where the force of gravity is not vertical i.e. towards the centre of the earth, but it is inclined at some angle, much away from vertical. At these places one cannot stand vertical from ground, but has to align body inclined in the direction of gravity. In China one has to accelerate the engine of his car to go downward and has to apply breaks to go upwards at these places of abnormal gravity. These natural phenomenons are mysterious and still un-explained by the scientists.

❑ The mysterious huge construction of China Wall, whose length is 1500 kms and 15 to 20 ft high, visible from Moon.

- Amar-Nath Cave of Lord Shiva in The Himalayas in India.
- The existence of *Vedas, Puranas* and other *Shastras* prove the existence of highly advanced culture in India, much before lord Krishna (5320 B.C.) and much before Lord Rama (9,56,000 B.C.). These do not fit in the mind of the Historians. They cannot ignore them simply by calling them myths.

- So many ruins of pre-historic temples and idols of God, found in 'Maya' and other civilizations in US and other countries. Some of the idols of gods are at least 10,000 yrs B.C. proves the hollowness of the historical scientists.

- There are always thousands of cases of rebirths throughout the world. They remember their history of many past incarnations. They are able to narrate the mysterious events of their past lives. So many persons get life again after their death. They tell us their mysterious experiences of life after death. Some saints have the ability to predict their next birth accurately.

- So many persons have the ability of the exact prediction by analyzing the dreams, palmistry and horoscopes etc. Some can predict even their next births and tell about previous lives.

- So many cases of witnessing of UFO's (unidentified flying objects) observed by thousands of people at different times in different countries all over the world. Some have been able to take the video films of these flying objects. All the observers cannot be declared wrong or mischievous. These UFOs are still mysteries.

❑ So many people have actually seen the ghosts in their lives. The ghosts have the ability to change their body to different forms at their will. They can appear and disappear at their will. They have the freedom of physical matter slaveness like food, transportation, injuries etc. All such observations and stories cannot be baseless. Science must do something for research in this field.

❑ Many persons are found all over the world, who have the miraculous ability of eating iron, steel, glass, ceramics, blades, bulbs, swords and so many other things without any difficulty. Later the scientists have confirmed the presence of these items in their stomach with the help of endoscopes and X-ray photographs. The persons eating these items have no knowledge of the mystery they are doing. They have no training of any trick to eat these items. These items are digested or do not create any problems to these persons. How it is possible? Science has failed to answer. If we do efforts to know the answer to this strange phenomenon, it will open a Pandora box of vast knowledge in a new field. It will be very useful to us but still unknown to us.

❑ At the time of Ramayana and Mahabharata we come to know about some of the miraculous herbal medicines. These had the miraculous power to cure the injuries overnight. The worriers who were injured in the battlefield used to take this herbal ointment at night. Their injuries were used to heal immediately and their pain also vanished overnight. Next day the worriers were fresh and fit for further fights. How this knowledge of herbs has been lost?

❑ Some of the saints all over the world have the miraculous spiritual power to cure the patients instantly like

Jesus Christ and Sri Sathya Sai Baba and others. Some even can give life to dead.

❑ Recently, the archeologists have discovered a human skull from Botswana near South Africa. This human skull is nearly seven million years old. By this single discovery the whole structure of the development of human civilization by the historians till now, has fallen to ground and it is a further proof of the events stated in the *Ramayana* nearly one million year ago.

❑ The basic difference in scientific view & spiritual view is that science does not believe in the existence of *ether* (*Akasha*), which is present throughout the universe, even between the nucleolus & electrons inside and outside of the atom. According to spiritual view the universe is suspended in ether and every material thing has come out of *ether*. It is true that the science has failed in detecting ether, but it does not mean *ether* does not exist. It is the limitation of science to detect *ether*. As per science if the space is vacuum (contains nothing) or the there is vacuum inside & outside the atoms and other particles. It means even God does not exist in vacuum and therefore God is not an omnipresent entity. It seems to be an absurd view. God & *ether* are "no things" and 'no thing' does not mean 'nothing'. Science cannot detect pain, joy, bliss, anger & depression etc. by any physical instruments. Does it means these do not exist?

How the science will be able to fit all these strange phenomenons in their system, without accepting themselves wrong and without accepting the existence of God and Self-Realization? This is true that most of the scientists have a faith in God, but are silent to bring out the changes and transformation in scientific philosophy

and thinking, due to their helplessness. The science on earth is still in its childhood stage. Very soon there will be further explosion of scientific knowledge. In future both the yoga and the science will work together in consonance with each other to find the absolute truth & God. And then a New Age will begin.

¶"*See in Me yourself… for I see Myself in all of you.*
You are My life, My breath, My soul …
You are all My forms.
When I love you, I love Myself …
When you love yourself, you love Me.
I separated Myself from Myself … so that I may be Myself.
I separated Myself from Myself and became all of this …
so that I may be Myself.
I wanted to be Myself … that is anandaswarup… premaswarup…that is what I am, and I wanted to be that…
How can I be anandaswarup … and premaswarup…
and get ananda … and give ananda …
and get prema … and give prema …
and to whom am I give ananda …
and to whom am I give prema …
so I did this …
I separated Myself from Myself and became all this."¶

¶… By Sri Sathya Sai Baba, originally published in 'Spirit & the Mind' by Samuel H. Sandweiss.

!Om ! Peace ! Peace ! Peace !

14

God's Advice to His Children (Not to Worry)

The following is the text of one of the kind advice given by God to His children for not to worry. We know that when a child is born, he has a total surrender to his parents, he gets their love & everything he needs from his parents. He is not to worry at all for himself, his present & future needs. The child demands only such things, which are needed at present. The child gets satisfied, as soon as his demands are fulfilled. It is a fact that whatever belongs to the parents will naturally go to their children. But as the child grows older he begins to worry & doubt on his parents due to the impact of *Maya.* He begins to think that he will not get everything from his parents. Similarly, we starts doubting upon God & begin to afraid that we will not get everything we need in our future, although God has given us everything at present. God Father is advising us as follows:

"O, my dear child, it appears that you are too much afraid of every thing. Probably you do not realize that I am always with you. This is the only reason for your baseless fear. I assure you that I am always with you, and if you are convinced of this, you must become fearless now."

"You are un-necessary worried of everything, because you do not know that I am your savoir of life & always with you. I have given you all the things such as Sun, the Moon, the Air, the Water, the Earth, light, heat, sound, animals, food and vegetation etc. for the sustenance of your life, without your asking. Why do you doubt that I will not provide you, your petty food? I always have everything with Me for all your needs and will have everything for you in future too. Do not doubt upon Me. If you are convinced that My eternai storehouse is full of everything, then do not doubt that you will not get any thing out of it, required for your daily needs."

"My dear little one, I assure you that I am your supreme Savior, well-wisher, true Friend & true Companion during your sorrows and worse times. Does my supreme love for you do not force you to love Me back? Does my mercy upon you do not grow your faith in Me? My dear child, why don't you love Me too, after experiencing my eternal Love for you? Become Mine after you are convinccd of My mercies upon you. My child, do not act and misbehave in the world against My will so that I would forced to call you back from this world. If I call you back, you will be in trouble & pain, due to your great grief & sorrows."

"O, My child, you must realize My eternal Beauty behind all My creation. I have got everything with Me except your love. Therefore if you love Me, I shall always be with you, and will provide you all the happiness of life you need forever. I am the beauty behind all the beauties. Remember that all the worldly material things can give you happiness only if, you become mine, and otherwise it will not. I warn you, do not ignore or forget Me for the worldly petty things. I have created everything in the world only for you but you will get all the things for you at the right time you need. If you remember Me always in your every breath, I assure, I will give you everything you need."

"My little child, due to my supreme powers I did not face any problem or difficulty in creating this world for you. I created the universe, just from My single Thought of My Will. Do you think, I may face sōme difficulty, in providing you any petty thing, for the sustenance of your life? However, when I act opposite to your needless desires, you become against and angry to Me. But have you ever tried to guide and control, your mind and senses, which generally act opposite to My desires & wishes for you. Don't you know that the people of the world love you only to fulfill their selfishness? But remember that I love you only to fulfill your desires. I expect nothing to take from you. Due to love and mercy I am willing to give you so many things in life. Why don't you come to Me, with your empty hands, so that I may fill them fully as per your needs."

"My dear baby, you should renounce the worldly enchanting things. You should love and meditate upon Me. It is also your righteous duty of *Dharma.* I assure you as per my planning whatever I have made and to be done for you, I have always done it without fail, and I will continue to do so, for you. I have always cared and looked after you, even during your sleep & when you were in the womb of your mother and when you were a child and not able to look after yourself. Don't you know for Me you are always My little child. Believe Me, I will make you free from all your worries, if you simply love Me too."

"As I do not demand your tomorrow's worship, meditation and devotion today, you should also not demand your tomorrow's needs today from Me. This is as per My choice and wish, that I fulfill your today's need today, and tomorrow's need tomorrow. When you think that I am not giving you any thing, even then, I ought to give you so many things hiddenly, which you do not know. For Me the thorns are as good and beautiful as the flowers. Whatever I give you, you should always accept it always silently & gladly with pleasure. Since I know your future, I know better than you, about your tomorrow's needs and whatever is best for you. I wish you to make you a great man."

"Whatever I give to you, you should always be happy and satisfied with that. Do not try to oppose it, otherwise you will be in trouble. Remember you will not be able to change it with your limited capabilities. Also if you oppose, it will further reduce your love and devotion to Mc. As per My wish, you should always remain satisfied with the things I have given to you. It will provide peace to your mind and rest to your body & will increase your wealth."

"O My child, meditate upon Me & realize My vastness and greatness. If you realize My vastness & greatness you will be convinced that you are just nothing and have insignificant existence in the vast universe. You should meditate upon My infinite omnipotent powers, great aura of My light and you should be fully convinced that you are always with Me. Then there is no doubt that you will become fearless & worriless. Remember when you will sit along with me, you will not remain a little insignificant creature in the universe but you will be merged back in Me at My mercy."

"O my dear baby, I assure you that if you surrender all of your desires at My feet, control and tame your mind to become desireless, then your heart will become pure and the curtains of your ignorance will be removed. This will also remove the burden of fulfilling your desires from your mind. Then I will direct the world to take care of all your needs, and the world will assist you in solving all your problems and hardships. Remember if the whole world would not able to solve your difficulties, then I with all my super omnipotent powers will come and free you from your difficulties. Believe Me, it is really a truth."

"If you give all and surrender to Me, I will guard you and guide you. I know the agitations of your heart and its aspirations, but you do not know my heart. I am always in your heart and react to the pain and joy you feel. Do not lose the contact of my company. Cultivate nearness with Me always and you will be rewarded with My supreme love. Be confident that you will be liberated."

"In this way you will be free from all of your worries. You will get all the pleasures and peace of your mind. This world is Mine and I will give every thing to you. I assure you that I will always fulfill all your needs of this world and of the other worlds also. So do not worry any more and be happy."

With Blessings & Supreme Love
Your Supreme Father

!Om Anandam Om!

> "*When I am afraid, I will trust in You.*
> *Record my lament;*
> *list my tears on your scroll-*
> *are they not in your records?*
> *In God I trust: I will not be afraid.*
> *What can man do to me?*
>
> **--- Psalm 56:3, 8, 11**

Jesus Christ also warned against obsessive worry.

"*Therefore I tell you, do not worry about your life, what you will eat or drink; or about your body, what you will wear. Is not life more important than food, and the body more important than clothes? Look at the birds of the air; they do not sow or reap or store away in barns, and yet your heavenly father feeds them. Are you not much more valuable than they? Who of you by worrying can add a single hour to his life?*"

"*And why do you worry about clothes? See how the lilies of the field grow. They do not labour or spin. Yet I tell you that not even Solomon in all his splendour was dressed like one of these. If that is how God clothes the grass of the field, which is here today and tomorrow is thrown into the fire, will he not much more clothe you, O you of little faith? So do not worry, saying, 'What shall we eat?' or 'What shall we drink?' or 'What shall we wear?' For the pagans run after all these things, and your heavenly Father knows that you need them. But seek first His kingdom and His righteousness, and all these things will be given to you as well. Therefore do not worry about tomorrow, for tomorrow will worry about itself. Each day has enough trouble about of its own.*"

--- Matthew 6:25-34

Glossary

Abhisheka	Ablution, ritual washing.
Advaita or Adwait	The viewpoint that consciousness can transcend duality and man can merge with God. There is only Brahman & nothing else. God & I are one & the same thing.
Aggyia Chakra	The Chakra between eye brows.
Ahankar	Ego or 'I' associated with physical body. Also the false pride of ego.
Aham-Brahmashmi	I am God. God and 'I' are one.
Ahimsa	Non-injury, avoidance of violence, harmless.
Akasa or ether	Ether or space, first of five elements evolved from *Brahman (Om),* the subtlest form of matter.
Amrita	Nectar of the gods, which makes the body immortal, an ambrosial liquid sometimes materialized by Sai Baba.
Anahat Chakra	The Chakra behind the throat. One listens Anahat sounds on its opening.
Anahat Sounds	The inner sounds without any viberation of physical thing, audible even if you close your ears.
Ananda	Bliss, joy. Bliss is considered to be the very substance of God (God is bliss, not has bliss).
Ananda-swarupa	The very form of nature of bliss and *Ananda.*
Andhakoop	Dark well.
Angad	The monkey disciple of Lord Rama.
Antiparticle	Each of the matter particles has a corresponding antiparticle. When a particle collides with antiparticle, both annihilate and leave only

energy.

Arjuna The disciple of Lord *Krishna* to whom *Krishna* revealed the truth of human existence just prior to the opening battle of the *Mahabharata* war. The divine is course is known as the *Bhagavad-Gita.*

Asana Easy, comfortable sitting pose. *Hatha yoga* posture of human body.

Asanthi Grief, anxiety (absence of peace).

Ashram Hermitage or monastery.

Astral body Man's subtle body of light or prana or life force; Man has got three bodies: causal body, astral body and physical body. The astral body has nineteen elements: intelligence ego, feeling, mind, five senses, five instruments of actions, and five instruments of life force.

Astral- world The subtle sphere of lord's creation, A universe of light and color composed of life energy or lifetrons. Thc subtlest aspect of one's being. That which is without any changes, unmodified, unaffected and timeless.

Atma Individual soul; atma is the unseen basis, the substance of the entire objective world. It is the reality behind the appearance, universal and immanent in every being.

Atam-Shakti The force and the power of the soul.

Atom Basic unit of elements of ordinary matter

Avatar or Avatara An incarnation of God. When God takes human form and play lila.

Avataran The embodied lifetime of the *Avatar.* Descent of God in human form.

Avidya or Maya Ignorence. Non-Knowledge.

Aum (Om) The Cosmic sound Aum, which creates and

	sustains every thing. It is the Word or Holy Ghost or Hum or Amin.
Ayodhiyia	The birthplace of Lord Rama.
Baba	Grand Father. A holy saint or *Sanyiasi.*
Belief	A hypothesis assumed to be true without verifying it's truth.
Bhagavad-Gita or Geeta	This means "Song of the Lord". This is the renowned ancient scripture of India & part of the great epic *Mahabharata.* It has eighteen chapters and 700 *slokas.* It contains the spiritual teachings in the form of a dialogue between Lord *Krishna* to *Arjuna* (his disciple) *nearly 3250* years B.C., and is meant for all mankind. A must for all Yogis.
Bhagavan	Lord. God. "He who possesses all opulences".
Bhajan	Devotional songs.
Bhakta bhakti	A *bhakta* is a devotee, one who has *bhakti* (devotion)*,* virtue, self-control, faith, and devotion to God.
Bharat	India, the land that has *rathi i.e.* attachment to *Bha* or *Bhagwan,* the Lord.
Big-bang	The big explosion at the beginning of the universe in the singularity at the beginning of the universe in which the matter of the whole universe was condensed at a point of infinite density and gravitation. It was the beginning of the time.
Big-crunch	The singularity at the end of the universe, when the matter of the whole universe is began to concentrate at infinite density and gravitation at a point.
Black hole	A region of space-time from which nothing can escape out, even the light and other waves cannot escape due to the huge force of

gravitation.

Brahma The creator God of the Hindu Trinity, the other two being Vishnu and Shiva.

Brahman The ultimate, unchanging, Absolute Spirit composed of pure being and consciousness before the creation. The immanent principle, said to have three aspects: creation, preservation, and destruction. The absolute supreme reality Brahman is behind the apparent multiplicity of the phenomenal world.

Brindavan The name of a town on the banks of the Yamuna river, near Mathura, associated with Sri *Krishna's* childhood. It is also the name of the place, where Sri Sathya Sai Baba frequently resides when away from *Parasanthi Nilayam,* his *ashram.*

Buddhi The discriminating faculty of mind, intellect, or intelligence.

Causal body The man as a soul is a causal bodied being. The causal body is composed of 35 idea elements: 19 elements of the astral body + 16 basic elements of the physical body

Chakra Seven centers or 'lotuses' of potential energy arrayed upward in man's ethereal or astral body from the base of the spine to the crown of the head.

Darshan	To see a great person and receive his blessing.
Death	When soul leaves the body permanently & four pranas also leave the body.
Deepawali	A Festival of lights, celebrated in the memory of Lord Rama, becoming the king of Auodhiyia.
Delusion	Dual-vision, An illusion suffered by the whole humanity.
Desires	Wish for, longing
Devotion	Love for seeking God.
Dharma	Religion of God, Righteousness, duty, code of conduct one of the four ends of human pursuit.
Dhritrashtra	Father of Kaurvas in Mahabharata.
Dhyana	Meditation. The state of thoughtless consciousness with awareness of ego 'I'.
Diksha	Spiritual initiation, to dedicate oneself.
Dream	When mind completely detach itself from physical body and the ego creates another body & universe for itself.
Dus-karmas	Misdeeds, Bad-karmas.
Dussraha	Festival in India celebrating the victory of Lord Rama over Ravana, king of Lanka.
Dwapara Yuga	See Treta Yugas.
Electron	A very small particle, which have negative charge that orbits the nucleus of the atom with a great velocity.
Elementary or subatomic particles	The particles which are believed to be further undivided like electron, proton, neutron, photon and many others.
Ether	It does not mean the ordinary organic chemical. The space between the heavenly bodies and the sub-atomic particles is not vacuum but it is filled with something throughout the universe

and even inside the matter and particles. The whole universe is suspended in ether. Electromagnetic waves or light waves cannot travel in vacuum, needs a medium, which is ether. It is the first and finest manifestation of God in the form of matter and all the subatomic particles has come out of it. It is still undetectable by the scientists.

Faith	An unshakable hypothesis presumed to be true, even it is failed.
Field	Something that exists throughout space and time, as opposed to a particle that exist at only one point at a time.
Frequency	No. of complete cycles per second.
Fitzgerald contraction	The contraction in length of an object with increase of velocity.
Gamma rays	Waves of very short wave lengths.
Galaxy	A group of billions of stars like our sun.
Geodesic	The shortest or the longest path between two points in space.
Ganesha	Names for the elephant-headed God, son of Lord Shiva.
Ganapathi	Lord Ganesha.
Ganga	The holy river Ganges.
Gopa	The cowherd boys of *Brindavan,* playmates of Sri *Krishna.*
Gopis or Gopika	The milkmaids of *Brindavan,* companions and devotees of Sri *Krishna.*
Gunas	Primary qualities of a human being: peaceful (*sathva),* active *(rajas)* and dull *(tamas).*
Grahasthi	Married man who lives with his family.
Guru	Spiritual teacher and a guide to spiritual path for a God seeker.
Hanuman	One of the most miraculous and devoted *bhakta*

of Lord Rama represented as monkey man, mentioned in the *Ramayana.* He is still alive and gives His *Darshan* to His disciples.

Hatha yoga School of yoga, which gives more importance to a*sanas* or yoga postures for the purpose of physical well-being and for awakening of the spiritual centers.

Indra The king of the gods.

Involution Involution means going back of the creation back to God. For every process of evolution (going away from God) there is a process of involution. The process of involution is going at all the time. At the end of the universe the whole creation will dissolve back in God. That will be a complete involution of the universe.

Jagat The objective, transitory, untrue world.

Japa, japam Recitation or repetition of the name of the Lord continuously.

Japamala A religious necklace of 108 beads used *in japa* & repetition of the name of God with reverence and devotion.

Jatayu The vulture disciple of Lord Rama.

Janam-asthmi Festival in memory of the birth of Lord Krishna.

Karma Material activities with fruits of actions.

Karmic-law The fruits of human actions are as per law of karma. The actions of God (lila) are without any fruits.

Karamphal The fruits of actions.

Knowledge Opposite of *Maya* or ignorance, helps in knowing God and absolute truth.

Kriya Yoga A scientific technique of special pranayam in seeking God promoted by Mahavtar Babaji.

Kurukchetra	The battlefield of Mahabharata.
Jal	Spiritually pure water like Ganga-Jal.
Ji	A syllable added to a word to denote respect, e.g., *Swamiji, Babaji.*
Jivan-mukthi or Moksha or Nirvana	The God-realized person in whom only the divine vision is active. He no longer has any identification whatsoever with his body. He is one with God.
Jnana or Gyana	Knowledge. The *yoga* path in which emphasis is laid on knowledge and discrimination, leading to wisdom, and the awareness of one's identity with the divine.
Jnani	One who has direct knowledge of the highest wisdom. One who follows the path of yoga. The word is also used to denote: one who has reached awareness of his divine identity.
Jyoti	The light and form of a flame.
Kailas	A peak of the Himalayas regarded as the sacred abode of Lord *Shiva.*
Kali or Mahakali	A name of the divine goddess mother; the Primal energy.
Karma & Karmic-Law	Action; the law that governs all action and its inevitable consequences on the doer; the law of cause and effect, or moral compensation for acts done in the past.
Kirtan	Singing of spiritual songs by a group of devotees in the glory of God.
Kosas	The five sheaths of embodiment.
Krishna	An *Avatar (incarnation)* of *Vishnu.* Born nearly 5320 years ago in the end of Dwapara yuga.
Kundalini	Spiritual energy lying dormant in individuals at the lowest point of the spinal cord. It is different from *prana.* Without awakening Kundalini, there cannot be any process of involution

	(journey back to God)
Law of Cause & Effect	Every effect or an event must have a cause. There cannot be any event without any cause.
Laya Yoga	The techniques of concentration on *Anahat* sounds to achieve self-realization.
Leela (lila)	Divine play of God or His actions, which are without the fruits of karmas. The word is used to mean divine miracles also. But the whole of creation, being regarded as an inexplicable miracle, sometimes called the Lord's *lila.*
Life Energy or prana	Prana, Intelligent cosmic energy responsible for creation and organization of life and matter.
Light Year	Distance traveled by light in one year.
Maha-Samadhi	Willfully leaving the body by the soul of a Yogi (willful death).
Mahatma	A great purified soul.
Mahavtar Babaji	The great grand guru of Sri Paramhansa Yogananda. The Eternal Himalayan Yogi.
Magic	A mysterious performance by using hidden tricks to deceive the viewers.
Mahima	The praise of superhuman power.
Manas	The mind.
Manav	Man. Human.
Mandir	Temple. A monument for the worship of God.
Manipur Chakra	A Chakra near the novel centre in the spine.
Mantra	Sacred words or verse repeated during meditation or Vedic hymn.
Margi	Path, road, way, course.
Mass	The quantity of matter in a body; its inertia; or resistance to acceleration.
Mauna	Observing silence.

Maya	Ignorance obscuring the vision of God; the primal enticing illusion appearing as duality and called the world; creates attachment with world.
Medulla Oblongata	The top end of spine in the centre of skull.
Mind	The cosmic energy by which the brain functions
Miracle	A mysterious phenomenon generally seems to defy the known laws of sciences.
Mukti or Moksha or Nirvana	Salvation or Liberation of soul free from material existence of birth and rebirth.
Muladhar Chakra	A Chakra at the lower end of the spine. Seat of Kundalini.
Nadis	The nerves in the astral body. Main Nadis are Ida, Pingla & Sushumana.
Nagara-sankirtan	Nagar means city. Sankirtan means singing *bhajans or songs along with dance in the glory of God,* in a group while walking slowly through the streets; done in the early hours before dawn.
Narada	The ancient *rishi* or seer who wrote the classic of *bhakti yoga,* called *Narada Bhakti Sutras.*
Neutrino	An extremely light elementary particle of negligible mass.
Neutron	Neutral particles like protons in the nucleus of an atom.
Neutron star	A cold star of mass little more then sun, which have a radius of few kilometers with a density of hundreds of millions of tons per cubic inch.
Nirbhikalpa Samadhi	When experiences total oneness with God & Truth after the death of ego 'I'.
Nirgun & Sugun	Nirgun means devoid of any properties (Brahman). Sugun means which have some

	properties.
Nirvana or Moksha	Freedom from material existence. But still may be separate from God.
Nostradamus	A French doctor, who predicted thousands of major world events. He dreamed the future of the world.
Om or Aum	The primeval *Anahat* sound by which God sustains the cosmos.
Padmasana	A cross-legged posture for long meditation.
Paramatma	The pure *atma* viewed in its universal aspect as God.
Paramhansa	The highest degree of spiritual achievement of Nirbhikalpa Samadhi. Higher then Swami.
Patanjali	The name of the ancient sage who wrote the basic guide to Y*oga,* known as *Patanjali Yoga Sutras.*
Photon	A quantum of light energy.
Positron	Positively charged antiparticle of electron.
Prakiriti	Primordial Nature, which in association with *Purusha* (eternal conscious principle) creates the universe.
Prana	The vital force or cosmic energy that sustains life in the physical body in all living beings. There are five types of *prana.*
Prasanthi Nilayam	The abode of undisturbed peace. The name of Sathya Sai Baba's *ashram* in India.
Prahalad	A great disciple of Lord Vishnu.
Prema	Divine love of the most intense kind, universal unconditional unblemished love. It is different from sexual lust generally called love.
Premarasa	The flavor of *prema*
Proton	Positively charged particle, which resides inside the nucleus of the atom.
Pundit	Scholar of the knowledge of God.
Puranas	Eighteen Holy Books of Hindu *Shastras*, which describes historical events and are supplements

	to Vedas. These are not mythology as said by some western Historians having no knowledge of Hindu *Shastras.*
Purusha	Eternal conscious principle; Soul.
Puttaparthi	The village in southern India where Sathya Sai Baba was born (November 23, 1926) and where he has his *ashram known as Prasanthi Nilayam.*
Quantam	The minimum possible unit particle of energy or any material thing, e.g. light is discrete & can't be less then a photon or quanta.
Radha	The beloved & devotee of Lord *Krishna.*
Rajsic	The active, passionate aspect like king.
Rakshasas	The human race having *tamsic* characteristics.
Rama	An *Avatar* of God Vishnu in Treta-Yuga, a divine being. An *Avatar* whose name means, he who pleases; he who fills with *ananda* (bliss).
Ramakrishan Paramhansa	1836-1886: A great saint of Bengal. He was the spiritual guru of Swami Vivekananda.
Rishi	A sage, one leading a life without desires, with attachments only to the a*tma.* A seer of truth.
Sabhikalpa Samadhi	The initial state of samadhi in which the yogi is aware of his ego 'I' separate from God.
Sadhaka	A spiritual aspirant engaged in conquering his egoism and greed, the sense of 'I' and 'mine'.
Sadhana	Spiritual discipline or practice through activities such as meditation and recitation of holy names.
Sadhu	A holy-man, generally used with reference to a monk.
Sahasrar	The thousand-patelled chakra in the forehead, which is the reservoir of life energy.
Sai	The divine mother of all.
Sakhya	One of the five attitudes cherished by the dualistic worshipper toward his chosen ideal:

	the attitude of one friend to another.
Samadhi	Trance, perfect equanimity, untouched by joy, sorrows and communion with God. Complete absorption in God consciousness.
Sankhya	One of the six systems of Hindu philosophy.
Samsara or Sansara	The sensory world, which captures consciousness and gives rise to craving, attachment and suffering.
Samskaras	The tendencies inherent from previous births.
Sanathana Dharma	The ancient wisdom, the eternal path of righteousness.
Sankalpa	God's resolved or will.
Sankirtan	Reciting or singing devotional songs with joy.
Sanyiasi or Sanyias	A Hindu ascetic; one who has adopted the monastic, celibate life. Wears saffron clothes. Do not live in any family.
Satan	*Maya.* The power by which God has separated Him from His creation.
Sathya Sai Baba	The most miraculous Avatara saint at Puttaparthy in India.
Self-Realization	When the human soul experiences & merges with God and *Maya* vanishes.
Shastras	The scripture that illumines, the moral code, directly transferred to humanity from God. Ordinary human mind cannot write *Shastras*, without the grace of God. Only superhuman man writes the Shastras. Shastras are the authority in the spiritual field.
Sat-chit-Ananda	The supreme state, usually translated as existence, knowledge, bliss.
Satwic	Pure, good, pious; the principle of balance or wisdom.
Sathya	Truth that which is always the same no matter

	past, present, future or circumstance
Samadhi	An ecstatic state in deep meditation. It is the highest step on the eightfold path of Patanjal-Yoga. Shuttle experiences beyond delusion and Maya. Samadhi is attained when the meditator or observer, the process of meditation and the object of meditation (God) becomes the same.
Sampati	Yogi vulture with super powers at time of Rama
Satsang	Being in the society of good, spiritual people.
Satwa, rajas, Tamas	The three *gunas* or characteristics of embodied beings, translated roughly as peaceful, active and dull.
Savak	Who is dedicated to the service of God.
Self	*Atman* or soul.
Self-realization	The state of knowing God, the absolute state achieved by Yogis when the body, mind and soul become one with God, the soul merges in God and all the powers of God like omnipresent, omnipotent and omniscient are achieved The soul is in permanent Bliss or Happiness or Joy.
Shankar-acharaya Adi	India's most advance self-realized saint. A great scholar, thinker and spiritual philosopher. He founded great four *Maths* (monastic centers of spiritual education) in India. The Head of the Math is known as *Jagadguru* (world teacher) Shankaracharaya.
Shakti	The creative divine power; a name of the divine mother; the feminine aspect of God, representing His power and energy.
Shanti	
Shirdi-Sai	Undisturbed peace, eternal peace.

Baba Great Indian holy man, worshiped both by Hindus and Muslims, from whom Sathya Sai Baba of Puttaparthy says he was reincarnated.

Shiva Adi-Purusha. The destroyer God of the Hindu trinity, the other two being *Brahma* and *Vishnu.*

Siddha/ Sidhpurusha *A siddha* is one who has attained *siddhies* (yogic *powers).* Individualized Spirit.

Spiritual eye The third eye of Shiva or the single eye of intuition and omnipresent perception at the Aggyia chakra or between the eyebrows. When a yogi is under deep meditation the spiritual eye is visible. This is not present in the physical body.

Soham So means He, and ham means I. Soham means He is I or I am He. This mantra is realized in Nirbhikalpa samadhi.

Soul Atma

Maharishi Aurobindo 1872-1950: His ashram at Pondicherri, in Southern India, was turned into a community of spiritual seekers from all over the world, called Auraville. A prolific writer, his works include *The Life Divine, Essays on the Gita, The Synthesis of* Yoga, *Letters* on Yoga, and many others.

Sri Raman Maharishi 1879-1950: He was an illumined *rishi* of southern India; taught non-duality through self-inquiry one should constantly ask himself, "Who am I". His *ashram* is located on a sacred hill called Arunachala.

Sub-atomic particles The elementary particles smaller then atom. There are more then 100 such elementary particles in the universe.

Sudarshan

Chakra The miraculous weapon (a revolving wheel) of Lord Vishnu.

Sukhasana A cross-legged easy posture for meditation.

Swami Lord, spiritual preceptor, a member of India's most ancient monastic order.

Swadhisthan Chakra The chakra near the Lumber in spine.

Swarupa Form, body.

Tapa or Tapasia Religious austerity, sacrifice, asceticism designed to weaken the conviction that man is body.

Tatvamasi Tatvam means You (God) and asi means 'I'. This mantra means You and I are one. No duality.

Treta Dwapara & Kali Yugas The second of the four *yugas* or cycles of world periods. Hindu Shastras divides the duration of the world into four *yugas, Satya, Treta,* D*wapara* and Kali. The first is known as the Golden Age as there is a great prepondcrancc of virtue among men, but with each succeeding *yuga* virtue diminishes and vice increases. In the Kali yuga there is a minimum of virtue and-a great excess of vice. We are supposedly in the Kali *yuga* now. It was started after Lord Krishna approx. 5300 years ago.

Upadesh Spiritual instruction.

Upanishad A category of Indian scriptures. 108 philosophical treatises that appear within the *Vedas.*

Vedanta Anta means end of Vedas or later portion of Vedas"; Adi Shankaracharaya was the chief exponent of Vedanta.

Yoga Yoga means communion of *atma* (soul) with

	God. Yoga is that science by which the soul gains mastery over the instruments of body and mind and uses them to attain Self-realization—the reawakened consciousness of its transcendent, immortal nature, one with Spirit.
Veda	The Knowledge of God. The oldest scriptures about God are known as Veda.
Vedanta	One of the six systems of Hindu philosophy, formulated by Bhagwan Ved-Vyas.
Vedas	The most sacred scriptures of the Hindu religion, regarded as revelations to great seers and not of human origin. There are four *Vedas:* The *Rig-Veda,* the *Yajur-Veda,* the *Sam-Veda* and the *Atharw-Veda.*
Vedic	Which is derived from Vedas.
Vibhuti	Sacred ash, frequently materialized by Sri Sathya Sai Baba.
Vishnu	The preserver God of the Hindu Trinity, the other two being *Brahma* and *Shiva*
Visuddha chakra	The chakra in the spine near the cervical.
White dwarf	A stable cold star supported by, exclusion principal repulsion between electrons.
Whitefield	*A* township about thirteen miles from the city of Banglore, where Sathya Sai Baba casually lives.
Yoga or Yog	Union of the individual soul with God; also the technique by which to realize this union. It is the general term for the several types of devotional practice that the disciplines used to

	control the mind and transforms it into an instrument for God-realization.
Yogi	The devotional spiritual aspirant who seeks union with God by means of one or more specific mental and physical disciplines which are traditional and which are known by the title of *yoga.*
Yugas	The four phases of world through which life moves to complete a world cycle. Sat-Yuga, Treta Yuga, Dwapara-Yuga and Kali-Yuga

REFFERED-BOOKS

The Name of Book	*Author*	*Publisher*
Autobiography of a Yogi	Sri Paramhansa Yogananda	Jaico Publishing House, India.
The Men's Eternal Quest	-Do-	Yogoda Satsang Society of India, Ranchi,, India & Self-Realization Fellowship, USA.
The Divine Romance	-Do-	-Do-
Journey to Self-Realization	-Do-	-Do-
Metaphysical Meditation	-Do-	-Do-
Science of Religion	-Do-	-Do-
Spirit and the Mind.	Samuel H. Sandweiss	Sri Sathya Sai Books Publcn. Trust, Prasanthi Nilium-515134, India
Geeta Vahini	Sri Sathya Sai Baba	-Do-
Jnana Vahini	-Do-	-Do-
Dhyan Vahini	-Do-	-Do-
Sai Baba: Man of Miracles	Howard Murphet	-Do-
Bhagwad Geeta	Bhagwan Ved-Vyas	Geeta-Press Gorakhpur, U.P. India
Sri Mahabharata	-Do-	-Do-
Sri Ramayana	-Do-	-Do-

Srimad Bhagwat	-Do-	-Do-
Manu-Smarity	Maharishi Patanjali	-Do-
Kaliyan Bhavishiya Puran	Ved-Vyas	-Do-
How to be Self-Reliant	Swami Ram Sukh Das	-Do-
Prana	Swami Vivekananda	Sri Ram-Krishan Mission, India.
Ananda	Swami Ram Thirtha	Ram Thirth Mission.
Holy Bible	New King James Version	India Bible Literature 67, Beracah Road, Kilpauk, Madras.
Way to Self-Realization	Sh.N.C. Kancil	Educational Publisher 8606, Model Basti, New Delhi-5, India.
The Urantia Book	Urantia Foundation	533 Diversey Parkway Chicago, Illinois 60614 U.S.A.
Bhagavad-Gita	Swami Prabhupada	The Bhaktivedanta Book Trust

ILLUSIONS

Unconceivable Triangle
which is not possible

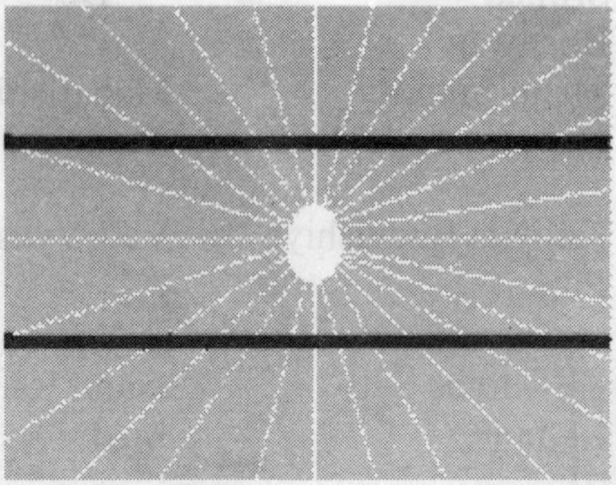

Two horizontal lines does
not seem parallel

A young woman & an old lady
makes the illusion

If concentrate at the centre the
surrounding seems revolving Our
Sahasrar Chakra looks like it